Starting Out Right

Beginning-Band Pedagogy

J. Si Millican

THE SCARECROW PRESS, INC.
Lanham • *Toronto* • *Plymouth, UK*
2012

Published by Scarecrow Press, Inc.
A wholly owned subsidiary of The Rowman & Littlefield Publishing Group, Inc.
4501 Forbes Boulevard, Suite 200, Lanham, Maryland 20706
www.rowman.com

10 Thornbury Road, Plymouth PL6 7PP, United Kingdom

British Library Cataloguing in Publication Information Available

Library of Congress Cataloging-in-Publication Data

Millican, J. Si (John Si), 1968-
  Starting out right : beginning-band pedagogy / J. Si Millican.
      p. cm.
  Includes bibliographical references and index.
  ISBN 978-0-8108-8301-7 (cloth : alk. paper) — ISBN 978-0-8108-8302-4
(ebook)
  1. Bands (Music)—Instruction and study. I. Title.
  MT733.M564 2012
  784.071—dc23

                                                            2012008391

Printed in the United States of America

To Sherry, Miles, and Alison

Contents

Preface

This book is my humble attempt to meld the ideas of the *sound-to-sign-to-theory* approach of learning music that was introduced to me in my formal training at the University of North Texas and the University of Oklahoma with the knowledge and skills that I gathered from the great teachers and colleagues I had an opportunity to work with as a public school band director. On one hand, this book has its roots in the technical aspects of teaching beginners of all ages—assembling and playing each instrument, making the initial sounds on each horn, selecting equipment, recruiting, planning, managing a classroom, and all of the myriad tasks that band directors all over the world encounter each day.

In addition to this kind of "nuts and bolts" information, this book presents what I call a *language-based approach* to teaching the skills of playing, reading, and writing music. The governing philosophy of this approach is that learning the language of music is a lot like the way we learn our native tongue: we learn to speak, then read, and then write. A language-based approach to developing musical literacy and performance skills proceeds in a similar manner: students hear music, they then imitate what they have heard, they learn how what they hear and play is notated, and then they learn the rules and labels for the things they have heard, played, and read.

The book is also guided by my research into the knowledge and skills that great music teachers use in their day-to-day teaching. My initial research brought the work of Lee Shulman to my attention. Professor Shulman, along with his colleagues, proposed that great teachers understand their subjects *differently*. Teachers, as opposed to other professionals in their field, understand their subject matter in such a way that they are able to communicate the many aspects and intricacies of topics to students.

Let's look at an example to illustrate the differences between the way a professional and a teacher might view concepts in their various fields. A physics teacher, we would hope, understands the *content* of physics, but she needs to understand this content in such a way as to *explain it effectively* to her students. A rocket scientist probably has even greater (and arguably more practical) knowledge of the concepts of matter and motion than our physics teacher, but does this knowledge make him a better educator? Without knowing what students at a particular level are capable of conceptualizing, without knowing the common misconceptions students have about physics or knowing the mistakes they commonly make, without knowing the best order or techniques in which to present material, or without having good speaking, presentation, or organizational skills, our rocket scientist will be less effective in communicating even the most basic ideas of physics to students than the physics teacher who has all of these attributes in place.

We have all had the experience of taking a class led by a person who obviously has a great deal of knowledge on the subject but is unable to effectively communicate those concepts. These people seem to get frustrated easily and may even become exasperated when we cannot grasp what, to them, seem to be the most basic concepts or skills. Perhaps you have had a music teacher who was a brilliant performer but was less than capable in communicating his or her knowledge or building your skill.

Shulman (1987) uses the term *pedagogical content knowledge* for this amalgam of content knowledge, curricular knowledge, general pedagogical knowledge, and knowledge of students (fig. P.1). Subject matter knowledge is not, in itself, enough to guarantee success as a teacher. Professional educators need a different kind of knowledge of their subjects in order to convey concepts, skills, and ideas to their students. Beyond subject-matter knowledge, a teacher needs to have curricular knowledge (what order to present material, what textbooks are best, what visualizations or activities convey concepts best), knowledge of students (what students like, what they find challenging, common misconceptions or misrepresentations they have about particular topics), and general pedagogical knowledge (the general classroom and presentation skills teachers of any subject need to have).

In this book, I make an attempt to outline specific elements of content knowledge, curricular knowledge, general pedagogical knowledge, and knowledge of students as they relate to acquiring musical literacy skills. Part I of the book outlines some of the underlying concepts of how students best learn the language of music. Chapter 1 looks into the nature of both middle-school students and older beginners and addresses the special needs of students with disabilities. The second chapter presents how musical literacy may be directly related to language acquisition.

Part II takes these general ideas and presents how we might put the language-based approach into action. Chapters 3 and 4 discuss ways to produce the first sounds on each instrument using imitation and rote-based in-

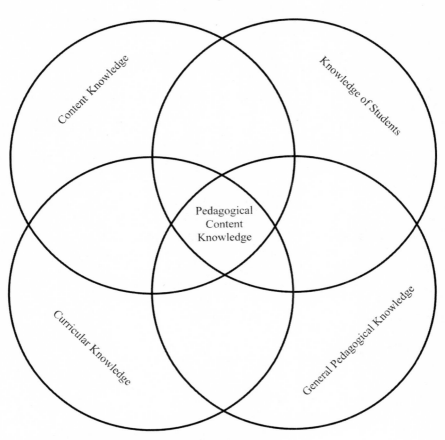

Figure P.1. Pedagogical content knowledge model

struction. Chapter 5 includes information on how we should move beyond rote-based teaching and on to reading musical notation. This approach can be applied to any standard band method book, and chapter 6 talks about these and other materials and how you might most effectively use them with your young instrumentalists.

After the fundamentals of playing with a great sound have been introduced and after our students learn to read and label basic, beginner-level music, it is time to move on to more advanced topics and techniques. Chapter 7 introduces some of the first advanced pedagogical issues young instrumentalists will come across as they dig into the music they will encounter in their second and third years of playing. Specific ways to rehearse and present this material are presented in chapter 8. This book is intended to be a jumping-off point in many regards, so chapter 9 offers suggestions on ways to move forward in your development as a teacher by utilizing resources such as mentors, private lesson teachers, and other professionals in the music community.

The final part of this book deals with some of the important structural elements of leading a band program. Some of this information is general pedagogical information, including recruiting and classroom management (chapters 10 and 13). Specific content knowledge, such as selecting great instruments, mouthpieces, and care supplies (chapter 11), and some specific tools for assessing your students' progress are included as well (chapter 14).

It is my sincere hope that the material presented in this book will give you some ideas about how you can present musical concepts to your students, the sequencing of the materials we use, and the nature of the students in your care. I hope that you will find sufficient content knowledge, curriculum knowledge, knowledge of students, and general pedagogical knowledge presented here to strengthen your pedagogical content knowledge such that you are the most effective teacher you can possibly be. What we do is vitally important, and how we go about what we do can make a tremendous difference in the lives of our students.

REFERENCES

Shulman, L. S. 1987. Knowledge and teaching: Foundations of the new reform. *Harvard Educational Review* 57 (1): 1–22.

Acknowledgments

As I mentioned in the preface, this work is an integration of the many great ideas and concepts that I've been able to encounter through my formal education and from my experience as a public school teacher. As an undergraduate student at the University of North Texas, I had the opportunity to study in a wonderfully enriching musical environment. I am indebted to Roger Warner, John C. Scott, and Dennis Fisher for their introduction to the practical and theoretical concepts and skills that have become a part of my teaching. In graduate school at UNT and at the University of Oklahoma, I was able to receive kind guidance, assistance, and mentorship from Will May, Hildegard Froehlich, Michael Raiber, Nancy Barry, William Wakefield, Brian Britt, Roland Barrett, and Charlene Dell. Each of these individuals planted seeds that have borne fruit in many places in my teaching career and in this text, and I am forever in their debt for their kind mentorship and caring guidance.

Along the way, I was fortunate to work with many wonderfully knowledgeable and talented music educators who selflessly shared their time and expertise with me. My first mentor at Hutcheson Junior High School in Arlington, Texas, was Carol Allen. She saved me countless years of trial and error and helped set me off on the right path by illuminating the human side of what we do. I absorbed a tremendous amount of information from my fantastic colleagues in the Lewisville Independent School District. Some of the wonderful directors and private teachers who inspired and enlightened me include Cheryl Pittman, Mark Biggs, Kennan Wylie, Steve White, Debra Haburay, Becca Hargis-Smith, Cathy Johnson, Dick Clardy, John Benzer, Mary Ellen Cavitt, Steve and Lynn Seibert, Brad Kent, Mike Brown, Melissa Townsend, Danna Rothlisberger, Clay Paul, and Jennifer Vaerewyck. In the

Belton, Texas, schools, I was able to work with and learn so much from Mark and Karen Nalley, Scott Dudley, Bruce Hurley, Brent Mathesen, Kim Flowers, and James Whitis. Many of the ideas presented in this book are modifications and adaptations of ideas these people have shared with me throughout our years together. Great teachers "steal" great ideas from each other and make them work for their particular situations, and I have taken a lot of information from the people listed above and modified it to work in my teaching. If I have used something in this book that is your original work and have not given you proper credit, please let me know.

I'd also like to recognize the impact of my own teachers. Ann Chamlee was the first of my music teachers to really connect with me in a special way. Her inspiration and encouragement, along with her limitless vision for whom I could become, continues to propel me in my artistic and creative pursuits. My band directors, Benjamin Timmons, Debbie Brock, Mark Nalley, Durward Howard, and David Pennington left lasting marks on me as a person and as a teacher. Special thanks to professor Sherry Rubins for her kind remarks and editing of the percussion chapter of this book.

Finally, I'd like to thank my family. My mother and father continually supported my musical endeavors and always told me that I could choose any career that I wanted, as long as it made me happy. My children, Miles and Alison, are a constant reminder of what is really important in the world. My wife, Sherry, is a caring mother, a trusted friend, and my life-support system.

In the end, it matters little how much money we earn, what awards we win, or what we accomplish in our professional lives; what is important is the people we meet and the impact we have on each other as human beings. Thank you all for helping me improve my knowledge and skill as a teacher, but thank you most for making me a better person.

I

FOUNDATIONS

1

Who Are We Teaching?

Miles McGee, a lanky, sixth-grade trombonist at Andrew Jackson Middle School, found himself sprawled out across the band hall floor just inside the entrance. He looked up to see his trombone case had flown open, and now the disassembled sections of his bright, new instrument were splayed across the band hall. Miles imagined that the entire class had seen him collide with the doorjamb, which suddenly seemed much narrower than it had last week. Was everyone pointing and laughing?

"Oh man! I hope Nina Reston didn't see that!" Nina was the eighth-grade class president and was the leader of a particular clique of girls who seemed to rule the hallways of Jackson Middle School. These girls were suddenly looking more and more attractive to Miles.

"Nice entrance!" commented Mrs. Sanchez. "You have grace as well as talent, I see! Gather up your things, and come join us." Mrs. Sanchez shot Miles a wink as she continued preparing for class. "You're just in time for warm-up."

"You know me—light on my feet," said Miles as he gathered up his things trying to save face to anyone who had noticed his big arrival in the band room that morning. Miles was becoming a bit of a class clown, and his sense of humor often earned him positive attention when he wanted it and often lightened things during awkward or embarrassing moments such as these.

Miles had just gone through a growth spurt and suddenly felt as if the simple task of walking down the hallway without bumping into things was a major chore. This whole middle-school experience was a lot different from the cozy confines of Cedar Park Elementary School, where he had spent the first five years of his schooling. Now, instead of one teacher for most of his classes, as he had in elementary school, he scurried from room to room moving between different classes with different teachers. It seemed as if his schedule took him from one end of the seemingly giant school building to the other for each different class.

"Welcome to middle school," Miles sighed as he collected his instrument sections and placed them carefully back into his trombone case.

Knowing our students is one of the most important things we can do in order to be effective teachers. In this chapter, we'll look at some of the physical, emotional, psychological, and cognitive changes typical middle-school students encounter. We'll investigate how our knowledge of students' development can help us teach music more efficiently and effectively, and we'll also look at the important modifications we can make in order to help students with developmental differences. Finally, we'll take a look at important differences in teaching older beginners.

While we may teach beginners of any age, the majority of beginning-band instruction in the United States happens in what might charitably be called the "exciting" years of middle school. During that time, students undergo amazing changes in their physical, emotional, psychological, and cognitive development with many of these changes happening all at once! The physical processes of puberty, combined with rapid changes in emotional and psychological development, expansion of social relationships, a heightened awareness of the opposite sex, and emerging personalities, all interact with an amazing increase in cognitive development in which students' minds and thought processes change significantly. A basic understanding of the changes that many students experience during this time can help us teach music more effectively.

Keep in mind that, while much of this information applies to a majority of the students walking the hallways of middle schools across the country, the characteristics we'll explore in this chapter are merely guidelines. We must leave room for individual differences in the timing and degree of change that our students will experience. In fact, differing timelines for development is one of the sometimes-exasperating features of the adolescent experience. Differences in individual students' family structure, community, school environments, and peer influence, all are important factors to consider as they influence the development of individual students. Even variances in child nutrition—the types and amount of food that a child eats—can impact students' development. Additionally, there are cultural factors to consider as we try to make generalizations about the development of middle-school students. Recent immigrants or families with strong cultural traditions may exhibit different characteristics from those described here.

Educators are continuing to find more ways to include students with developmental differences. More and more students with physical, emotional, social, cognitive, and neurological disabilities are able to join mainstream music classrooms. We're also finding ways to reconnect with older beginners, and several programs have emerged that help adult beginners discover the joys of making music.

DEVELOPMENT OF MIDDLE-SCHOOL STUDENTS

Ages and Stages

Most of our students will start learning an instrument during the late elementary or early middle-school years between the ages of ten and twelve. The transitions from elementary to middle school, between middle school and high school, and even the transition from high school into adulthood involve a myriad of physical, emotional, psychological, hormonal, and cognitive changes. The middle-school experience can be especially stressful in that many of these changes occur simultaneously or rapidly. Think about some of the things a typical middle-school student goes through as she transitions from elementary school to middle school. Typically, she might move from a smaller elementary school, with one primary teacher, to a larger middle school, with multiple teachers, different classes throughout the day, and a mix of new students from different elementary schools. Some of these students, thanks to typical variations in the onset of puberty, may physically resemble the average elementary-school student or may be developing rapidly into full adult size.

MULTIPLE ENTRY POINTS INTO INSTRUMENTAL MUSIC STUDY?

Can students begin studying an instrument in public schools after the "beginning band" year is over? In many band programs, the only time a student may elect to begin instrumental music instruction is in beginning band—typically in the fifth or sixth grade. Many times, if students fail to choose to join band at the same time as their peers, they are

locked out of instrumental music study, at least in a formal school setting, for the remainder of their academic careers. Why not provide extra opportunities for the students to join instrumental music programs
at a later date? What are some issues that prevent directors from being
able to provide this opportunity? What are some scheduling concerns
that might keep directors from offering beginning-band classes for
older students? How might a high-school beginning-band class affect
the overall band program? What are some reasons some students fail
to take advantage of opportunities to start later in their lives? How
might your philosophy of music education influence your decision on
whether or not to provide opportunities for older beginners?

Physical Development

For middle-school students, one of the most amazing catalysts for
physical change is the biological process known as puberty. These changes
brought on by hormonal development affect different individuals at different times. Some students mature earlier while some students take longer to
develop and grow. Looking at a typical middle-school band class, many of
the girls may seem more mature physically while most males may appear—
and even act—more boyish.

Both girls and boys at this age often go through periods of accelerated,
dramatic growth spurts. These growth spurts occur a year and a half to two
years earlier for girls than for boys (Wigfield, Burnes, and Eccles 2006). It's
not uncommon for teachers to wave goodbye to a tiny sixth-grade boy at
the end of the school year and then greet a much different young man when
he returns after the summer break. As music teachers, we need to help our
students cope with these changes; we can help them realize that the correct positioning of their saxophone neck straps may have changed or that
the feeling of the trombone slide positions might be a little different after
they've been through a period of rapid physical growth.

Most students have gotten their permanent teeth by the time they start
middle school. This also means that orthodontists may have begun tin-
kering with the alignment of teeth by adding braces, retainers, and other
foreign objects into our students' mouths. This can be quite a challenge for
woodwind and brass players as they adjust to the addition, adjustment, and
removal of these new mouth accessories.

Developmental changes are also important when helping students and
their families select instruments. As we'll see later, it is helpful to match a
student's physical characteristics to the instrument he or she might play.
Students may or may not "grow into" an instrument; the student who looks
too small to hold a euphonium might be able to handle that instrument

quite well in six months. Generally, boys and girls become stronger as they continue to mature through middle school. While it's important to note that, while arm lengths may change or torsos may stretch as students grow and develop, some characteristics remain relatively stable. For instance, students with skinny fingers tend to keep that general characteristic even as they continue to grow taller. A student with full lips will tend to keep those full lips even as he becomes a lanky teenager. It sometimes helps to make a note of the physical characteristics of parents or older siblings to get an idea of how a student might develop.

Students' abilities to control their bodies also develop throughout the middle years. Elementary-age students generally have more trouble starting wind instruments because they lack development in certain types of motor control. Both *gross-motor control*, the ability to control the larger muscles of the torso and the limbs, and *fine-motor control*, the ability to control the smaller muscles of the fingers and toes, become more reliable and stable as students reach the middle-school years. Improvements in gross-motor control during this time frame can help students develop a stronger feeling of rhythm and pulse even though this improvement in whole-body coordination is sometimes thrown off track by growth spurts. Developments in fine-motor control allow beginners to execute intricate movements with the fingers and hands. They also become more adept at using hands separately, which is particularly helpful when learning woodwind and percussion instruments.

Emotional and Psychological Development

When many people think back to their adolescent years, the emotional aspects of moving through middle school often stand out vividly. While the overly dramatic, emotionally unstable student with wild mood changes may come to mind, this stereotype is an exaggerated version of the reality for the experience of most middle-school students. That's not to say that sometimes the minds and emotions of middle-school students can't be mysterious. One minute a student may be crying over the results of a chair test; the next minute she is giggling happily with her best friend.

Three of the most dramatic changes in the emotional and psychological development of middle-school students are that they begin to notice the opposite sex, develop different types of friends, and their relationships with parents often change as students become more independent. Social relationships become very important during these years. Loyalty and friendship are particularly valued. While boys tend to value group activities and games, girls value personal intimacy and deeper interaction with their friends. Good friends have a tremendous power of persuasion over the personal experience of middle-school students and may even influence what instruments students choose to play. Friendships can be an important factor in retaining students between middle and high school or even whether students elect to join the band at all.

Middle-school students also begin to function more as independent adults and move away from the influence of their parents. As they become more involved with school and extracurricular activities, students spend less and less time with their parents. Often, they spend more time with their teachers than they do their own families! Some students will develop strong bonds with you and view you as a combination of "best friend" and "surrogate parent." These roles can be particularly tricky for young teachers to manage. It is important that teachers remain open, kind, and supportive without crossing the line of professional adult-student interactions.

Students often start to develop and expand features of their personalities during puberty. These emerging personalities may influence instrument selection, as we'll see later. Students also begin to take on various social roles. For instance, students may begin to visualize themselves as a "flute player" or "percussionist" and to start to take on characteristics that they perceive represent those roles. They may begin to identify themselves as "band students," or they may experience conflict as they struggle to choose between seemingly conflicting roles, such as "athlete" or "musician." Teachers can be important in helping students develop healthy role images and self-esteem. Successful experiences in music, positive social involvement with other classmates, supportive interactions with adults, and the unique activities of band help students develop positive identities as band students. If most of these experiences are positive, then students will have an easier time developing a positive self-image and positive role identification as a member of the band. Remember that the opposite can also be true: negative experiences, lack of success, and negative interactions with classmates can lead to less than positive experiences, a poor self-image, and a negative impression of the band experience.

Cognitive Development

Students also undergo changes in their thinking, reasoning, problem solving, and learning styles during their middle-school years. Students' thinking becomes more organized, and they are capable of thinking in multiple layers. As they develop, they are capable of more abstract thinking and rely less on concrete examples. Students at this stage also develop the ability to engage in hypothetical thinking and can use *concepts* to apply what they learn in one area to different situations. For instance, if a middle-school student really understands the concept of playing with a separated, march style, then note-length issues don't need to reintroduced to the same degree whenever the band pulls up a different march.

On the other hand, students also start to form *mis*conceptions and *mis*-representations that are just as important for teachers to understand. For example, a student may have the misconception that the most efficient way to move from the lower octave to a higher octave on the flute is to blow harder into the headjoint. While this method of changing registers may work initially, this student fails to understand that tone quality and intonation will suffer by merely blowing faster air and that there are more efficient ways to move between octaves. Discovering common misconceptions and misrepresentations that students have is an important part of developing as a teacher.

Remember that all of your students are unique; as teachers we must work to connect to students on a range of developmental levels and by presenting material in a variety of different ways. During the middle-school years, students begin to favor a particular learning style. These styles include *auditory, visual,* and *kinesthetic* learning styles. It's important to note that all students engage material using *all three* of these modes to some degree; however, most of us favor one particular learning style over the others. Auditory learners learn best by listening to explanations and appreciate modeling concepts using instruments and with the voice. The most efficient way to communicate note lengths to an auditory learner is to model by playing or singing the style for them. Visual learners prefer printed words and appreciate diagrams. When discussing note lengths, they would rather see a picture of what the note should "look" like rather than hear explanation. Visual learners like to take notes and draw pictures of concepts and value illustrations and visual models. Kinesthetic learners process information and concepts by feeling and moving. While one would think that the physical movement associated with instrumental music performance would be beneficial to kinesthetic learners, Mixon (2011) points out that they may need to understand concepts by moving and feeling concepts away from instruments first. A kinesthetic learner might appreciate demonstrating note-length concepts by conducting or through holding their hands together and apart to emulate different durations of notes.

APPLICATION TO MUSIC TEACHING

So how does knowing how students develop physically, emotionally, psychologically, and cognitively help us teach beginning band? If we truly understand how our students' minds and bodies work and continue to develop over time, we can adapt how and when we present musical concepts to their developmental levels. Here are a few ways that you can apply knowledge of your students to your music teaching. Many of these are explored throughout the remainder of this book.

1. *Match your expectations of what a student can achieve physically to his or her developmental level.* Don't expect your tiny, sixth-grade trombone section to immediately be able to reach seventh position with perfect intonation. A student who cannot coordinate his or her hands to play paradiddles fluently on the snare drum today may be your best player in a year. While it's important to have high expectations, the limitations of students' bodies may delay them from achieving what you've asked them to do. Be sure whatever your students perform is done very well utilizing correct and efficient playing fundamentals.

2. *Be aware of the possibilities of future physical growth and development as you guide students in selecting instruments.* While general characteristics, such as lip shape and finger width, remain fairly consistent as students grow, keep in mind that a smaller student may "grow into" a larger instrument. Making a note of a student's parents or older sibling's physical stature may provide some clues that help you make these decisions.

3. *Keep in mind that students are just beginning to develop fine-motor skills as you help them develop these skills.* Finger movements must be deliberate, consistent, and regularly practiced in order to develop. Make finger movements precise and quick (always using correct technique) to help develop fine-motor facility and muscle memory. Try to work some exercises for fine-motor skills every day.

4. *Let your knowledge of your students' emotional and psychological development guide your classroom-management decisions.* Embarrassing a student by calling her out in front of her peers may be one of the worst things you can do in a classroom-management situation in a middle-school setting. Don't take emotional displays personally, and remember that middle-school students are resilient and subject to change emotionally. Work to develop a sense of community, and establish a strong, positive group identity within each section and within the band program.

5. *Utilize peer (and near-peer) teachers to help younger or less-developed students develop their skills.* A great way to utilize your advanced students is to have them help weaker players. Pairing students in this way helps keep your strong students from becoming bored while helping your weaker students improve through individual attention. Many successful band programs utilize older students as mentor teachers for their beginner classes. For instance, you may have a talented eighth-grade clarinet player serve as a "band aide" during the beginning-clarinet class. This arrangement can be motivational for the older students and may provide a wonderful role model for the younger students.

6. *Present musical concepts and content in as many different ways as possible.* The many ways in which you teach concepts should be informed by the cognitive abilities and learning styles of all of your students. Kevin Mixon's (2011) book *Reaching and Teaching* All *Instrumental Music Students* contains excellent examples of presenting concepts to students with various learning styles.

7. *Help students connect what goes on in the band room with what goes on in their math, English, social studies, and science classes.* Middle-school students are at an exciting place in their cognitive development. They are finally able to begin to consider the many connections between subjects. By bringing in concepts from subjects outside of the band room, you help the students process those concepts in different ways that may make them more meaningful to the students. Some of your students will *only* understand these subjects if you present them in a musical context!

8. *Make your band class a positive and supportive learning environment.* Friendship and students' desire for the approval from valued groups often leads to stress in the lives of middle schoolers. The middle-school students can also sometimes be cruel in their exclusion of individuals from groups. Try to keep group dynamics positive in your band classes. Pay attention that nobody is ostracized or ridiculed in your class. You can model positive feedback on performances and insist that others use positive comments to each other. Model and expect courteous communication in the classroom.

One of the leading researchers in cognitive development during the early twentieth century was Lev Vygotsky. His work has influenced the way teachers present material and can be useful to teachers of all grade levels and all subjects. Vygotsky proposed that our students progress most efficiently when they work within what he called the *zone of proximal development*. In order to work in this zone, the student should work on tasks that are just difficult enough to need a little help from the teacher (or a more-accomplished student) in order to be successful. If the student can perform the activity without the teachers help, then the activity becomes too easy, and the student becomes bored. If the student cannot perform the task, even with the teacher's help, then the activity is too difficult, and the student becomes frustrated. The help that the teacher or the more-skilled student gives the student is called *scaffolding*. The teacher serves as a scaffold, or a support, that helps the student learn a particular concept. It is up to us as teachers to design meaningful learning activities based on the physical, emotional, and cognitive abilities of our students. Operating in the zone of proximal development allows us to most efficiently present concepts to our students.

DEVELOPMENTAL DIFFERENCES

Some of our students experience more profound developmental differences than those normally encountered in the middle-school years. Thanks to the introduction of the Individuals with Disabilities Education Act (IDEA) in the 1970s, more and more of these students are able to participate in regular classrooms. The principal theme of IDEA was that students with disabilities should be given the opportunity to be included in as many regular classrooms and school activities that other students participate in as they are able. In the words of the act, they are to function as best they can in the least restrictive environment (LRE). If a student's abilities allow him, he should not be restricted from participating in any activity that other students are able to enjoy.

A student who has been officially identified with a disability will most likely be referred to a specialist in the school district who will coordinate an annual admission, review, and dismissal (ARD) meeting involving parents, teachers, and other professional staff. This review, conducted annually, will determine what modifications or special services these students require in order to have the chance to be successful. In the annual ARD, the team will develop an individualized education plan (IEP) for the student, which describes these modifications. These modifications may be specific or general and may or may not include specific directions for music instruction. It is important to note that the modifications listed on the IEP are not optional. These modifications are requirements of federal law and should be carefully followed.

ALPHABET SOUP!

Educators working with students with disabilities are confronted with a myriad of abbreviations. See if you can discover the definitions for these common abbreviations often used when working with students with disabilities. Knowledge of these terms will be important as you work with other professionals on your campus.

504	FERPA
ADD	IDEA
ADHD	LRE
ARD	ODD
ED	OHI

It is important to remember that individuals identified with any disability function along a continuum of the disability from low to high functioning. For instance, a student who has been diagnosed as hearing impaired may be totally deaf or have only a partial hearing loss. Disabilities may be physical, such as a vision impairment, muscular dystrophy, cerebral palsy, muscular sclerosis, or spina bifida. Other disabilities are emotional in nature, such as emotionally disturbed or oppositional defiant disorder. There are also cognitive and neurological disabilities, including mental retardation, Tourette syndrome, and other developmental delays. Some learning disabilities prevent individuals from perceiving or processing information in the brain, causing the disability to manifest itself in physical, cognitive, or emotional ways. Dyslexia is a common example of a specific learning disability and can be quite problematic to a student's ability to process music notation if not addressed.

Modifying Instruction to Help Students with Disabilities

So how can we help students with disabilities be successful in band class? The most important thing to remember is that we cannot let the student's condition define the person. A student is not ADHD (attention deficit hyperactive disorder); she *has* ADHD. Treat each student as an important individual, just as you would any other student, and give the students what they need to be successful in your class.

Here are some guidelines that may help students with disabilities be more successful in your band class:

1. *Get help!* Your campus likely has specialists, paraprofessionals, and other aides that can provide you with more information and materials to help your students be successful. They can assist you in enlarging music for a vision-impaired student or help you decide the best way to work out a behavior modification plan with an emotionally disturbed student. These people are there to help you teach these students; take advantage of them!
2. *Assign instruments matched to each student's potential for success.* A severely hearing-impaired student might be more successful on a percussion instrument, where the vibrations of the instrument may help her perceive the music, than she would be on French horn, where she would need to perceive fine differences in pitch. A student with one arm might be quite successful manipulating three valves on a brass instrument but would struggle with using all ten fingers on a woodwind instrument. Focus carefully on the possibilities for success for each

student rather than on the limitations that may seem overwhelming with a disability.

3. *Make modifications to instruments if possible.* Add a strap to help students hold a euphonium. Lower a snare drum stand to help a student in a wheelchair. Crafty parents or even the industrial technology class at the school might be able to help build equipment and modify instruments to help your students.

4. *Make modifications to assignments as appropriate.* Don't be afraid to change the requirements of an assignment so that a student can be successful. That doesn't mean that you should dilute assignments or embarrass or degrade a student who could otherwise be successful. Making appropriate modifications is especially important if they are required as a part of a student's IEP.

5. *Include the student in the same activities, and give your student the same amount and types of feedback you give other students.* Use age-appropriate speech, and provide feedback in the same way that you would to any other student. Talking down to a student with a disability diminishes that student as a person. Remember, you are modeling the manner in which your students should communicate with persons with disabilities. Include students with disabilities in small group work and classroom activities as much as possible.

The University of Texas Center for Music Learning website has a wealth of information for working with students with disabilities. The web address is listed at the end of this chapter.

ADULT BEGINNERS

Many teachers are discovering the opportunity to teach adult beginners. You may think that teaching trombone to a sixth-grade beginner is fundamentally the same as teaching a sixty-year-old beginner. In reality, there are some important differences to consider. While these older learners participate in some of the same activities as younger beginners, these students are in a different place in their physical, cognitive, and social lives than our middle-school learners. The New Horizons International Music Association is one of the leading adult music education organizations in the United States. New Horizons groups started at the Eastman School of Music and have spread across the United States. These groups are made up of adult musicians who have either played all their lives, played as a younger person but have not touched their instruments in a while, or adults who have never played an instrument. The musical experiences in these groups vary from small ensembles to jazz bands to full concert bands. More information on the New Horizons International Music Association can be found on their website.

One of the leaders in adult education, Malcolm Knowles, developed a set of attitudes and approaches that he found worked best with adult learners. We can apply many of these principles to teaching beginning instruments to adults:

1. *Adult learners want to know the reasons behind learning activities.* While younger students may go through activities and exercises just because they are the routines of the class, older students want to know how they'll benefit from the material and activities you present to them.

2. *Adult learners often have commitments outside of the class, such as family and work.* While middle-school students may be busy with a variety of extracurricular and academic pursuits, many adult learners juggle job and family commitments or may have many other interests and activities outside of music lessons. Keep your expectations aligned with the adult students' outside lives, and make music an enriching activity that supplements their daily experience.

3. *Adult learners prefer to work in an autonomous environment.* A typical leadership arrangement in which the conductor or teacher makes all of the musical and procedural decisions may not sit well with older learners. Adults want to be involved in decision making and planning. This may mean that the group might wish to decide the location and time of the next concert rather than leaving those decisions solely to the director. You may wish to give the students a selection of eight songs and have them pick four for the concert. Remember that many of your students may have served for a long time as leaders themselves. Use their desire to make decisions, and plan to your advantage. This does not mean that older students want a weak leader; you should still provide strong *musical* leadership.

4. *Adult learners learn best by solving problems and completing tasks rather than memorizing rules and principles.* All students learn best through experience, but adults are even more likely to learn best through active participation. Memorizing a list of key signatures may be less effective than learning to play tunes in which those same key signatures are utilized.

5. *Adult learners use their life experiences and pre-existing knowledge as they develop new learning.* All students build upon their prior knowledge to develop new learning, but adult learners have a wealth of pre-existing knowledge that they call upon to help them give structure to new ideas and concepts. This prior learning may be from their professional lives or from other events in their past. It's important to get to know

your students in order to help them make connections between their life experiences and the musical concepts you wish to communicate.

The middle-school and adolescent years are some of the most exciting and important years in the development of young people. In many ways, these can be the years that help determine what kind of humans our students will become. If we match the physical, cognitive, psychological, and emotional development of our students to our musical instruction, we can open these windows to a wonderful world of musical knowledge and a high level of achievement. Our efficient musical instruction reinforces maturation in all of these areas. Much of the remainder of this book specifically addresses the particulars of middle-school students and how we can best match our instruction to allow them to achieve their full potential.

FIELD EXPERIENCE CONNECTIONS

1. Visit the school lunchroom during a student mealtime. Make a note of the physical, psychological, emotional, and cognitive differences you observe. Share your observations with your cooperating teacher or with your classmates.
2. If you've taken a child development or educational psychology class, look over your notes and thumb through your textbook to see how you might apply those concepts to music teaching.
3. Take a look at the different instrument sections in the bands or beginner classes at your field experience school. Make a note of any personality differences you see between the players on different instruments. What roles do you see taking shape in the students in each section? Does the flute section have a personality type different from the low-brass section? Explain your reasoning, and provide some specific observations to support your ideas.
4. Think of a concept that you might present to a beginning-band class (keeping a steady beat, playing a new note, counting a particular rhythm, etc.). Develop some different ways to present those concepts. See if you can develop one way to address visual learners, one way to help auditory learners, and another way to target kinesthetic learners.
5. Ask some middle-school students why they chose to play their instrument.
6. Ask your cooperating teacher if there is a gang problem at your school. How does gaining membership in any group reinforce adolescents' need for acceptance in a peer group? What might gang members get from the group that they may not be getting elsewhere?

7. Ask your cooperating teacher if she ever assumes the role of a parent for her students. How does this make her feel?
8. What support does your cooperating teacher get from the school for working with students with disabilities?

REFERENCES

Adamek, M. S. 2005. *Music in special education*. Silver Spring, MD: American Music Therapy Association.

Dabback, W. M. 2005. Toward andragogy in music: Examining the gap between theory and emerging practice in the instrumental music education of older adults. *International Journal of Community Music*. http://www.intellectbooks.co.uk/Media-Manager/Archive/IJCM/Volume%20B/03%20Dabback.pdf

Gerber, T. 1994. The adolescent learner. In *Music at the middle level: Building strong programs*, pp. 5–12. Reston, VA: Music Educators National Conference.

Jensen, E. 2006. *Enriching the brain: How to maximize every learner's potential*. San Francisco: Jossey-Bass.

Mixon, K. 2011. *Reaching and teaching all instrumental music students*. Lanham, MD: Rowman and Littlefield Education.

Wigfield, A., J. P. Burnes, and J. S. Eccles. 2006. Development during early and middle adolescence. In *Handbook of educational psychology*, 2nd ed, ed. P. A. Alexander and P. H. Winne, eds., pp. 87–113. Mahwah, NJ: Lawrence Erlbaum Associates.

WEBSITES

New Horizons International Music Association. www.newhorizonsmusic.org.

University of Texas Center for Music Learning. Disabilities information. www.cml.music.utexas.edu/DisabilitiesArchive/DisabilitiesOpener.htm.

2

Learning the Language of Music

Estella was worried about her beginning-trumpet class. They were good students, very attentive, and eager to follow her every instruction. They were, in many ways, a dream class. Each of the students was so polite and respectful, and they seemed to be practicing diligently and consistently every week.

Nevertheless, Estella was worried.

"These kids just cannot *read* anything!" she confessed to her friend Jackie, another first-year teacher in the school district. Jackie and Estella had become fast friends at the district's new-teacher orientation sessions just prior to the start of the school year.

"What do you mean, Stella? You said your trumpet class was rocking!" asked Jackie.

"I mean, we seem to take all period to work through reading a line of music, then we get to a line that is just as easy, and they act like they have never read music before!" explained Estella. "We have to go over every line note-by-note it seems. The other day, I asked my best student what the name of the last note in the first measure was, and do you know what she said?"

"Did she give you a fingering instead of a note name?" asked Jackie.

"Yes!" Estella exclaimed. "That drives me crazy! Another thing that bothers me is that they don't seem to hear it when they miss notes! I mean, if you're playing 'Mary Had a Little Lamb,' and you play wrong notes, you ought to *hear* that, right?"

"I know," answered Jackie. "It's like they are just pushing down buttons instead of playing music. You have a class of button pushers."

"Well, I don't know what I'm going to do," said Estella. "I wish my kids could read music, play by ear . . . you know, all the fun stuff. Looks like I've got a bunch of button pushers instead of musicians."

You wouldn't get upset with a three-year-old if she were not able to read a passage from Shakespeare. You wouldn't expect a baby to recite a famous poem. We don't expect preschoolers to be able to have the penmanship or composition skills necessary to construct a college essay. Learning to speak and read and write a language occurs along fairly predictable lines of development. There are many parallels between learning a spoken language and learning the language of music. We can take our knowledge of how we learn a language—how we learn to speak, read, and how we begin to learn to write—and apply that information to how we learn those skills in music. While the development of speaking, reading, and writing English are fairly well documented and understood, some of the common procedures in teaching musical reading and writing are in direct conflict with these precepts.

Consider a notation-based band class where the students begin their instruction by opening up their method books and reading a page of whole notes and half notes. A teacher using this approach might begin by explaining, "This note is an F, and you play it by pushing down your first valve." This is somewhat like putting a book in front of a pre-kindergartner and saying, "These are the letters of the alphabet, and they go together to make words, and this first big bunch of words is called a paragraph. Now let's read." Of course, this is an exaggerated example, but it illustrates one of the conceptual flaws in the notation-based method of presenting musical concepts.

Drawing upon the work of reading specialists, psychologists, and music educators, we can discover the most important commonalities in learning to speak and read text and learning to perform and read musical notation. Just as children first learn to speak, then read, then write in a particular language, these philosophies help our students learn to first play, then read, and then compose music. This approach of moving from musical sound to notation to theory sets up our students to be musically literate performers and lifelong participants in the arts.

MUSIC AS A LANGUAGE

When we learn a language, we learn first to interpret the sounds and then speak the language before we learn to read. After we can speak and read, we learn to write what we have spoken and read. An understanding of the basic concepts about how we develop language skills, both aurally, verbally, and through text, can help us uncover some useful guidelines that can help us teach musical concepts. Reading text and reading music are not completely alike, but several important educators throughout history have used the concepts of learning to speak and read to help us teach music more effectively.

How Reading Text and Reading Music Are Similar

Let's take a look at some of the ways in which reading music and reading text are similar. When we learn a new language, we usually learn to speak, then read, and then write the language. As a language learner, we do not "finish" learning to speak and then move to reading; each one of these skills develops along separate tracks, each advancing from basic to more complex skills while the other skills continue to grow and develop. At any given time when we are learning a language, our writing skill may not be as advanced as our reading skill, or our speaking skill may be more advanced than our reading skill. If you have ever tried to learn a foreign language, you may have had the experience of being able to understand a sentence if you see it in print but not recognizing that same sentence if you heard someone speak it to you. Perhaps you may understand what someone has asked you in a foreign language, but you can't come up with the proper answer. All of these are examples of the three tracks of speaking, reading, and writing a language developing at different rates simultaneously. Hopefully you'll develop enough skill in all three of these areas that you'll become fluent in the language. Developing speaking, reading, and writing skills are all a little bit different, so we'll take a look at each one individually and talk about how musical development might evolve along similar lines.

How We Learn to Speak

In order to understand how speech develops, we can look back to our experiences as infants and babies as we developed our own language skills. Even before we are born, we have been exposed to the sounds and the language of our environment. After birth, we continue to listen to all of the sounds of our surroundings. As babies, we begin to babble and make nonsense sounds in an effort to develop the physical linguistic skills necessary to communicate. All of the time, we are *imitating* the sounds we hear from the people in our environment. This process is interactive: baby makes a sound, and the parent reacts. Picture a proud father leaning over the crib repeating "Da-da" in an effort to get his daughter to say his name. When the baby finally does react by saying "Da-da," the father responds by smiling and laughing, thereby reinforcing the child's utterings by exclaiming, "Yes! Yes! Da-da!" As our band students are beginning to "babble" by experimenting with their first sounds, it is important for us to reinforce their attempts and to let them know if the sounds they are making are what we're looking for.

The next step in language development includes the formation of a small collection of single words. Short, basic words, such as "ball" or "dog," are our first attempts at making sense of our world through language. As developing musicians, we may begin to produce single notes of different pitch or make characteristic sounds on our mouthpieces at this stage. Certainly, these are not what we might call "music" any more than we might call a baby's babble "speech," but this step is vitally important in laying the foundation for future development. Here again, the teacher's feedback is vitally important as our students develop these "babbles" of our musical language.

Next, we begin to put words together in very short sentences as our speaking vocabulary expands. Now we might say, "big dog" or "my ball." We begin to develop our own rules for combining words and showing meaning. In music, we begin to string notes together into more meaningful bits. Perhaps we play two whole notes a half step apart or three half notes moving between brass partials. When we begin to string notes together, we are adding more and more musical meaning to their relationships; a pattern of three quarter notes followed by two eighth notes *means* something in common time.

This stage of language development is more than imitative; we gradually develop and apply informal rules as we combine words to create new, meaningful sentences that we've not heard before (Temple, et al. 1988). Our beginners are also working to create rules for themselves and combining what they learn in our classes into their own new ideas. Often, this experimentation takes place outside of the band room in bedrooms or garages during home practice. It is important to help our students develop these skills by showing them healthy and productive ways of experimenting that do not interfere with their growth.

As we continue to develop our speaking skills, we start to pick up on things such as dialect and grammar as we begin to learn more complex formal and informal rules and customs. If you grew up in rural Georgia, you may develop a different accent from that of a student growing up in Brooklyn. Perhaps your family members may use nonstandard grammar in their speech, and you begin to pick up on those patterns and informal "rules" of speech. In the music classroom, our students also absorb the sounds and structure they hear during class. It is important for us to provide great models of characteristic tone quality and accurate pulse and rhythm, for instance, as they sponge up everything they see and hear from the examples we provide through our playing or through recordings of great performances. If you're teaching a beginning-trombone class, for instance, your students would benefit most if you could provide a model of an excellent sound on the trombone—or at least provide great recordings of trombone players for your students to listen to frequently. Even models of more advanced students could help your students develop superior tonal concepts.

If we apply the principles of learning a language to how we might naturally learn musical skills, we might come up with a few basic guidelines:

1. Start with simple building blocks, in isolation, following a natural progression of
   a. Babbling—first sounds and guided "experimentation" on the instruments
   b. Words—isolated notes and rhythms, and
   c. Patterns of words—related notes and rhythms.
2. Learn combinations of notes and rhythms in context with a tonality or meter rather than in isolation.
3. Feedback and modeling are particularly important in guiding the development of our students. Model what you want to see and hear, and give immediate, specific feedback on what your students perform.
4. Help students develop "rules" of performance. Important concepts such as "hold notes out full value" or "sit as you stand" are very difficult to add later on in their development. Establish the foundations of playing efficiently and accurately early on.

How We Learn to Read

In the initial stages of learning to read text, we learn the individual letters and the sounds they make. Next, we begin to combine letters into words and begin to build a reading vocabulary. We notice that the patterns of letters make up words, and these words represent people, places, and things. In music, we learn individual notes and rhythmic figures and then put them together into more meaningful combinations of small micro-phrases or rhythmic patterns.

During this stage, children learn to pick out the differences between similar letters, such as *q*, *p*, *d*, and *b*, and individual words, such as *dog* and *cat* (Lapp and Flood 1986). Similarly, in music class, we help our students identify concepts such as "same and different," "shorter and longer," and "higher and lower." Developing these discrimination skills is important for comprehension in the musical world when it comes to relating what we read in musical notation to what we hear musically.

Eventually, we began to combine our written words into simple sentences. We learn to read sentences like, "See Jane run." Notice that our speaking vocabularies are often very far ahead of our reading vocabularies as we learn these new skills. This is an important consideration for music instruction; our playing abilities may, at first, far outpace our reading abilities. When we start to combine these words into sentences, we also learn to read new, unfamiliar words using context; we anticipate what words will come next based on our familiarity with what we've learned through speaking in our environment. We also learn to decode new words using rules we've learned about the basic sounds of letter combinations. It is this combination of a basic vocabulary of "sight words" and knowledge of how letter combinations usually sound that allow us to quickly develop our reading skill.

When we learn to read, we move from the known to the unknown; we first learn to read or decode words that we already know (Lapp and Flood 1986). When we begin to write, we also begin with words we already know. In most English-speaking countries, we also have stories read to us, which is an important part of reading development (Temple, et al. 1988). These two factors are important for us as music teachers; when we introduce notation, we should most likely begin by reading music that matches what we already know how to play. It can also be beneficial to have our students look at musical notation as it is being played as they develop their reading skill. Encourage students to read along as either you or other students play through familiar or unfamiliar music.

So how does our knowledge of reading letters, combining those letters into words, and then combining those words into sentences guide us as we make decisions about teaching musical literacy? First of all, notice that we learn to speak before we read, and we read before we write. In music class, we might follow that procedure in the following way:

1. Learn many tunes by rote (without music).
2. View the tunes *we've already learned by rote* as we listen to and perform them.
3. Learn the names of the notes, and label musical ideas after we are comfortable with the first two steps.
4. After we can read many familiar songs (those we've learned by rote), we can begin to read familiar rote songs *that we have not seen before*. This initial stage of decoding helps us associate the symbols of the music to the sounds in our ears.
5. After we read tunes that we know by ear, we can start to read new music that is totally unknown to us (we can read any "book" on our own).

We Also Learn to Write!

Eventually, after we have developed the skill of reading and writing many different words, we begin to be able to communicate our thoughts and ideas on paper through writing. As it turns out, learning to write is a bit more mysterious than learning to read. Discovery learning plays a huge role in acquiring the skills as we are given samples of writing to read and many opportunities to write as children. We begin by writing individual letters symbolizing small units of sound. We then begin writing complete words using combinations of letters and then later move on to writing complete sentences. Eventually, we are even able to use our writing to express our thoughts and feelings (Temple, et al. 1988).

So, as we ponder how reading text and music are alike, we are left to consider how writing text and writing music may be similar. We probably already give our students plenty of chances to see written music, but how often do we give our students opportunities to write music? Remember, as we begin to write music, we should initially begin notating sounds that we've already played. If we consider that we first write individual letters, we may begin by writing individual notes, then move on to writing meaningful patterns (combinations of notes or rhythms), and then move on to writing musical phrases of some type. Of course, as with writing, our creative writing abilities emerge only after a rather formulaic approach to developing mechanical-writing skills, and our writing usually lags behind our spoken (or playing) abilities. The important thing is that we give our students experience in writing music at the early stages and systematically work toward giving them a creative outlet through writing and arranging their own pieces.

How Reading Text and Reading Music Are Different

Of course, reading text and reading music are different in several important ways. First of all, unless you're dealing with a language such as Mandarin Chinese, there is a pitch element to reading music that is absent when reading text. In addition, characteristic tone quality is an important factor in the performance of music and is not necessarily an essential factor in conversational English. The elements of rhythm and meter are usually only encountered in poetry in the written and spoken word, but they are essential to most music. Another important difference between English and music is the fact that tonal music is based on a standard scale or a collection of notes in a particular mode. The *tonic note* is an important concept in tonal music; functional harmony helps us find "aural landmarks" that give us hints as to what notes might come next. Scale degrees within a given tonality have implied movement and direction in a tonal system that help knowledgeable players anticipate what notes might come next in a given passage. When compared to prose, music relies on repetition and familiarity, using patterns, both tonally and rhythmically, more than does the spoken word.

Another difference between letter decoding and musical interpretation is that some musical notation represents an *idea* rather than a *sound*. In music, a staccato symbol implies something stylistically, depending on the context. For instance, a staccato marking in a jazz chart would be played differently from a staccato in a Mozart serenade. The context makes all the difference.

Music Reading Philosophies

While the differences between learning to speak a language and learning the language of music may be complicating factors, we still can use principles taken from the language acquisition model and apply them to music teaching. Historically, music was taught much as language was taught. Musicians were taught using an apprenticeship model where a teacher would hand down the traditions and techniques of performance and would serve as a model for his students in the development of all aspects of his musicianship. In the 1850s, the use and availability of printing presses led to a widespread increase of publication of instrumental music methods. Some of the materials that teachers used in the apprenticeship model began to be written down and published on a mass scale for others to use. What was lost in the process of converting the oral tradition to written "methods" was the detail of the personal interaction between the mentor and the apprentice and the information that took place *beyond* the musical notation. Musical modeling was vital to the apprenticeship approach. Emphasis switched to finger drills and technical exercises in many of these publications, and fingerings began to be associated with notation rather than being associated with sounds. This type of arrangement continues to exist in some forms today. Only recently have band method books begun to include recordings and videos of great teachers playing as a supplement to written instruction. While most publishers of beginning methods probably assumed that teachers would model for their students and develop playing skills outside of the method books, some teachers undoubtedly just placed the books in front of their students, turned to page 1 of the book, and then worked line by line through the remainder of the book. The result of that process was that many students became "button pushers" who associated notation with the pressing down of buttons or closing of tone holes instead of with sounds they heard. If you've ever asked a student, "What's the name of that note?" and have had them respond, "First valve," then you've encountered a button pusher. Presenting a method book and beginning with page 1, without having taught a student how to produce a characteristic sound or by playing a few tunes by ear before reading tunes from the method book, would be like placing a novel in a baby's crib and expecting her to start learning how to read. As we have learned from language acquisition, babies learn to babble, they learn to speak, then they learn to read, and then they learn to write. As musicians, we should learn to perform without notation first, then learn to read music, and then learn to notate the music we play and imagine.

It may seem as if teaching musicians how to play first and then learning how to read musical notation is a relatively new idea. In reality, this approach has been used regularly for more than three hundred years. One of the first philosophers to emphasize experience through performance before learning the rules and terminology of a subject was John Heinrich Pestalozzi. His ideas were applied to music and brought to the United States by Joseph H. Naef and Lowell Mason in the late 1700s and early 1800s. Some of the main points from Pestalozzi and his advocates include the following:

1. Teach sounds before signs.
2. Children should sing before learning written notes and note names.
3. Teachers should lead children to active participation by teaching them to listen to and imitate sounds.
4. Students should talk about similarities and differences in what they hear and perform.
5. Teach students one new thing at a time; separate elements such as rhythm, melody, and expression before combining them.
6. Master one skill thoroughly before moving on to the next.
7. Theory and principles should grow out of experience through performance; teach the terminology and theoretical material after students have experienced them through playing. (Abeles, Hoffer, and Klotman 1994)

Another influential music teacher of the late nineteenth century was John Curwen in England. Many of Curwen's ideas about music learning mirror those of Pestalozzi, Naef, and Mason:

1. Let the easy come before the difficult.
2. Introduce the real and concrete before the ideal or abstract.
3. Teach the elemental before the compound, and do one thing at a time.
4. Introduce, both for explanation and practice, the common before the uncommon.
5. Teach the thing before the sign, and when the thing is apprehended, attach it to a distinct sign.
6. Let each step, as far as possible, rise out of that which goes before, and lead up to that which comes after.
7. Call in the understanding to assist the skill at every stage.[1]

Three great musicians and teachers, Emilie Jaques-Dalcroze, Zoltán Kodály, and Carl Orff, were particularly influenced by these approaches to teaching music. Each took these ideas and fashioned them to particular learning styles or teaching techniques that he found most effective.[2] Jaques-Dalcroze applied Pestalozzian principles to music teaching with an emphasis on the kinesthetic and aural learning styles. He believed that each student should be able to express musical ideas through *movement* before moving on to instruments, voice, or notation (Choksy, et al. 2001). Jaques-Dalcroze felt that the combined use of the ear and the body were the best vehicle for introducing and developing musical ideas.

Kodály emphasized a singing approach as the primary vehicle through which students developed musical literacy. In Kodály's view, musical skill is taken *to* instruments, after being developed through the voice, rather than learned from instruments. Kodály might have said, "If you can't sing it, you can't really play it!" Kodály emphasized use of functional solfège and familiar folk tunes to learn musical concepts (Choksy, et al. 2001).

Carl Orff thought that students learned best from experience through ensemble and individual performances. He felt that musical concepts were best solidified through imitation first, then experimentation, then creation. As with Pestalozzi, Mason, Jaques-Dalcroze, and Kodály, he felt strongly that the imitation, experimentation, and creative activities should happen *before* musical notation and theory were formally introduced (Choksy, et al. 2001).

Another important teacher whose philosophies were in line with these principles was Shinichi Suzuki. In the early twentieth century, Suzuki introduced what he called the "mother tongue" approach. He pointed out that Japanese children all learned how to speak Japanese, so we may gain an insight into musical learning from the ways these children learned to speak their language. Suzuki felt that it was early, informal education through experience and an aural approach that language skills naturally developed. Suzuki applied those thoughts to musical instruction and insisted that exposure to lessons should begin as early as possible and should be centered on the memorization of rote melodies. Suzuki felt that musical notation should only be introduced when absolutely necessary—when the notation would help students rather than inhibit their performances.

These ideas were expanded upon and codified in a very detailed way by Edwin Gordon in what he called "music learning theory" (Grunow, Gordon, and Azzara 2001). Gordon believes that each student should be taught to *audiate* music—to hear musical sound when no physical sound is present—when she looks at or thinks of a musical passage. Close your eyes and think of a group of your friends singing "Happy Birthday." Now try to imagine the sound of a tuning note being played on your instrument. If you can hear that music in your "mind's ear" you are audiating. Gordon believes that a specific sequence of deliberate, tonal, and rhythmic skill-development exercises can help students learn to audiate and become fluent, creative, literate musicians.

Gordon's skill-learning sequence is shown below in a simplified form in order to explore his philosophy:

1. Students hear musical patterns (aural), and then they sing it back to the teacher (oral). This stage, completed with the teacher and students singing neutral rhythmic and tonal syllables, is called the *aural/oral* stage.

2. Students assign a meaningful association between the words being spoken and the *function* of the notes through solfège and rhythmic syllables. For example, we label the interval C and E in the key of C major *do* and *mi*. Gordon calls this the *verbal association* stage.

3. The teacher then presents two- and three-note cells into meaningful rhythmic and tonal patterns (see figure 5.6 for an example of tonal patterns derived from the folk song "Lightly Row"). In this stage, students begin to experience the patterns they learned in the previous two stages in a meaningful context; for instance, the tonal patterns may move back and forth between tonic and dominant chords. This level is called *partial synthesis*.

4. Students are next called upon to audiate while they look at printed music as they perform the tonal and rhythmic patterns they have learned so far. At this stage, the students aren't reading the music, per se, but they are watching the music go by and are being asked to think about what the notes will sound like before they are played (Feldman and Contzius 2011). This stage is called *symbolic association*.

5. Students are now working to recognize tonality and meter as they perform, read, and write music. This is called *composite synthesis*.

The five stages outlined above work to help students recognize common melodic and rhythmic patterns—the "building blocks" of common-practice music—and pick out the meter and tonality of each. This entire process outlined above is referred to as *discrimination learning*. From here, students begin to learn new patterns, building on the patterns previously learned, to develop their reading skills. Creativity and improvisation become natural extensions of the learning process once the students have acquired these building blocks and become aurally familiar with them. Theoretical issues are only addressed after all of the above have been mastered.[3]

Most Important Commonalities among Philosophies of Musical Development

By looking at the ideas of Pestalozzi, Curwen, Jaques-Dalcroze, Kodály, Orff, Suzuki, and Gordon and considering how students learn to acquire

spoken and written language, nine themes emerge as important commonalities among all of these philosophies.

1. *Move from sound to sign to theory.* Just as we first learn to speak, then
   to read, then to write our spoken language, we should first play, then
   read, then write our musical language. What begins as rote imitation
   leads to meaningful interpretation. Training the ear is the primary way
   to enlighten the musical mind. Start with rote tunes, and then introduce notation as students develop.
2. *Sing it before you play it.* If you can truly audiate the music—if you can
   hear it in your mind's ear—then you should be able to reproduce the
   music with your voice. Students can demonstrate their musical understanding through their voices in this way.
3. *Learn many songs by rote.* To emulate the ways we absorb the spoken
   communication that leads to our ability to speak and read and write,
   we should establish a solid background of familiar songs that teach us
   about playing our instruments. What kind of tunes should you play?
   Where can you find these tunes? Begin by examining the material in
   the many beginning-band method books that are available. If you use
   a beginning-band method, find the most familiar and popular tunes
   in the book, and begin to teach those to your students before encoun-
   tering musical notation. Find out what tunes your students know and
   enjoy from elementary school or summer camp. Even popular songs
   or television themes can be adapted and learned by rote. You'll find
   that your students already know a lot of tunes; your job is to sequence
   them appropriately.
4. *Teach one new thing at a time.* It may sound obvious, but teach easy
   skills before moving on to complex skills. What makes this difficult is
   being able to identify which skills are easy and which are complex; it's
   not always as obvious as it seems. Breaking down a musical skill into
   its individual parts, particularly those skills that you may execute automatically as an accomplished performer, is sometimes difficult. Consider assembling your instrument. You probably flip open your case
   and grab the sections of your instrument and assemble them in a few
   seconds. Breaking that fairly complex skill into its parts takes some
   thought and consideration of the viewpoint of the inexperienced
   beginner (and consideration of the typical middle-school student's
   coordination and development of fine-motor skills). We might first
   need to know how to identify if our case is facing up or not. We then
   might need to know the names of the various parts of the instrument.
   We might also need to know about where to grasp each of the parts
   so that we don't damage the instrument. When you analyze all of the

skills involved, a task as "simple" as opening your case and putting your instrument together becomes a fairly complex activity.

Isolate elements before putting them together; the "putting to-gether" part is one new thing that teachers sometimes forget. Let's say you decided to isolate a difficult measure in one of your beginning-band tunes into three steps. You might (1) have your students clap and count the measure in question, (2) have them play the rhythm on their starting note from that measure, and (3) have them finger through the notes of that measure while counting. If you just moved from clapping and counting to playing, you might pass one or more important steps and lose some of your students.

5. *Move from the known to the unknown.* Build on what your students can already do or what they already know. Try to relate new material to skills they can already perform or to concepts they already under-stand. When I first started teaching beginners, I assumed that I was teaching my students how to count rhythms for the first time. My eyes were opened when I went to visit one of the elementary schools whose students would attend my middle school and saw that the music teacher, who had formal training in the Kodály method, was teaching the students how to count the same rhythms to her fifth-grade students (using ta and ti-ti) that I was "introducing" to my sixth graders (using numbers and "ands" for the down- and up-beats). Teaching rhythms to my sixth graders the next year was so much easier because I related the "new way" of counting to what they had already been taught (quite skillfully, I might add) in elementary school. By starting on solid ground, you help ensure that students are successful when they start a new activity, and then you can build off that success to the new knowledge or skill.

6. *Teach whole-part-whole.* This concept is based on the ideas of intro-ducing one new thing at a time and moving from the known to the unknown. Present the entire piece of music first so students will understand what they're learning; then divide that tune into smaller, digestible sections that can be easily taught to the students. Finally, help your students recombine the parts to perform the whole piece. We'll look into the whole-part-whole model later on in this chapter.

7. *Master a skill before moving on.* Many young teachers make the mistake of trying to move too quickly. These teachers are often afraid that their students will become bored or that they won't be able to get to all of the necessary material their students need to know. Moving quickly may force students to move forward before important fundamentals are established. Take your time so that each student can be successful and build upon a solid foundation.

8. *Make frequent use of models.* Another common mistake many teachers make is that they talk too much. If a picture is worth a thousand words, then a musical model is worth a million. Don't talk about a musical concept when you could model it instead. You'll find that speaking less and playing more will communicate your musical ideas in a shorter amount of time. If you're able, model on the student's instrument with a great sound and solid technique. A great way to do this is with the call-and-response technique; the teacher models first, and then the students imitate the teacher's model. It's best to do this without explanation first. After students master imitating the teacher's model, then the teacher can go back and explain whatever concept they're working toward.

Experienced students make great models as well. While students might be impressed with your playing, they may view the accomplishments of an experienced student a more achievable goal. Younger students may think, "Gee, if she can play that, maybe I can do that next year." Peer modeling is a great teaching tool as well. As long as your students have been taught the proper way to give positive feedback, they can listen to and comment upon their peers playing in a constructive way. Playing the "same/different" game (for instance, select a student with a steady tone versus a student who has a wobbly sound) is a positive way to use peer models. If you're not a great performer on the instrument that you're teaching, you can utilize great recordings that feature professional technique and tone. It's best to develop the ability to play a few simple notes, with great tone quality and accuracy, on every instrument you intend to teach.

9. *Engage your classes using different learning styles.* Get up and move to connect with your kinesthetic learners. Provide diagrams and draw pictures for your visual learners. Make sure your aural learners are hearing you, as well as others; play as much as possible so that they absorb the ideas you're trying to get across in the most efficient way.

STARTING WITH SOUND

If we accept the premise that students learn to read and write music most efficiently if they experience activities that allow them to learn how to read and write text, then it stands to reason that we should approach beginning-band instruction with the introduction of simple sounds of the musical language. Since we learn to speak before we learn to interpret the sounds that letters and combinations of letters represent, we should learn a large repertoire of songs by rote before we learn the names of notes and what they look like on the page. Even before we touch our instruments in the band class, we can begin to develop a common repertoire of easy rote tunes that will help us transition from playing by ear to reading music. To recap, the most efficient and natural progression of teaching beginners to play, read, and write music is to

1. Learn many tunes by rote (sound)
2. Learn how to read those rote tunes (sign)
3. Learn the "rules" involved in reading those tunes (theory)
4. Discover how to apply the rules of note reading to learn other tunes and how to begin to notate the sounds we hear in our minds and play on our instruments (musical literacy)

Chapter 7 addresses setting up your students for success by teaching them the fundamentals of breathing, posture, and the first notes on their instruments. The remainder of this chapter addresses the process of teaching rote tunes to students after they can produce individual notes and small combinations of notes with a characteristic tone quality.

The process of beginning with rote tunes without music also helps prevent information overload for our students. Imagine the frustration of a beginner trying to manipulate his completely assembled instrument, his music, a music stand, all the while trying to sit with great posture, good hand position, breathe correctly, form an embouchure . . . It's just a lot to think about all at once!

Teaching Rote Tunes

One of the most efficient ways of teaching rote tunes to beginners is by utilizing a *whole-part-whole* approach. Using this method, we begin by singing the entire piece (the first *whole*), then we break the larger piece to learn more manageable parts (two or more *parts*), and then put all of the pieces back together to perform the final *whole*. We'll break this procedure down into seven steps.

1. *Select an appropriate tune.* This tune may be a popular song, a tune students already know, or a selection from the beginning-band method book that they may encounter at a later date. When selecting an appropriate tune, keep in mind the Pestalozzian principles discussed in the first part of the chapter: start with simple tunes, move slowly by adding new concepts gradually, and build on what students know to introduce new ideas and skills. We'll use the folk tune "Hot Cross Buns" as an example to illustrate the following steps.
2. *Establish tonality.* Before teaching the first notes of the tune, you'll need to place them into the context of a tonality by singing a few notes

Figure 2.1. "Hot Cross Buns"

to establish the tonal "home base" for the piece. You might sing the tonic triad or a simple scale, but be sure to place the starting notes of the tune into context. Our "Hot Cross Buns" example begins on the third scale degree (*mi*), so we should precede the first notes by singing something like that shown in fig. 2.1.

3. *Sing through the entire piece* (*whole*). Singing through the entire piece provides the students with an overview of the tune. As students develop, they will begin to notice more of the structural and musical elements in the initial run-through of the *whole*. They'll start to say things like, "I've heard this song before," or "The last part of this song sounds like the first part." At first, they may only perceive these things on a subliminal level, but even in the initial stages, they begin to assemble a structure for the entire piece with minimal formal instruction or explanation.

   Use solfège to teach the rote tunes so that students begin to learn how the notes relate to each other in a given tonality. Using the words of the folk song or neutral syllables, such as "doo," does not help them learn the function of each degree of the scale, which is important when learning to improvise, compose, or to play music by ear. Using specific note names prevents them from applying their functional knowledge of the piece to different keys and creates confusion when teaching transposing instruments in the same class.

4. *Divide the song into logical musical segments* (*part*). This tune naturally breaks down in to four segments of two bars each. Notice that the first two measures, bars 3 and 4, and the last two bars are identical; measures 5 and 6 are the only musical material that is different. Realizing this helps you as a teacher understand that you really only have to teach four different measures to your students in order for them to be able to perform the piece (fig. 2.2).

   As you move through this process, you might use some probing questions such as, "Have we heard these three notes together like this before? Is this a new pattern or a different one?" or "Does this chunk

Figure 2.2. "Hot Cross Buns" echo style

of music begin on the same note?" in order to help your students create structure for their understanding.

Selecting the "parts" of the music you want to teach is sometimes challenging. Keep your students' cognitive and musical abilities in mind as you decide how long or short the "parts" should be. Short-term memory is not always as developed for younger students, so keeping the segments shorter is usually better. Usually, your tune will provide you with musical clues that help you decide how long the "chunks" will be; four-bar phrases break down into two-bar parts, or you may get clues from the text of the song. Keep in mind that musical phrases do not always align with the bar lines of the printed music.

Once you've selected your small segments, don't be afraid to make adjustments as you teach. Your students may be struggling to get the parts as you've presented them because the segments you have selected are too long to memorize or for them to process, or the students may be learning the tune more quickly than you imagined. Start with a plan, but feel free to adjust your plan to suit your students.

5. *Review the parts as necessary.* If you are teaching a complex tune with many parts, you may need to go back and review segments you've worked on earlier to reestablish the music in the students' minds. If you find that your students do not comprehend the parts when you review, feel free to make adjustments so that they understand and can be successful with the parts before you combine the parts into larger chunks.

6. *Combine smaller parts into larger segments.* Once your students can successfully perform the smallest units of your piece, begin to combine those parts into larger "chunks." The first four bars of "Hot Cross Buns" can be combined into one large chunk of material, and the last four bars can be combined into a second large chunk. The second large chunk begins differently from the first large chunk but ends

the same. Once again, ask some probing questions of your students to help them notice the similarities and differences between the two larger chunks to help your students make sense of the musical structure and start to develop the "rules" that guide musical performance and composition.

7. *Sing through the entire piece (whole)*. Now that your students can perform the smallest parts and can combine those small chunks into larger segments, they are ready to sing through the entire piece. The whole-part-whole process is complete. If your students can sing this tune using solfège, they can more easily apply this tune to the first notes they learn on their instruments and can later play this tune in a variety of different keys as their technique and range develop. If your students know a lot of tunes by ear, using solfège, the transition to playing their instruments and reading music will be easier.

Applying Rote Tunes to Instruments

After your students are able to recall and sing a wide variety of tunes by ear using solfège and after they are able to play the notes used in the tune you wish to play with centered, characteristic sounds, the students are ready to move those tunes onto their instruments (see chapter 7). You will have taught each of the notes in the song in isolation—one at a time—until the students can reliably master starting and stopping each note. Also consider how you'll handle consecutive notes on the same pitch for the woodwind and brass performers; if your students will articulate each note, they'll need to be able to use their tongues to distinguish between consecutive notes on the same pitch (such as bar 5 of "Hot Cross Buns").

Carefully study your rote tune, and think about the aural skills, the rhythmic skills, and the executive skills your students will need in order to perform the piece successfully. Identifying the challenges in these three areas will help you make decisions about how to introduce the song to your students.

AURAL SKILLS, RHYTHMIC SKILLS, AND EXECUTIVE SKILLS

Breaking down the fundamentals of musical performance involves three broad categories of aural, rhythmic, and executive skills. Each of these is discussed in more depth in chapter 7.

Aural skills relate to the students' ability to audiate and interpret what they hear in a functional way. Audiation, as you will recall, is the ability to hear music in the mind's ear when no music is present. The key to audiation is that it contains a functional component—in other words, you not only hear the tune to "Happy Birthday" as you hear it in your mind's ear, but also you understand that the first four notes of that song *function* as *sol-sol-la-sol* in the key in which you are singing. Our students' ability to audiate can help them play more accurately and helps them make musical sense of what they are playing.

Rhythmic skills involve the ability to perform the rhythmic challenges of the piece. When working on rhythmic skills, it often helps to play the rhythms involved in a particular passage on one note. In this way, you can isolate the rhythms by eliminating any note changes.

Executive skills involve the physical manipulation of the fingers and/ or the embouchure in order to play a given passage. Executive-skills issues can also be effectively addressed through isolation. Perform the passage in question by removing the rhythmic element of the passage and playing only the notes in question. See chapter 8 for more ideas on rehearsing aural, rhythmic, and executive skills.

Scan the Piece for Executive-Skill Challenges

Realize that, as we develop the fine-motor skills of manipulating the fingers on a wind instrument, musical steps are easier than skips or leaps. Teachers generally introduce consecutive notes (E, F, G) before they start to change the order of notes. Identify any places in the tune where the students encounter notes "out of order" from the musical alphabet. Even when we change the order of consecutive, stepwise notes, we increase the difficulty of the executive skill: *mi, re, do* actually *feels* different for the young performer from *do, re, mi.* Moving fingers quickly is a part of developing fine-motor skill on all the instruments. In general, moving notes with faster rhythms are more challenging than slower rhythms.

Consider the folk tune "Long, Long Ago" as an example (fig. 2.3). The tune begins with consecutive, stepwise notes up the scale, but in bar 2, we change directions from ascending to descending. Bar 2 also features a downward skip of a third. Bar 4 concludes with an upward leap of a perfect

Figure 2.3. "Long, Long Ago"

fifth. Each of these elements presents executive-skill challenges for the fingers and for brass embouchures.

Scan the Piece for Aural-Skill Challenges

Sometimes our students miss notes not because they have trouble with fingerings of the notes but because they cannot audiate the correct pitches. If students cannot sing or audiate the music, they may have trouble performing the same music with their instruments. As with the students' executive skills, consecutive notes with stepwise motion are easier to audiate and sing than are skips or leaps. Leaps can be particularly challenging for brass players when those leaps skip notes in the harmonic series. If a trumpet player moves from a first-space F in the treble clef to a fourth-line D (both fingered with the first-valve), she has to skip the B♭ in the first-valve harmonic series. If she has the ability to audiate and sing a major sixth (F to D), she will be more successful moving between those two notes and may also be *more aware that she is playing the major sixth* that she hears in her mind's ear. What may seem to be executive-skill errors are often aural-skills challenges in disguise; if a student cannot play a particular passage, check to see if he can sing it before turning your attention to potential executive-skill problems.

Scan the Piece for Rhythmic Challenges

At first glance, identifying rhythmic challenges may seem fairly simple. New rhythms and "fast notes" are difficult, but there are other issues that often give students trouble rhythmically. Long notes often give performers trouble; be sure that students hold all notes with longer rhythmic values out to the very end of the note. This is especially true for notes at the ends of phrases or long notes followed by rests. If your students have developed a strong habit of holding individual notes out full value before they learn tunes, this will be easier to reinforce. Rests are often a challenge for younger performers as well; remind them that silence is as important as sound in music. Be certain students hold notes before rests their full value to prevent students from rushing through the rests. Pickup notes are often rhythmically challenging. Finally, be aware of any syncopations or other places where the rhythm of the music moves in opposition to the natural rhythms of our bodies and limbs as we move through space.

Once you've identified areas that might present challenges for aural, rhythmic, and executive skills, isolate these spots, and work on the individual issues prior to introducing the piece. Using the "Long, Long Ago" example, you might isolate the *do-sol* skip in bar 4 by singing, then singing and fingering, and finally by playing those two notes in isolation. If the students can successfully play through those two notes separately, they are more likely to pick up this "tricky" combination more quickly when they learn the tune on their instruments.

After you've identified and isolated these spots, it is time to introduce the rote tune to your class on their instruments. The procedure is much the same as teaching a rote tune to your students using their voices, but the added manipulation of the instruments, coupled with the physical skills needed to perform on the instruments, leaves us with a few more details to fill in. The procedures outlined below assume you're teaching a song that the students already know and can sing through easily using solfège. If they have not learned the song before, you'll need to follow the steps outlined earlier in the "Teaching Rote Tunes" section (see p. 33).

1. *Establish tonality.*
2. *Sing through the entire piece (whole).* As with your presentation of the song before, you'll want your students to know the entire large form of the piece.
3. *Point out where any aural, rhythmic, or executive skills you worked on earlier occur.* If you worked on fingering a particular combination of notes, you might point out that they occur in a particular place in the music. This helps your students connect the "new" song with the skill they just worked on prior to starting the piece.
4. *Sing and finger through the parts.* The teacher sings each part; then the students echo by singing and fingering the notes as they sing. Singing while fingering helps the students connect what their fingers do with the musical sounds they sing and will play.
5. *Play through the parts.* Once the students can successfully sing and manipulate their fingers while singing, it is time to play the small (one- or two-bar) segments. Be sure that almost every student can sing and finger with ease; if you spot anyone having trouble, isolate the problem areas, and move more slowly. It is usually helpful to hold out the first note of the tune so the students can "find" their beginning notes and start off the tune with a feeling of confidence. This is particularly helpful for brass players.
6. *Sing and finger through the entire piece (whole).*
7. *Play through the entire piece.*

This process may seem slow or overly simplified, but remember the developmental aspects of what we're asking our students to accomplish. The students must be able to hear, sing, and then perform simple to complex musical ideas all while manipulating their instruments using fine- and gross-motor skills that are, in many cases, undergoing an incredible period of development. The fairly complex skills that accomplished musicians take for granted are often very challenging for younger learners.

Moving in this way also helps develop some important musical-literacy skills. If students can really audiate these tunes, if they can sing them using solfège to help them understand the function of each note in the tune, if they understand what the notes they sing and play represent tonally, then they can perform these tunes in *any key* using notes they know. If they really develop this type of aural awareness and understanding, they can also figure out how to play *any song* that they are able to sing. This understanding opens up a door for your students to play tunes by ear and to improvise and compose more fluently. Share this information with your students to help keep them motivated to learn to sing and play by ear.

Three Myths about Rote Teaching

Some teachers are very skeptical about teaching by rote. There are three commonly held myths that prevent many teachers from utilizing this powerful teaching technique.

Myth number 1: My students will never learn to read music. Perhaps the greatest fear teachers have is that their students will never learn to read music if they learn to play by ear. It is true that if the connection between rote songs and melodies is never made with decoding notation, students may fail to develop music-reading skills. This is why it is important that teachers associate musical notation with what they are actually playing. Hold students accountable for being able to decode written music.

The traditional method of band instruction requires students to associate written notation with the pressing of buttons or closing of particular tone holes. This creates all sorts of problems later in the students' musical lives, such as not being able to hear missing key signature errors or being unaware if one is in the wrong octave on flute. When students learn to associate what they hear in their mind's ear with notation on the page, they have a greater chance of becoming *musical problem solvers* rather than *mechanical button pushers.*

Myth number 2: We'll never cover all the information in the beginning book if I teach this way; my students will be behind the students at XYZ school! In some ways, teaching rote songs before introducing the notation does take more time than the traditional approach to teaching band in the initial stages of instruction. However, the skills developed in the rote-teaching phase help to develop solid fundamental playing skills without the distraction of decoding notation. The aural skills developed in the initial stages of playing, if properly associated with note reading, will greatly *speed* progress when notation is introduced. The technical difficulties of each beginner line have already been addressed before the students are required to tackle the notational intricacies of each line, and the skills associated with each piece are reinforced when they are encountered a second time in the note-reading phase. Most teachers find that their students are able to read music and move *faster* through subsequent material than students taught in the traditional way.

Myth number 3: This is some radical new way of teaching. The rote-before-note teaching approach is neither radical nor new. Most teachers remember their own experience of starting on page one of a method book and then moving line by line through the book until they were finished. As we mentioned before, this approach not only introduces many new things at once (note reading, posture, hand position, embouchure formation, etc.), but it is completely disconnected from how people learn to read text. Imagine putting a page of "easy" words in front of a kindergarten student and working line by line through a book of text. No doubt some of the students might pick up on reading text this way, but a vast majority would likely fall behind from the very beginning.

As we have seen, the principles of sound-before-sign theory can be traced back to Lowell Mason in his guidelines for public-school music instruction written in the 1830s. The general concept of relating the skills of musical performance with those of learning a spoken language can be traced back to Shinichi Suzuki in the early 1900s. The primary method of teaching music up until the 1800s was through an apprentice system where the master teacher taught the young protégé skills and techniques through imitation. Many early jazz musicians learned their trade through the call-and-response techniques and by imitating more experienced players.

MOVING BEYOND SOUND TO SIGN AND THEORY

Your students can sing and play a select repertoire of music on their instruments, but how do you get your students to *read* new music? How do you prevent your students from being totally dependent on someone else to teach them all of the notes and rhythms in each song that they will need to learn? Again, we take our cues from the world of reading written text. After we have learned the basics of speaking a language, we can begin to associate the symbols of written text with *words and phrases we already know*. We then begin to pick up on the "rules" of language and the printed word so we can begin to read new sentences. Eventually, we codify the whole language-reading process into rules and develop a concept of the grammatical use of the language.

After your students know a great many rote tunes, you can begin to "read" the music associated with those tunes. At first, your students will only follow along as they play through these familiar tunes while they follow the musical notation, but eventually you can help them make the connections to reading the music. Begin to establish reading skills by asking leading questions such as, "On which note did we start this tune? Is it on a line or a space in the music?" or "Which way do the notes go on the staff as we play lower? Which way are we going in the musical alphabet as we play lower?" At this point, it is the teacher's job to connect what the students can play with the musical notation.

How can you be sure that your students are actually reading the music and not just playing from memory or by ear? One of the best ways is by calling on students to identify and discriminate between various musical passages or note combinations. For instance, show your students a set of four musical patterns made up of a few notes like the ones below. Play or sing one of the sets of notes for the class, and ask them to identify which one you played. The students must be able to "read" the music in order to answer correctly consistently (fig. 2.4).

Another activity is to have your students read a line of music silently and identify the name of the song. If we can develop this aural imagery in our students' minds, we are well on our way to developing strong musical-literacy skills in our beginning-band students. Keep in mind that, just as students read text that is simpler than what they are able to speak, the musical tunes your students read will initially be simpler than what they are able to play.

Introducing Music Theory

Even as students begin to learn to speak, they pick up many of the subtle "rules" of grammar and pronunciation. As they continue to learn to read, they pick up more and more of these rules as they become accustomed to reading. Eventually, students are guided in developing more formal rules for grammar and composition. As our students learn to play and read music, they are picking up on the subtle cues and "rules" of our musical language. Eventually, as students begin to read music, they will need to understand concepts of music theory.

Figure 2.4.   Discrimination of musical patterns

In a traditional, notation-based system, many music theory concepts are taught at the same time as the students are asked to decipher musical notation. In a sound-to-sign-to-theory model, students are asked to label and analyze only the most important items *after* they have encountered them in their playing. In this approach, theoretical concepts are only introduced when the students really need to know them; if a teacher can wait to introduce a term or the theoretical concept, she should do so.

This does *not* mean that we gloss over important musical concepts in order to learn a bunch of tunes! It would be educational malpractice to graduate a student from his or her first year of playing and not know the names of the notes on a staff or the definition of an embouchure. If we encounter a topic in our music or if we need to understand a particular musical issue in order to play our music better, then we need to introduce that concept to our students.

Let's look at a musical example to illustrate how this concept might work. The English nursery rhyme "Row, Row, Row Your Boat" is often performed as a round. When we first introduce this tune by rote, we might introduce our students to the term "round." When we then encounter this music in our beginning-band book, we might point out that, in order to perform this piece as a round, we might include a notated repeat sign. Each of these terms (*round* and *repeat sign*) is an important musical concept that we would want our students to understand. If they encounter these terms through performance—by *experiencing* the musical concept firsthand—they are more likely to understand and remember these concepts than if they write down the definitions before they have had a chance to play them.

As your students learn to perform by ear, read musical notation, and develop theoretical understanding, try to engage aural, visual, and kinesthetic learners as they develop each of these skills. Have each of your students keep a theory notebook as a part of his or her daily materials for class. As you encounter musical terms, have students write the term and definition, using age-appropriate language, in their notebooks. Print the notes on the board, and use diagrams and pictures to aid your visual learners. Play and sing musical examples for your aural learners. Think of ways to move to stimulate the kinesthetic learners. Specific music theory concepts that are important to include in your program are outlined in chapter 5.

REAL LIFE APPLICATION OF THE
SOUND-TO-SIGN-TO-THEORY APPROACH

In a perfect world, students learn a great body of rote songs, then how to assemble, hold, and play notes on their instruments, then play their repertoire of tunes on their instruments, next read familiar and new material, and finally develop their theoretical knowledge. In real life, we often teach the physical skills, aural skills, and theoretical knowledge in three separate streams that eventually converge during the first year of instruction. Here are a couple of examples of how we might teach in each of the three streams during different stages of a beginning-band class.

Beginner Class: Example One

1. Class enters the room with a listening activity (aural)
2. Posture review (physical)
3. Rhythm echo—teacher models the rhythm of the day; students echo (aural)
4. Breathing exercise (physical)
5. Teacher helps set each student's embouchure on mouthpieces; students play block notes on their mouthpieces (physical)
6. Draw block notes in notebook (theoretical)
7. Learn a new rote song (aural)
8. Sing a song we already know (aural)

Beginner Class: Example Two

1. Class enters the room with a listening activity (aural)
2. Breathing exercise (physical)
3. Review rote song we learned yesterday (aural)
4. Continue theory notes—*staff, bar line,* and *measure* (theoretical)
5. Students play through rote song learned yesterday, and the teachers asks questions to review how the bar lines work in this song (theoretical)
6. Play one of our favorite rote songs (aural, physical)

In the examples above we addressed a few physical skills, aural skills, and relevant theoretical skills in each lesson. Ideally, we'd want to construct activities that address each learning style during each of these activities. This variety helps keep students active and interested throughout the lessons.

Developmental Differences

Learning to play, read, and understand the theoretical concepts of music are complex activities. All of our students, being unique individuals, will excel at times and have difficulty at others, depending on their own strengths and weaknesses. Some of our students have profound developmental differences that may impact how they learn and progress. Some students have specific, identified disabilities and may have individual education plans with modifications that must be included in your instruction (see chapter 1 for details). The University of Texas Center for Music Learning website offers specific recommendations for helping students with a wide variety of developmental differences. Consider these strategies to help you work with students who are dealing with a few common developmental issues.

Hearing Impaired

It is important that you know the degree of hearing loss of students who have been identified as hearing impaired. It may also be helpful to understand particular frequencies that the student has trouble hearing or understanding. You may find that amplifying your voice is helpful in some situations, and you should consider how to best position loudspeakers for voice reinforcement and playing musical examples.

Many hearing-impaired students lip-read and need to be seated so they can see your mouth clearly. Avoid talking with a brass mouthpiece on your lips or a woodwind mouthpiece in your mouth. If a student has mild hearing loss, seat that student near you so she can hear you more easily. Provide written notes and outlines when possible, and be sure that videos you use have captions.

Some students might have a paraprofessional aide or a classroom buddy who helps take notes or interpret your speech through sign language. If any of these students use sign language, consider learning as much as you can.

Vision Impaired

Vision-impaired students can benefit from using music Braille. Many people are unaware that Louis Braille was a blind music teacher who developed systems to help blind students learn to read both text and music. Students who have only mild vision impairment may benefit from having music enlarged on a photocopier. These students can greatly benefit from having access to practice CDs or other recordings of the music. Students with more profound vision loss should be given the opportunity to visit the classroom before school begins in order to gain familiarity with the room setup, and you should avoid major adjustments to the layout of the room so that these students can maneuver safely. These students may need more time to set up and pack away their instruments and supplies and may require more time to move between classes (Lapp and Flood 1986).

Speech Impairment

Students with cognitive-speech or language-development impairments often have trouble relating aural speech skills to visual written skills. This same issue may arise in reading music; they may have trouble connecting what they hear to what they read. Since music activates more areas of the brain than does speech, some of these students may have *less* trouble learning to perform and read music. Remember that individuals may excel in the arts even if they are held back in other academic pursuits.

Dyslexia

More students are beginning to be diagnosed with a wide variety of specific learning disabilities related to dyslexia. These disabilities interfere with their ability to perceive or process information in the brain. Oglethorpe (2008) points out that dyslexia is a visual and aural phenomenon; the syndrome affects areas of vision, hearing, and speech.

Some people mistakenly believe that dyslexia only involves mixing up of letters or numbers. While this is true in some cases, others find that text (including musical notation) may appear thinner or thicker in places, may have rivers of white space between letters, words, or lines, or they may even perceive printed text as moving in space. Dyslexic students often have trouble shifting visual planes (Oglethorpe 2008). Moving focus from the music to a conductor and back or even shifting the focus from one line of music to the next may give these students trouble. Some dyslexic students have difficulty distinguishing between right and left hands and feet—a particular concern for our percussionists.

Different tools are available to aid students depending on the type and severity of their dyslexia. We can help some students by simply enlarging their music on a photocopier. Colored, acetate overlays and the use of colored highlighters help other students. Dyslexic students often need to be given more time to complete written assignments.

Bilingual and English Language Learners

Many communities have an abundance of immigrants who are new English speakers. These students and their families present special challenges to the music educator. If a majority of your English language learners speaks a particular language, it will help to learn some basic terminology and a few phrases in that language. Drawing upon their previous musical knowledge is especially helpful. Knowing that a *quaver* in Great Britain is the same thing as an *eighth note* in the United States may make your students more successful when that topic is discussed in class. Getting your Spanish-speaking students to equate *redonda* to the term *whole note* may make teaching these concepts easier.

If your school has an English language learner program, you can obtain data from the teachers to see how much English your students can read or speak. English learners are particularly appreciative of using written and verbal language along with diagrams and pictures when possible. Remember that a great deal of our musical concepts can be best taught without speaking at all! Learning the language of music may help some of our new students learn the English language easier.

FIELD EXPERIENCE CONNECTIONS

1. If you've taken a developmental reading class, take out your textbook or notes from that course, and see what topics or strategies you can apply to teaching music reading.
2. Teach a small section or beginner class a simple rote tune. Use the steps listed on page 39.
3. Flip open a beginning-band method book. Identify the first line that features a recognizable melody (one you might sing while walking down the hallway). What executive skills are needed to play this piece? Is this piece notated using the same rhythms one might use when singing? Why or why not?
4. Select a line from the first few pages of a beginner-band method book. Analyze the piece of music for what executive-skill, aural-skill, and rhythmic-skill challenges exist.

REFERENCES

Abeles, H. F., C. F. Hoffer, and R. H. Klotman. 1994. *Foundations of music education.* 2nd ed. New York: Schirmer.

Choksy, L., R. M. Abramson, A. Gillespie, D. Woods, and F. York. 2001. *Teaching music in the twenty-first century.* Englewood Cliffs, NJ: Prentice Hall.

Feldman, E., and A. Contzius. 2011. *Instrumental music education: Teaching with the musical and practical in harmony.* New York: Routledge.

Grunow, R. E, E. E. Gordon, and C. D. Azzara. 2001. *Jump right in: The instrumental series; Teacher's guide.* Books 1 and 2. Chicago: GIA. "Used by permission."

Haston, W. 2007. Modeling as an effective teaching strategy. *Music Educators Journal* 93 (4): 26–30.

Jordan-DeCarbo, J. 1997. A sound-to-symbol approach to learning music. *Music Educators Journal* 84 (2): 34–37, 54.

Landers, R. 1980. *The talent education school of Shinichi Suzuki: An analysis.* Athens, OH: Ability Development.

Lapp, D., and J. Flood. 1986. *Teaching students to read.* New York: Macmillan.

Oglethorpe, S. 2008. *Instrumental music for dyslexics: A teaching handbook.* 2nd ed. Hoboken, NJ: John Wiley.

Schleuter, S. 1997. *A sound approach to teaching instrumentalists.* 2nd ed. New York: Schirmer.

Suzuki, S. 1983. *Nurtured by love: The classical approach to talent education.* Princeton, NJ: Summy-Birchard.
Temple, C., R. Nathan, N. Burris, and F. Temple. 1988. *The beginnings of writing.* 2nd ed. Boston: Allyn and Bacon.

WEBSITES

University of Texas Center for Music Learning. Disabilities information. http://cml .music.utexas.edu/online-resources/disabilities-information/introduction/
Smaligo, M. A. 1999. *Resources for helping blind music students.* Available online at http://nfb.org/braille-music
Australian Music Education Information and Resources. The Curwen method. www. australian-music-ed.info/Curwen/Ped&TchngTechs.html.

NOTES

1. From John Curwen's *Teacher's manual* c. 1876. http://www.australian-music-ed.info/Curwen/Ped&TchngTechs.html.

2. Choksy, et al. (2001) provide excellent examples of applying the teaching methods of Jaques-Dalcroze, Kodály, and Orff to middle-school and older music students.

3. See Grunow, Gordon, and Azzara (2001) for detailed information on Gordon's music learning theory applied to instrumental instruction.

II

DEVELOPING FUNDAMENTAL SOUNDS AND MUSIC-DECODING SKILLS

3

First Sounds on Wind Instruments

Among the many "firsts" encountered in beginning band, the initial sounds produced on the instrument are perhaps the most important. Mistakes, misinformation, or incorrect embouchures are extremely difficult to correct after poor fundamentals have been established. Use the body as naturally as possible, introduce one new concept or skill at a time, and move from what students know to what they do not. Present the foundations of excellent posture and efficient breathing, then move on to the first sounds on the "small instruments," and finally move to making the first notes on the complete instrument. Each of these steps is presented in greater detail below.

POSTURE

The most fundamental concept of playing wind and percussion instruments is efficient posture. Students should stand in a lifted, balanced stance so that the mechanisms of breathing can work well. Introduce posture without instruments in the following steps:

1. Stand with *feet about shoulder width* apart with arms relaxed at the sides of the body.
2. *Balance your weight* evenly side to side and front to back. Help students find their "center" by shifting their weight forward, back, and side to side, then move back again to the middle, balanced position.
3. *Stand tall* with hips, shoulders, and head aligned but relaxed. Students might visualize themselves as a puppet hanging from a string attached to the top of their head.

4. Slightly *lift the upper body* to open up the chest cavity. Students might visualize an invisible puppet master gently lifting up on the imaginary string attached to the top of their head.
5. Keep the *shoulders relaxed and rounded*.
6. Have students memorize what their bodies feel like as they stand. Pay particular attention to what their upper bodies—the part of the body from their belt-line up—feel like. Keep this feeling when seated.

Insist on natural, relaxed, but lifted posture each time a new concept is introduced. This is our "home base" for great musicianship. Every time a new concept or skill is introduced, remember to check that each player demonstrates great posture.

EFFICIENT BREATHING

Establishing great posture is the first major step toward efficiency in breathing for wind players. With a lifted and aligned posture, the chest cavity is free and open to allow the lungs to expand to their fullest. Students can then work to develop efficient inflow and outflow of air and can develop capacity for taking in larger volumes of air. Efficient airflow is important as students fill up their lungs to play their instruments. Students will find it much easier to play if they fill up their "oxygen tanks" before the big mission. Efficient airflow into the body looks and sounds a particular way. Share these breathing checkpoints with your students and their parents so that they can monitor their practice:

1. *Efficient airflow is free of extra motion.* Keep the shoulders, head, and upper body relaxed and still when breathing in. Some students try to raise their shoulders when they take a breath to play an instrument. This movement causes all sorts of problems. In addition to being an inefficient use of the body, it often causes the embouchure to move in relationship to the instrument.
2. *Efficient airflow is quiet.* The throat should be relaxed, and the tongue should be out of the way as breath moves into the body. Have your students yawn; if the students keep their upper bodies still, this natural action is most like breathing for playing instruments.
3. *Efficient airflow is low in the upper body.* Many students will try to inhale by expanding the upper chest cavity as they take more and more air in. Students should be instructed to fill their lungs from the bottom up much as you would fill a bucket of water. Expanding the stomach first allows more air to move into the lungs more freely.

After students are able to inhale smoothly, quietly, and low in their upper bodies, they can begin to focus their attention on the quality and quantity of the air moving out of their lungs. Have students choose a point on the wall in front of them and send their airstream to that point. This visualization helps students develop the concept of sending their sound (air) to a particular point in the room and helps set them up to move air through, and not just into, their instruments.

As students release air, insist that they follow these guidelines:

1. *Upper body and head relaxed and still*
2. *Cheeks flat*
3. *Lips even*
4. *Tongue in the "ooo" position to stay out of the way of the airstream*

Some teachers have their students form a preliminary "embouchure" without the instrument at this stage. There are many benefits to this approach. If you decide to form a pre-embouchure, be sure that you follow the embouchure guidelines listed later in this chapter.

THE BLOCK NOTE CONCEPT

Once students can produce a natural, relaxed breath in and out, it is time to introduce the block note concept. This concept is a representation of the default sound of each note played. The block is made up of three basic parts (fig. 3.1):

- The beginning of the note
- The middle of the note
- The end of the note

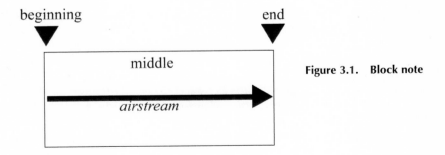

Figure 3.1. **Block note**

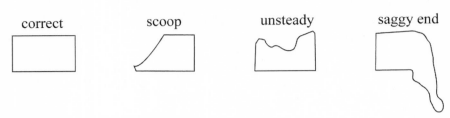

correct   scoop   unsteady   saggy end

Figure 3.2.   Block note variations

Notice that there is no difference in the airstream at the beginning, middle, or end of the note. Students should keep their air constant and their faces motionless at each checkpoint of the note. Teachers can illustrate poor beginnings, middles, or ends of the notes as they occur to help students to correct these problems. A couple of examples are diagramed in fig. 3.2.

As students aim their air at the imaginary point on the wall, have them place their hand between their mouth and the wall to feel the speed and consistency, or lack thereof, of each breath/note. Remind students to blow *through* their hand to the point on the wall. This concept will be important later as students add instruments; each time you add a new step toward playing the first note, have students keep the focus of the air on that imaginary target across the room.

Vary the number of counts that students exhale and inhale to gradually develop greater lung capacity. Students sometimes become less efficient as they work to develop the ability to exchange more air. Help your students remember the guidelines of quiet, still, relaxed, and efficient breathing as they increase their ability to take in and push out more air.

Breathing Games and Contests

Middle-school students love games. Friendly competition and games that develop breathing can help make developing these important fundamentals more fun. Be sure that students maintain proper posture and follow their breathing guidelines.

Bad posture crunch. This exercise exaggerates the negative effects of poor posture on efficient breathing. Have students sit with great posture, take in a big breath, hold it for a few seconds, and then release their air. Ask the students to notice how that felt. Next, while still seated, have students grab their ankles, take a big breath, and hold it for a few seconds. Ask the students to notice how that felt (very uncomfortable!). Point out that, even though this was an extreme example, their posture can either work to help or hinder efficient breathing.

Frankenstein breathers. This exercise helps students notice if they lift their shoulders while breathing—a definite no-no! Have students stand with feet shoulder width apart and extend their arms straight forward, palms to the floor. It is very difficult to raise your shoulders without also raising your hands. If your students are mature enough to handle it, you might have them place their hands on each other's shoulders and repeat this exercise.

Heavy suitcase breath. This is a variation on the *Frankenstein breathers* exercise. Instead of extending the arm straight out, have students drop their arms to their sides and stand comfortably with good posture. Have them pick up two imaginary suitcases—one in each hand—and take a breath normally. The students should imagine that the suitcases are full of heavy items so that their shoulders cannot lift at all when they breathe in. Be sure that they do not over-exaggerate in such a way as to bring their posture out of alignment!

Book on the stomach. If you have students think of a baby or a puppy breathing, they will tell you that their stomachs do most of the work when they breathe. This exercise shows that we do the same thing when we breathe efficiently. Have one student lie down on his back. Place a heavy textbook on the student's stomach, and ask the student to breathe deeply. Have the other students notice how the book moves up and down as he breathes. Also note that no other part of the body moves!

Sticky paper. This can be a good game to demonstrate moving air efficiently. Have a student stand about one foot away from a smooth wall, mirror, chalkboard, or other surface. Have the student take a deep, efficient breath and then hold a piece of paper up against the wall using only his or her breath. After students are able to hold the paper against the wall, they can compete to see who can hold the paper there the longest (as long as they breathe efficiently!).

SMALL INSTRUMENTS

Using small instruments for woodwind and brass players is a logical next step in introducing the first sounds on each instrument after efficient breathing has been established. The small instruments for brass players are the various brass mouthpieces. Small instruments for woodwinds include the flute headjoint, the reed for oboe and bassoon, the mouthpiece and barrel for clarinet, and the mouthpiece and neck for saxophone. This intermediate step in introducing the first notes prior to assembling the large instruments is an extremely important one. Using small instruments allows the students to focus only on producing a sound correctly and efficiently without the distraction of holding or manipulating the fully assembled instrument. Producing a good sound on the small instrument helps students set up a solid playing foundation that can be easily transferred to the large instrument.

Poor habits developed in the initial stages of playing the instruments are difficult to correct. The teacher should initially help each student form the proper angle and pressure by placing each small instrument on the embouchure. After students can form the embouchure and place the mouthpiece consistently, the teacher can monitor each student rather than placing the mouthpiece each time. Have each student use a mirror so that he or she can see exactly what is going on with the small instrument–embouchure combination. Establish great fundamentals on the small instruments so that the students' first experience on the large instruments is successful.

INSTRUMENT CASES

There are some important details related to instrument cases that should be addressed before students can begin to make sounds on the instruments. The first step when assembling each instrument is to learn how to manage the operation and opening of the instrument case. Many directors recommend that students sit on the floor so that there is less chance of damaging an instrument by dropping the various pieces. Have students place their instrument cases with the latches facing them. Help the students discover how they can tell if their case is facing up:

1. The handle is on the bottom part of the case (not on the lid of the case)
2. The latches flip UP from the bottom to the top
3. The name of the instrument is often printed on the top
4. The lid of the case is often thinner than the bottom

Have the students unlatch their cases without opening them. Point out that the lid of the case remains completely closed. When the students return the parts of their instruments into the cases correctly, the cases will close completely. If a student notices that her case does not close completely, it may indicate that some part of the instrument has been returned to the case incorrectly or that something else is obstructing the case lid.

After the cases have been unlatched, have the students open their cases and identify the parts of the instrument. Have them notice that each part fits into the case in only one way. Have them carefully pull each individual piece out and then return each piece to the case (see special notes for manipulating woodwind instruments below). After the students have returned each of the instrument pieces, have the students close their cases without latching the latches and check to see that the lids close completely. If the lids do not close, help the students find the obstruction. Some teachers find that a quick quiz on instrument part identification is a motivating activity for the students.

Small Instruments for Woodwinds

The small instruments for woodwinds include the headjoint for flute, reeds for oboe and bassoon, and the mouthpiece and barrel or neck for clarinet and saxophone respectively. While some small instruments in the woodwind family are easily assembled, others need careful instruction and monitoring. Ruining a reed on the first day of playing has disappointed many a double-reed player.

Assembly

Clarinet and saxophone students produce a sound easier and are able to manipulate their small instruments easier when they use their mouthpiece and barrel or neck. Be sure that the corks are well lubricated before assembling these instruments, especially if they are new. It takes a few days to compact new corks, so students may need help assembling their small instruments the first few times. Some teachers take the time to lubricate the corks before students assemble their instruments for the first time.

Have students soak their reeds as they assemble the mouthpiece and barrel or neck. This ensures that the reeds are thoroughly soaked when the small instrument is completely assembled, and having reeds in mouths prevents students from talking during your instructions. Instruct students to be careful with the reed as it is very thin. You can show students how thin a reed is by placing a soaked reed over a page of text; you can actually read text through the tip of the reed!

Assemble the mouthpiece and the neck or barrel before adding the ligature and reed. This procedure keeps these delicate parts protected. Hold the mouthpiece in the left hand and the barrel or neck in the right hand. The clarinet barrel has a wide end and a narrow end; the narrow end attaches to the mouthpiece. Avoid grabbing the octave key of the saxophone neck. Align the two parts and, with gentle twists back and forth, push the two parts together. Do not screw the mouthpiece on like a lightbulb. The opening of the saxophone mouthpiece should be on the opposite side of the neck from the octave key vent and on the same side as the curved part of the neck.

1. *Slip the ligature over the mouthpiece.* There is a wide end and a narrow end on each ligature; the wide end slips over the mouthpiece first.
2. *Loosen the ligature screw(s) a few turns to allow space for the reed.*
3. *Push the ligature up slightly with your thumb.*
4. *Insert the thick end of the reed under the ligature so that the flat side rests on the table of the mouthpiece.*
5. *Align the tip of the reed with the tip of the mouthpiece.* You should be able to see a *tiny* bit of the mouthpiece sticking out over the top of the reed.
6. *Check to see that the reed is aligned evenly as it rests on the table of the mouthpiece.*
7. *Slide the ligature down to the correct spot on the mouthpiece.* Some mouthpieces have lines that aid in guiding the placement of the ligature. You may need to loosen the ligature screw(s) a few more turns. Most ligatures are designed so that the adjustment screws are to the player's right.
8. *Tighten the ligature screws only enough to gently hold the reed against the mouthpiece.* Over-tightening will prevent the reed from vibrating freely.

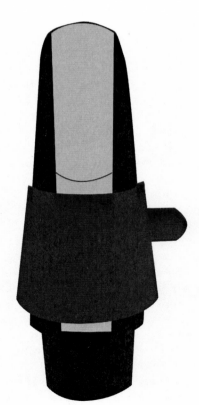

Figure 3.3. Reed placement on the mouthpiece

First Sounds on the Small Instruments

Flute

Flute players begin with the headjoint of the flute as their small instrument. Hold the instrument with the end plug to the player's left and the open end to the player's right. The student should hold the headjoint with the left hand near the end plug and seal up the opening on the right side with the flat palm of the right hand.

Remind your students of the following embouchure guidelines:

1. *Lips together.* Say "em" so that the upper and lower lips are even.
2. *Small aperture.* Say "pooh" to form a football-shaped opening in the lips (see figure 7.3).
3. *Corners firm.* Visualize keeping the corners of the mouth close to the sharp canine teeth.
4. *Bottom lip relaxed.* Let the bottom lip lay on the embouchure plate. Some teachers have their students wiggle the headjoint horizontally to check if the bottom lip moves freely with the embouchure plate.

To make a sound, aim your air at the back of the embouchure plate so that about half of your air goes into the flute and half of your air goes outside the flute by saying the syllable "hoo." Be sure to use the same air speed you used when you aimed your air at the imaginary target on the wall earlier. Making the initial sound will take some experimentation. Try some of the following adjustments to find your best sound:

1. Roll the headjoint slightly in and out.
2. Move the headjoint left and right horizontally.
3. Aim your air slightly higher and lower.

You'll know you have your instrument in the best position when the sound opens up with a full, strong tone. When everything is aligned perfectly, a small triangle of condensation often appears on the headjoint.

Oboe and Bassoon

Double-reed students begin with the reed as their small instruments. The reed must be soaked in order to vibrate correctly, but reeds that are soaked too long are often too stiff to play. Soak the entire portion of the reed (not the string) for about three minutes in a small container of water. Many students use an empty prescription pill container for this purpose since they feature waterproof caps. A properly soaked reed looks like a slightly elongated football when viewed from the end (fig. 3.4).

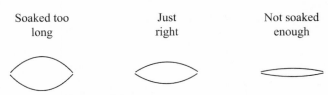

Figure 3.4.   Three reeds

Have the student follow these steps to form the initial embouchure:

1. *Roll the bottom lip just over the bottom teeth.*
2. *Place the tip of the reed on the bottom lip.*
3. *Roll the top lip over the top teeth.*
4. *Close the lips around the reed and draw the reed into the mouth.* See below for important differences between oboe and bassoon.
5. *Support the reed with lip pressure from all sides.* Some students visualize a rubber band wrapped around a rolled-up newspaper.
6. *Corners firm.* Visualize keeping the corners of the mouth near the canine teeth.
7. *Keep the teeth open.* Support the reed by using the lip muscles.

The major difference between playing the small instrument of the bassoon and the oboe is the amount of reed taken into the mouth. Oboe students should be instructed to place only a small amount of reed in their mouth. Bassoon students take more reed into the mouth—almost to the first wire. Both oboes and bassoons will often "crow" when the reed and embouchure are both set up properly. This "crow" is not a definite pitch—it sounds more like a buzz.

Be sure students use the same air as they did when they aimed their air at the imaginary spot on the wall earlier. For oboists, the opening that the air has to pass through is quite small, so there is a lot of backpressure when trying to play. Remind students to continue to visualize the imaginary target that they used during breathing exercises as they play small instruments.

Clarinet

Clarinet players use the mouthpiece and barrel as their small instrument. Hold the barrel with the right hand so that the end is completely open. If students hold their barrel with the fingers covering the end, the pitch will be affected.

Remind your students of the following embouchure guidelines:

1. *Bottom lip rolled slightly over the bottom teeth.*
2. *Top teeth touch the mouthpiece.*
3. *Corners firm.* Close up the sides of the mouth around the mouthpiece.
4. *Flat chin.* The chin is pointed so that an upside-down "U" forms.
5. *Angle check.* Hold the small instrument so that it is slightly forward. Think of blowing *across* the reed, not *into* the barrel.

Place the mouthpiece in the mouth so that the bottom teeth are aligned with the spot where the reed first makes contact with the mouthpiece. To make a sound, blow across the mouthpiece to the imaginary point across the room saying the syllable "hoo." If the embouchure is correct, the small instrument should sound a concert F♯.

Saxophone

Saxophone players use the mouthpiece and neck as their small instrument. Hold the neck with the right hand so that the end is completely open. If students hold their neck with the fingers covering the end, the pitch will be affected. Avoid grasping or opening the octave key vent.

Remind your students of the following embouchure guidelines:

1. *Bottom lip rolled slightly over the bottom teeth.*
2. *Top teeth touch the mouthpiece.*
3. *Close up the mouth around the mouthpiece.* Apply equal pressure from all sides. Some students visualize a rubber band wrapped around a newspaper.
4. *Flat chin.* The chin is pointed so that an upside-down "U" forms.

Place the mouthpiece in the mouth so that the bottom teeth are aligned with the spot where the reed first makes contact with the mouthpiece.

To make a sound, blow into the mouthpiece toward the imaginary point across the room, saying the syllable "hoo." You'll know you have your instrument and embouchure adjusted correctly when your small instrument plays a concert A♭.

Small Instruments for Brass

Brass players use the mouthpiece for their small instrument. As with woodwind instruments, setting up correct fundamentals through the use of small instruments allows brass students to work on the fundamentals of playing without having being distracted by holding and manipulating the entire instrument.

Have your students remember the following embouchure guidelines:

1. *Lips together.* Say "em" to keep the top and bottom lip aligned.
2. *Flat chin.* Point the chin toward the ground, forming an inverted "U" shape at the bottom of the chin.
3. *Firm corners.* Keep the corners of the mouth near the canine teeth—avoid a "smile" embouchure.
4. *Flat cheeks.*
5. *Teeth apart.* About the same space between the top and bottom teeth as the width of the shank of the mouthpiece.
6. *Wet the lips.*

Placement of the Mouthpiece

For all brasses except the French horn, the mouthpiece should be placed so that half the mouthpiece rests on the top lip and half covers the bottom. French horn players usually align the mouthpiece so that two-thirds of the top lip and one-third of the lower lip rests on the mouthpiece. Most students should start with the mouthpiece centered side to side on the lips (fig. 3.5).

There are two common ways to help students align the mouthpiece properly on the lips. In the first method, have your students place the rim of the mouthpiece along the bottom of the bottom lip with the shank of the mouthpiece facing down. Next, rotate the shank of the mouthpiece up so that the rest of the mouthpiece comes to rest of the lips (fig. 3.6).

Another way that some teachers help students find their mouthpiece placement is to have students blow a steady airstream to an imaginary target on the wall while holding their mouthpieces away from their lips at arm's length. Line up the middle of the mouthpiece with where you visualize the airstream. Gradually bring the mouthpiece closer and closer to the face while you keep the shank of the mouthpiece aligned with the air column. This method helps align the student's airstream with the center of the mouthpiece.

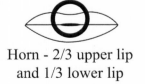

Horn - 2/3 upper lip
and 1/3 lower lip

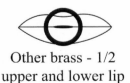

Other brass - 1/2
upper and lower lip

Figure 3.5.   Mouthpiece placement for horn vs. other brass

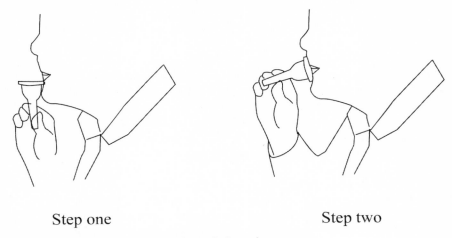

Step one   Step two

Figure 3.6. Step one, step two of mouthpiece placement

IMPORTANT NOTE: Each student's mouth, lips, jaw structure, and teeth will be slightly different. It will take some experimentation to get the perfect placement for the mouthpiece. You will know you have gotten the mouthpiece in the correct spot when the tone is free and open and produces the best sound.

Some teachers find it useful to use mouthpiece visualizers to help align the aperture of the lips to the center of the mouthpiece. Vizualizers consist of a normal brass mouthpiece with the cup removed so that the placement of the lips can be seen inside the rim. These visualizers are available in many different sizes through music stores or online.

In keeping with the concept of moving from the known to the unknown, start small-instrument work by just blowing air through the mouthpiece. Use only enough pressure to make an airtight seal for the lips on the mouthpiece. Remember to aim the air at the imaginary target across the room. Bring the lips gradually closer together while maintaining a steady airstream until the lips start to buzz. Many students will be startled when their lips first buzz. After the initial surprise has worn off, have students attempt to sustain the buzz. Remind students of the checkpoints for a great brass embouchure (see above); many students will slow down their air, become tense, or close their teeth as they begin to buzz their lips. Focus students' attention on producing a relaxed but full buzzing sound.

MOVING FROM THE KNOWN TO THE
UNKNOWN: BLOCK NOTES REVISITED

Once students are able to make a sound on their small instruments, it is time to start refining the beginnings, middles, and endings of their sounds by applying the block note concept. As we discussed earlier, the block note concept emphasizes a steady airstream and embouchure; this is the default model for tone production on each instrument. There are several common errors that students make that can all be related to this model. Several of these problems are related to the beginnings of notes:

1. *Embouchure is not set or steady at the beginning of the note.* Breathe through the corners of the mouth with as little motion as possible in the body. Keep the entire body still as you begin the note. Visualize a full glass of water or a book carefully balanced on your head as you begin each note to help keep your body as still as possible.
2. *Airstream is not fast enough at the beginning of the note.* The air should move at the same speed at the beginning of the note as it does in the middle and end of the note. If you have established this habit in the pre-instrument breathing phase, this issue should be easily addressed.
3. *Airstream is too fast at the beginning of the note.* Some students use an "explosion" of air to start notes. Remember to use the "hoo" syllable to start the note. Starting with a breath sound keeps the tongue from being a complicating factor in the first stages of tone production.

Students often find it helpful to visualize these incorrect starts of notes by relating them to the block note model (see figure 3.2).

Students should balance the resistance of the instrument with the airstream they produce and the firmness of the embouchure. The instrument and embouchure muscles produce backpressure that must be counterbalanced by the air the student produces. If the students blow too lightly, the result is a stuffy or small sound. In this case, the air pressure of the embouchure/instrument combination pushes back against the air the student is attempting to move through the instrument. If the student blows too hard, the sound is raspy and wild. The air pressure the student blows outweighs the resistance of the instrument/embouchure combination (fig. 3.7).

Problems with the middles of notes include:

1. *Airstream or embouchure does not remain steady.* Keep the air moving forward steadily, and keep the muscles of the embouchure and jaw steady while playing.
2. *Airstream too fast.* The sound is wild and out of control; use a little less air pressure to allow the instrument to speak clearly. Some brass play-

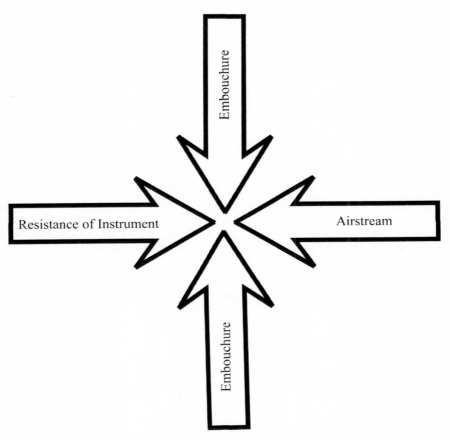

Figure 3.7.   Balance of embouchure to air stream

ers blow so much air across their embouchures that the lips pooch
out into the cup of the mouthpiece. Remind these students to use
enough embouchure pressure to balance the air moving through the
instrument.

3. *Airstream is too slow.* The sound is weak or stuffy; use a little more air
to balance the backpressure of the instrument/embouchure combination. Remind students to aim their air all the way to an imaginary
target on the wall across the room.

4. *Embouchure pressure is too tight.* Sound is stuffy and muffled. Clinch-
ing the embouchure muscles too tightly prevents the lips or reed
and the air from vibrating. Single- and double-reed players can even
close off the airstream completely by biting down too much. Use

only enough pressure to make a consistent sound. Check also that the tongue is in a "hoo" position and out of the way of the airstream. Brass and flute players often sound stuffy when they clench their teeth together.

5. *Embouchure pressure too loose.* Stress the concept of *firmness* in the embouchure without *tension.* If the musculature of the face is too loose, the lips or reed will not have a firm foundation on which to vibrate. Clarinet players should hold on to the mouthpiece firmly enough so that you feel resistance if you try to wiggle their instruments from side to side as they play.

Problems with the ends of notes are similar to those at the beginnings of notes:

1. *Embouchure air relaxes before the end of the note.* Keep the embouchure steady until the note has ended and until the air stops. Stop the sound by stopping the air immediately—keep the air pressure steady until the note ends.
2. *Students release "extra" air at the ends of notes.* Students will usually have a little air left over in their lungs at the ends of notes. Let them know this is normal and they should not necessarily try to get rid of all the air in their lungs.
3. *Students stop the sound incorrectly.* Stop the sound by stopping the air. Avoid stopping the sound with the tongue (in the mouthpiece, between the lips, or on the reed) or by closing up the throat.

Reminder! The first notes on the small instruments are critically important in the development of playing fundamentals on each instrument. Be extremely meticulous in inspecting and correcting the playing of each individual player in your band. Have each student use a small mirror regularly to help them monitor and adjust their embouchures.

With a little guidance, you can invite students to critique each other as they play. Once you have given them specific things to listen and watch for, such as good beginnings, middles, and ends of notes, they can be excellent critics of each other's playing. Have students draw pictures of each other's "block notes" as they play.

Brass Small-Instrument Extras

Brass players can use the small instruments to help develop the air and embouchure control necessary for playing in various registers of their large instruments. Unlike the saxophone and clarinet, there is not a specific starting pitch that every student should produce on brass mouth-pieces. Start with whatever note each student naturally plays, and gradually expand higher and lower until most of the section plays in the same relative tessitura.

Brass players can play higher on the mouthpiece by:

1. Increasing the speed of the airstream
2. Increasing the air pressure
3. Firming up the muscles of the embouchure

Brass players can work to expand their range by gradually moving higher and lower as they play their small instruments. Have students start on their natural note and then gradually move lower like a descending siren. Next try starting on the natural note and moving higher. Students will be able to gradually expand how far they can play in each direction. Constantly monitor students to see if they are adding any unnecessary tension or movement as they play.

Brass players can also work to play rote songs on their mouthpieces, especially after you have introduced articulation concepts (see below). Start by modeling simple rote songs in an easy range using the call-and-response technique. Students also enjoy coming up with their own songs to share with the class.

Introducing Articulation Concepts on Small Instruments

The block note concept is an excellent way to introduce articulation concepts, especially when used first with small instruments. Start with a modified legato (connected) articulation based on the "hoo" starts that we began with, and then add a "too" articulation to the smooth, steady airstream of the basic block note. Gradually add more "too" articulated notes to the block airstream (fig. 3.8).

This approach keeps students from simultaneously having to concentrate on starting the initial sound with the tongue (a new concept) and articulating separate notes (another new concept). Coordinating the tongue and the airstream at the beginnings of notes is remarkably difficult for students at first. The "hoo, too" method starts with a concept that students have presumably already mastered.

The next logical step would be to introduce a "too" beginning to a long block note. This allows students to concentrate only on the coordination of the tongue with the initial air at the beginning of each note. Only after the "hoo, too" and the "too" beginnings have been mastered should they be combined. Students can then work on articulating notes of varying lengths (all initially without musical notation).

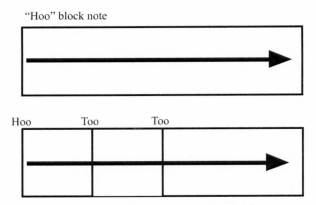

Figure 3.8. Block note and "hoo, too, too" blocks

LARGE INSTRUMENTS

After great fundamentals have been developed and every student can produce a characteristic sound on his or her small instrument, it is time to assemble and play the entire horn. If correct fundamentals have been established using the small instruments, adding the large instrument will be much less complicated for the students. Students should be instructed on proper assembly and correct hand position before beginning their first notes on the large instruments. Before assembling the instruments, be sure to review the important concepts related to opening and closing the instrument cases (see pp. 56–57).

Assembly of the Woodwind Instruments

The woodwind instruments are the most complicated to assemble. With their many sections, rods, and keys, it is easy to become confused or even damage the instruments. Instruct students to be *careful* but not *afraid* when assembling their instruments. The *rods* of woodwind instruments are particularly delicate. Rods are the long, cylindrical tubes of metal that run parallel to the body of the instrument that allow the keys to pivot up and down. Pressure applied to the rods may bend them and prevent the instrument from working properly.

Assemble each woodwind instrument from the bottom to the top, and disassemble them from the top to the bottom. This routine is important for the students as they develop good assembly habits and also helps the teacher monitor correct assembly. Until the students are comfortable assembling their instruments, it is important to have the class complete each step as a group. Some teachers have students who get ahead of the group sit out for the remainder of the class period. Since students are eager to assemble their instruments and play, most teachers find they only have to use this classroom management technique once or twice.

Have a system of identifying the fingers of each hand: 1 = index finger, 2 = middle finger, 3 = ring ringer. The "pinkie" refers to the little finger of each hand. The thumb is also used on each woodwind instrument.

Flute Assembly

Begin by identifying the foot joint, the main body, and the headjoint. Also help students identify the keys and rods. Remind students that the rods are particularly delicate.

1. Hold the main body of the flute with the left hand so that the palm rests underneath the flute near the bottom of the joint. Avoid contact with the rods.
2. Hold the foot joint in the palm of the right hand.
3. Slip the foot joint onto the main body by carefully pressing the parts together as you gently twist the parts back and forth with a rocking motion.
4. Align the rod of the foot joint with the center of the last key on the main body of the flute.
5. With the assembled foot joint and main body in the left hand, grasp the headjoint in the right hand. Assemble the main body and the headjoint using gentle twists back and forth.
6. Align the center of the embouchure hole with the center of the small key at the top of the main body of the flute. Some directors like to put a drop of colored fingernail polish on the headjoint and main body to help students align these two parts. The fingernail polish can be easily removed.

If the sections of the flute become dirty, they can be difficult to put together. Wipe each part of the instrument with a soft, cotton cloth to remove any dirt or oil. Never lubricate the sections of the instrument with oil or grease; this will only attract dirt and grime and make the instrument more difficult to assemble.

Flute Hand Position

Begin with the instrument in the vertical "rest" position with the head-joint pointed to the ceiling with the keys facing away from the body. Slide the first joint of the index finger of the left hand along the side of the main body of the flute. *It is important that the first joint of the first finger always remains in contact with the flute!* Place the left thumb on the B♭ button on the back of the flute. Fingers 1, 2, and 3 are placed on the B, A, and G keys respectively. Gently curve the fingers so that the pads of each finger touch the center of each key. Let the pinky rest on top of the G♯/A♭ key. Check to see if the first joint of the first finger is still contacting the side of the flute.

Allow your right hand to form a relaxed C shape by allowing it to rest along your side. Bring your relaxed hand up to the lower part of the main body of the flute, and allow the first, second, and third fingers to find the F, E, and D keys respectively. The side of the right thumb rests on the back of the main body of the instrument opposite the first finger and keeping the relaxed C shape in the hand. Let your pinky rest on top of the D♯/E♭ key.

Moving from rest position to playing position involves balancing the flute on three contact points: the lip plate, the first joint of the left index finger, and the right pinky. Place the headjoint on the lips so that it feels just like it did when playing the small instrument.

Disassemble the flute from the top to the bottom in the same manner as you assembled the flute using careful twists back and forth while pulling each section apart. Avoid pressing the rods as you disassemble the parts, and put each part in the correct space inside the case.

Oboe Assembly

If you are going to play the large instrument, have the students soak their reeds beforehand so that the reeds will be ready to play after assembly. Help students identify the upper joint, the lower joint, and the bell. As with the other woodwind instruments, help students identify the keys and rods. Remind students that the rods are particularly delicate.

1. Hold the lower joint of the oboe with the left hand so that the palm rests underneath the instrument. Grasp the lower joint so that pressure is not applied to the rods.
2. Hold the bell in the palm of the right hand.
3. Slip the bell onto the lower joint by carefully pressing the parts together as you gently twist back and forth. If your oboe has a B♭ key on the bell, press down on that key during assembly to raise the B♭ connecting lever to keep the lower bridge key safe.
4. With the assembled bell and lower joint in the left hand, grasp the upper joint in the right hand so that the bridge keys stay raised. Monitor

the bridge keys as you assemble the two pieces so that these keys do not get bent during assembly. Assemble these two pieces in the same manner with gentle twists back and forth.

5. Align the tone holes of the upper joint with the tone holes of the lower joint, and check to see that the bridge keys are aligned.

Oboe Hand Position

Begin with the instrument in the vertical "rest" position with the bell pointed to the floor and the tone holes facing away from the body. Place the left thumb on the back of the instrument at a 45° angle just beneath the octave key. The left thumb should be in a position so that it lightly touches, but does not press, the octave key. Fingers 1, 2, and 3 are placed on the B, A, and G keys respectively. Gently curve the fingers so that the pads of each finger touch the center of each key. Let the pinky rest on top of the G#/A♭ key.

Allow your right hand to form a relaxed C shape by allowing it to rest along your side. Bring your relaxed hand up to the lower part of the main body of the oboe, and allow the first, second, and third fingers to find the F#, E, and D keys respectively. The pad of the right thumb rests on the back of the main body of the instrument under the thumb rest halfway between the end of the thumbnail and the knuckle of the thumb. Watch that students do not let their thumbs slide to their left allowing the thumb rest to sit in the curve of the right hand. Let your pinky rest on top of the D#/E♭ key.

Bassoon Assembly

If you are going to play the large instrument, have the students soak their reeds before they put their horns together so that they will be properly soaked after assembly. Help students identify the seat strap, boot joint, tenor joint, long joint, bell, bocal, and hand rest. As with the other woodwind instruments, help students identify the keys and rods. Remind students that the rods and the bocal are particularly delicate.

1. Attach the seat strap to the boot joint.
2. Carefully grab the tenor joint with your left hand, and slide it into the smaller of the two holes in the boot joint using gentle twists back and forth.
3. Insert the long joint into the larger of the two holes in the boot joint. Align the bridge key between the long joint and the tenor joint, and attach the two joints using the locking mechanism.
4. Grasp the bell with your left hand. Use your thumb to close the key on the bell so that the bridge key raises, and attach the bell to the long joint using the same gentle twists back and forth.

5. Grasp the bocal near the corked end, and insert it into the small hole at the top of the tenor joint. The metal of the bocal is quite thin and is easily bent, so apply top-down pressure only to the corked end; pulling down on the thin end may bend or crack the bocal. Align the whisper key that extends from the top of the tenor joint with the speaker hole in the bocal.
6. Attach the hand rest (sometimes called a "crutch") to the rear of the boot joint.

Bassoon Hand Position

The student should sit near the front of the chair with the seat strap beneath the legs. Adjust the seat strap so that the bocal lines up with the embouchure when seated with relaxed, uplifted posture. The weight of the bassoon is primarily supported by the seat strap. Always adjust the seat strap to the body, not the body to the instrument. The instrument should sit diagonally in front of the torso much like the shoulder strap of a car seatbelt would cross the torso. The right thumb rests gently on the pancake key, and fingers 1, 2, and 3 cover the B, A, and G tone holes respectively. Let your right pinky rest lightly over the low E♭ key.

The left thumb rests lightly on the whisper key, and fingers 1, 2, and 3 cover the E, D, and C tone holes. Lightly rest your left pinky over the low F key. Keep a relaxed C shape with the hands.

Clarinet Assembly

If you are planning to play the large instruments, start by having your clarinet players soak their reeds. Help students identify the bell, the lower joint, the upper joint, and the barrel. Help students recognize major differences between the parts (for instance, the lower joint has three large keys and only one tenon cork). Also help students identify the keys and rods. Remind students that the rods are particularly delicate.

1. Hold the lower joint with the left hand so that the palm rests underneath the instrument. Grasp the main body so that pressure is not applied to the rods.
2. Hold the bell in the palm of the right hand. Slip the bell onto the lower joint by carefully pressing the parts together as you gently twist the parts back and forth using a rocking motion.
3. With the assembled lower joint and bell in the left hand, grasp the upper joint in the right hand. Press the ring of the D/A key with the fingers of the right hand to raise the bridge key. Raising the bridge key helps prevent bending this key during assembly. Connect these two pieces with gentle twists back and forth keeping a close watch on

the bridge key. Align the tone holes of the lower and upper joint, and notice if the bridge key sections are in line.

4. Grasp the barrel with the right hand. Notice again that there is wide end and a narrow end (students should remember this from their small instrument work). Carefully work the barrel onto the end of the upper joint with gentle twists back and forth. *See the section on small-instrument assembly for details on assembling the reed, ligature, mouthpiece, and barrel.*

Clarinet Hand Position

Begin with the instrument in the vertical "rest" position with the bell pointed to the floor with the tone holes facing away from the body. Gently grab the bottom joint of the clarinet with the right hand to support the instrument. Let your left arm hang to your side, and allow your hand to form a relaxed C shape. Gently lift your left hand, and position your left thumb on the F/C key on the back of the clarinet. If your hand is relaxed and in the correct position, your thumb will rest at a 45° angle to the instrument just beneath the register key. Position your thumb so that it contacts the register key lightly without depressing the key. Fingers 1, 2, and 3 are placed on the E, D, and C keys respectively. Gently curve the fingers so that the pads of each finger touch the center of each key. Let the pinky rest on top of the C#/G# key.

Allow your right hand to form a relaxed C shape by dropping it to your side. Bring your relaxed hand up to the lower joint, and place the first, second, and third fingers on the B♭, A, and G keys respectively. The pad of the right thumb rests on the back of the main body of the instrument, and the side of the thumb sits under the thumb rest halfway between the end of the thumbnail and the knuckle of the thumb. Watch that students do not let their thumbs slide over, allowing the thumb rest sit in the curve of the right hand. Let your pinky rest on top of the G#/D# key.

Saxophone Assembly

If you are planning to play the large instruments, start by having your saxophone players soak their reeds. Help students identify the neck, the neck strap, and the main body of the instrument. Also help students identify the keys and rods. Remind students that the rods are particularly delicate.

1. Loosen the neck strap, and slip it over your head.
2. Grasp the main body of the instrument by grabbing the bell with your right hand. Let the instrument sit across your body so that the bell rests on your right leg and the small end of the saxophone faces the player's left.

3. Connect the neck strap to the loop on the back of the main body.
4. Loosen the thumb screw on the main body where the neck attaches.
5. With the bell resting on the right leg, grasp the neck of the instrument. Avoid applying pressure to the octave key mechanism. With gentle back-and-forth twists, assemble the neck into the body of the instrument so that the neck points the opposite direction as the bell. Pay close attention to the octave key mechanism to avoid bending these delicate parts. *See the small-instrument assembly section for details about assembling the reed, ligature, and mouthpiece.*
6. Gently tighten the thumb screw on the main body to secure the neck.
7. Slide the neck strap so that the mouthpiece aligns with the embouchure when sitting in a relaxed, lifted posture. Always adjust the neck strap to the body, not the body to the instrument. Remind students that the neck strap is to *help support* the weight of the instrument while playing—it is not designed to hold the full weight of the instrument.

Saxophone Hand Position

Begin with the instrument in the vertical "rest" position with the bell pointed away from the body. Gently grab the bell of the saxophone with the right hand to support the instrument. Let your left arm hang to your side, and allow your hand to form a relaxed C shape. Gently lift your left hand, and position your left thumb on the thumb button on the back of the saxophone. If your hand is relaxed and in the correct position, your thumb will rest at a 45° angle to the instrument on the thumb button just beneath the octave key. Position the thumb so that it touches but does not depress the octave key.

Fingers 1, 2, and 3 are placed on the B, A, and G keys respectively. Gently curve the fingers so that the pads of each finger touch the center of each key. Let the pinky rest on top of the G♯ key.

Allow your right hand to form a relaxed C shape by allowing it to rest along your side. Bring your relaxed hand up to the instrument, and allow the first, second, and third fingers to find the F, E, and D keys respectively. The pad of the right thumb rests on the back of the main body of the instrument under the thumb rest halfway between the end of the thumbnail and the knuckle of the thumb. Watch that students do not let their thumbs slide over, allowing the thumb rest to sit in the curve of the right hand. Let your pinky rest on top of the E♭ key.

Assembly of the Brass Instruments

Compared to the woodwind instruments, brass instruments are relatively easy to assemble. With the exception of the trombone, most brass instruments require only the addition of the mouthpiece in order to start playing. Add the mouthpiece by inserting the shank of the mouthpiece into the receiver, giving it a slight twist with gentle, inward pressure to form a snug fit. Avoid popping the mouthpiece with the hand or pressing the mouthpiece too firmly into the receiver. This action may cause the mouthpiece to become stuck.

The horn angle of each brass instrument is determined by the structure of the teeth and embouchure as established in the first stages of playing the small instruments. If great fundamentals have been developed and reinforced when playing the small instruments, moving to the large instruments will be a smooth transfer of well-developed skills. While playing the large instruments, make the embouchure feel exactly as it did when playing the small instruments.

Trombone Assembly

Help students identify the mouthpiece, the slide, and the main body of the instrument.

1. Remove the slide from the case, and place the curved end on the floor so that the two open ends face up. The longer tube of the slide should face your right.
2. Lock the slide by turning the slide lock to the right. Double-check to see that the slide is locked by raising the slide slightly off the floor.
3. Hold the slide with your left hand, and grab the main body with your right hand.
4. Hold the main body so that the bell faces the floor, and attach the main body of the instrument to the longer of the two ends of the slide.
5. Rotate the main body so that the slide rests at a 90° angle to the slide.
6. Connect the two pieces with the locking mechanism at the base of the slide.
7. Carefully twist the mouthpiece into the mouthpiece receiver.

Trumpet/Cornet Hand Position

Start in "rest" position with your bell resting on your left leg. Place the thumb and fingers of the left hand around the trumpet valve casings. Place the third finger of the left hand in the third valve slide (players with different hand sizes may feel more comfortable using different fingers in the third valve slide). The left hand grasps and supports the weight of the instrument when playing.

Let your right hand hang to your side to form a relaxed C shape. Bring your right hand up to the instrument so that the pads of the first three fingers rest on the pearls of the valves. The thumb of the right hand rests between the first and second valve casing. Check to see that students do not place the pad of the right thumb under the lead pipe. Let the pinky of the right hand rest on top of the pinky ring. Check to see that the relaxed C shape is maintained. Bring your instrument up to your lips to move to playing position. Remember that most of the weight of the trumpet is supported with the left hand to allow the right hand to work the valves freely.

French Horn Hand Position

Let your bell rest on the thigh of your right leg. Grasp the underside of the bell with your right hand. (Many teachers allow their students to hold their horns in this way until they are more able to support the horn with their hand inside the bell.) Let your left hand hang to your side to form a relaxed C shape. The thumb of the left hand rests in the thumb ring or on the B♭ trigger. The pads of the first three fingers rest on the valves. Let the pinky of the left hand rest on top of the pinky ring. Check to see that the relaxed C shape is maintained. Bring your instrument up to your lips to move to playing position.

Trombone Hand Position

Start in "rest" position with your slide resting on the floor. Make an L shape with your left hand. Keeping that shape, place the left thumb under the bell brace and the left index finger along the side of the mouthpiece receiver. Wrap the other fingers of the left hand around the slide brace.

Let your right hand hang to your side to form a relaxed C shape. Bring your right hand up to the instrument, and grasp the slide gently between the thumb and first two fingers of the right hand. Bring your instrument up to your lips to move to playing position. Remember that most of the weight of the trombone is supported with the left hand to allow the right hand to work the slide freely.

Euphonium and Tuba Hand Position

There can be great variation in the ways that instrument manufacturers wrap the tubing of the euphonium and tuba. You may need to alter these instructions depending on the brand and model of the instruments you use. Try to keep the students' bodies as relaxed and as natural as possible regardless of what brand or model of instrument you use.

Place the instrument in your lap with the mouthpiece facing your lips. Wrap your left arm around the body of the instrument like you are carrying a sack of groceries. The weight of the instrument rests in the arm of the left hand and (perhaps) on one thigh.

Let your right hand hang to your side to form a relaxed C shape. Bring your right hand up to the instrument so that the pads of the first three fingers rest on the top of the valves. The thumb of the right hand rests between the first and second valves or beneath the lead pipe depending on the tubing arrangement of your particular instrument. Let the pinky of the right hand rest on top of the pinky ring. Check to see that the relaxed C shape is maintained. Remember that most of the weight of the instrument is supported with the left arm (and perhaps the thigh) to allow the right hand to work the valves freely.

Some teachers find that their euphonium players are more comfortable with the additional support of a rolled-up towel under the curved part of the bottom of their instrument. This relieves a little of the weight that students are required to hold. Many teachers use tuba cradles or stands to help support the weight of the instrument. These cradles can be an important aid to help young students—especially those playing full-sized instruments. Tuba cradles and stands can be found through major music instrument suppliers.

First Notes on Woodwind Instruments

The best first notes on the woodwind instruments balance ease of sound production with the ability to securely and comfortably support the weight of the instrument. Using a note with all the fingers closed provides a very secure feeling but may be difficult to play. Playing an "open" note with no fingers depressed might offer little resistance but is difficult to hold without potentially developing poor hand-position habits. The first notes on the large instruments should also work together harmonically to develop and connect our previous experiences with rote songs to allow students to jump right into playing music in your selected beginning method book. Some possible starting notes are given below. Regardless of which notes you chose to introduce your students to first, move on to new notes only after every student can produce a clear, pure tone on the old notes.

Flute players can start on fourth-line D, which is relatively stable and easy to finger for most players. Students can then move up to E♭ and then to F. Acoustically, fifth-line F is the first of these notes that requires students to use a good, focused airstream to avoid playing in the lower octave. Students can then fill in a B♭ tetrachord by adding C and B♭. Help your flute students focus on the fingers that change between notes. The finger manipulation required of the flute player for these five notes is quite involved. For instance, moving from D to C involves crossing the break of the flute. Much time should be devoted to solidifying these complex finger movements.

Oboists can start on third-space C. Complete an F tetrachord by adding B♭, A, G, and F. This selection of notes provides a solid, easily produced first note and few complex fingering swaps. Bassoon players can construct a B♭ tetrachord by starting on fourth-line F and then moving down to E♭, D, C, and B♭. Clarinet players find that their written first-line E is easy to produce and physically stable. Be sure to watch that students keep their nonplaying fingers hovering above the tone holes for each new note. Students can then work down to written D and C then back up from written E to F and G. Saxophone players can begin on their written third-line B and then move down to written A and G. Completing their written G tetrachord then involves adding C and D above their third-line B.

First Notes for Brass Instruments

As with the small instruments, the first notes for the large instruments for brasses should be selected based on the natural first notes produced by each individual student. Students can then work up or down to match the notes of the other members of the class. For instance, some trumpet beginners naturally play their second-line G as a first note while others might play C below the staff. Forcing the natural G players to play a C (or *vice versa*) may cause students to manipulate their embouchures in an unnatural fashion and produce poor fundamental habits.

All brass players should learn the basic chromatic fingering combinations. These combinations lower the pitch of the instrument by half steps. Starting with each open note, adding the second valve will lower the pitch by a half step. Switching to first valve lowers the open note another half step (or a whole step from open) and so on. The basic chromatic valve combinations are as follows:

OPEN   2   1   12   23   13   123   OPEN

For trombone players the basic chromatic positions are:

1   2   3   4   5   6   7   1

There are seven basic chromatic valve/slide combinations, and then the cycle repeats itself again. If a player knows the names of the open notes, she can figure out the fingerings or slide positions for any other note by using the chromatic combinations. Teach each of your brass players to memorize the basic combinations without playing at first (one new thing at a time). Students can even practice moving through valve combinations away from their instruments. After establishing a solid, natural first note on the large instruments, work to add the six other chromatic valve and slide combinations to the natural note. For instance, if the natural first note for a particular trombone player in your class is first-position B♭ at the top of the staff, have him move chromatically down to E♮ below that.

Block Notes Revisited

As soon as students can produce a great first note on the large instruments, it is time to apply the block note concept to playing other notes. Insist that students can play a clear beginning, consistent middle, and clear ending to each note (see above for block note checklists and potential problems). If you consistently reinforce the connections between breathing without the instrument, small instrument playing, and large instrument playing and if you move from what students already know and are able to do by introducing one new thing at a time, you will find yourself able to move through this phase with great efficiency.

As soon as students can produce a block note on their first note, it is time to start changing notes. At first, students will find it easier to have a rest between notes so that they can have time to find fingerings (fig. 3.9).

Students value this "think time" between notes to get their fingers ready to play.

As soon as students can play different notes in sequence with rests, it is time to move from note to note without rests. Relate these activities as best you can to what has come before: if you played descending whole notes chromatically with rests before, play descending whole notes without rests in the next exercise. Students will need to move their fingers or slides as fast as they can to make a smooth transition between notes. In keeping with the philosophy of adding one new thing at a time, practice moving between consecutive notes without playing first. This allows students to concentrate on manipulating their fingers and hands without worrying about what sounds are coming out of their instruments.

First Songs and Ear Training

Students are able to imitate and play various sequences by ear very quickly. As we discussed in chapter 2, this is how we learn any language—

Figure 3.9. Fingering switch

by imitating what we hear. As soon as students can play two different notes, start playing the notes in sequence by improvising various rhythms and combinations of notes. Students' ability to imitate will far outreach their ability to read music at this point, so don't be afraid to play rhythms that they may not need to "read" for many months.

Be sure that students are using their ears and not just watching your hands while you model for them. Some students may "cheat" by following your fingers and hand movements rather than using their ears. You might stand behind the class and model, or you may demonstrate with a different instrument.

Have other students model for the class, and take turns being the leader. Insist on a steady pulse from your players, whether they are modeling or responding to the leader. Keep a metronome going softly, and stop or redirect their playing if they stray too far from the pulse.

Begin modeling some of the simple lines from the beginner book including folk songs and melodies. Students will gradually associate pitches with fingerings, and you will lay the groundwork for reading music later on in the year. By starting students this way, you prevent them from becoming "button pushers" who respond to *notation* by pressing valves or moving to slide positions and promote associating what they see to the *sounds* that notation represents. This approach follows the philosophy of sound to sign to theory: first we hear and play the music, then we notate it, and then we define what we have played and heard.

QUESTIONS FOR DISCUSSION

1. What percentage of students needs to be able to perform a task correctly before moving on to a new concept? Should you wait for everyone to be successful? Are there times you should move on before a student has not mastered a certain fundamental skill?
2. Share some of your favorite breathing or note playing games with the class.

FIELD EXPERIENCE CONNECTIONS

1. Ask your cooperating teacher about some of his or her classes' favorite breathing games or exercises.
2. Ask your cooperating teacher if you can work with some small groups of students on breathing and block note concepts.
3. How does your cooperating teacher reinforce great playing fundamentals? Is there a particular time during the lesson that these fundamentals are emphasized?

4. Create an innovative breathing or block note game, and share it with your students. Evaluate what went well and what you might do differently. Ask permission to record your presentation of the game, and share it with the rest of your class for feedback.

REFERENCES

Bluestine, E. 2000. *The ways children learn music.* Chicago: GIA.

Colwell, R. J., and T. W. Gooslby. 2002. *The teaching of instrumental music.* 3rd ed. Upper Saddle River, NJ: Prentice Hall.

Fraedrich, E. 1997. *The art of elementary band directing.* Galesville, MD: Meredith Music.

Green, E., J. Benzer, D. Bertman, and E. Villarreal. 2004. *Essential musicianship for band: Ensemble concepts.* Milwaukee: Hal Leonard.

Griswald, H. G. 2008. *Teaching woodwinds.* Upper Saddle River, NJ: Pearson Education.

Johnson, K. 2002. *Brass performance and pedagogy.* Upper Saddle River, NJ: Prentice Hall.

Pilafian, S. and P. Sheridan. 2002. *The breathing gym.* Fort Wayne, IN: Focus on Excellence.

Whitener, S. 2006. *A complete guide to brass.* 3rd ed with DVD. New York: Schirmer Books.

Williams, R., and J. King. 1998. *Foundations for superior performance: Warm-ups and technique for band.* San Diego: Neil A. Kjos Music.

Williams, R., J. King, and D. Logozzo. 2001. *The complete instrument reference guide for band directors.* San Diego: Neil A. Kjos Music.

4

Developing Solid
Percussion Foundations

The beginning-percussion section needs particular attention in the first few days, weeks, and months of development in order to help the students master the fundamental performance skills on both battery and melodic instruments. After you have selected students with aptitudes that would help them be successful playing percussion instruments and after you've helped the students acquire the proper equipment, it is your task to help your students build the foundations of great, relaxed playing of the five basic strokes used in the percussion section, a familiarity with the melodic keyboard instruments, and basic playing techniques of other important instruments commonly used in young bands. Your knowledge of the fundamentals for each of these instruments will help you guide your students in developing great foundations for future growth.

Students and families who are interested in studying percussion instruments need special guidance. (In chapter 10 we present methods for helping students choose the instruments on which they might be most successful.) Many parents believe that, just because their son or daughter likes to beat on things around the house or play drums on a video game, they would make great percussionists. Using the techniques outlined in chapter 10, you can help students and their parents identify the traits that would lead to success on percussion instruments. One of the most important factors contributing to success on percussion instruments is the ability to keep a steady pulse while completing coordination exercises at the instrument-demonstration night. You can also identify students with generally well-developed gross-motor coordination—particularly between right and left hands, right and left sides of the body, and hand to foot coordination—and guide those students toward percussion study. Remember that students playing percussion instruments will also need a good ear in order to successfully progress on the melodic keyboard instruments as well as to perform common tasks such as tuning timpani. For this reason, some directors prefer that their students have prior experience playing piano, but others do not make this a firm requirement. Familiarity with the piano not only serves to help students advance more quickly when working on the melodic keyboard instruments but also might indicate motivation to study and stick with a musical instrument.

As we discuss in chapter 11, percussion students and their families should be guided in the selection of beginning-percussion equipment and supplies. A standard beginning-band percussion kit typically includes a snare drum or a practice pad, a miniature bell set, a metronome, and some type of instrument stand. Many directors prefer that students purchase kits with practice drum pads rather than full-sized snare drums. Practice pads are easier to set up, transport, and maintain, and the sound from the practice pad is softer. The noise factor will be an important consideration to parents as their students practice at home and to directors with a band room full of percussionists playing all at once.

The miniature bell sets that are found in most beginning-percussion kits are not usually the best musical instruments. The keys on the bells are quite small, and the tone quality is often piercing and harsh. It is difficult to roll on the small keys, and it is often difficult to avoid striking the screws that are used to hold the keys in place. Nevertheless, the small size of the instrument allows students to have an instrument at home for practice. Some music stores offer rentals of small xylophones for home practice. The Adams Percussion Academy Series xylophone is particularly attractive as a relatively low-cost alternative to the traditional bell kit. Try to provide as many opportunities as possible for your beginners to play on full-sized instruments frequently during class time.

Developing responsibility and efficient classroom procedures are of particular importance to the percussionist (see chapter 13 for some specific recommendations). Help your percussionists develop the professional skills they'll need as members of an ensemble, such as keeping up with, organizing, and transporting equipment. Demonstrate and teach respect for each of the instruments used in the percussion section. The school owns many of the sticks, mallets, and instruments used in the percussion section, and you should make your expectations for the care of such equipment clear to each of your percussionists. One of the first things you'll want to address in the beginning-percussion classroom is when students are allowed to play and when they are not. Many directors develop a gesture or voice command that signifies that students should stop playing. Percussionists, like all other instrumentalists, want to play their instruments, but it can be distracting if students are playing while you're trying to teach. As we mention in chapter

13, use your students' desire to play their instruments to your advantage. If a student is not following a rule or is misbehaving, simply ask her to place her sticks on the floor for a few minutes. Usually, the student will be motivated to follow your directions after a few minutes of missing out on the fun the rest of the class is having.

ESTABLISHING FOUNDATIONS FOR GREAT SNARE PLAYING

Most beginning-band programs use the snare drum as the primary instrument to teach fundamentals that can be applied to all of the other percussion instruments. By teaching the proper grip, playing spot, and playing technique on the snare drum, teachers can help students transfer these fundamental skills to many of the other instruments. Both melodic keyboard instruments as well as snare drum should be taught in the beginning classes, and many of the basic fundamentals of playing the other instruments can be established by establishing efficient and relaxed playing on these two instruments. Teaching a relaxed, flexible grip, proper positioning of the body and instrument, the correct playing spot, and the basic strokes used on the snare drum will allow your students to move successfully to the keyboard instruments and will help them develop skills on all of the other percussion instruments.

Grip and Playing Position

One of the first things you'll have to decide is whether to teach your students matched or traditional grip for snare drum. With a matched grip, the students' left and right hands are basically mirror images of each other. The traditional grip grew out of military snare drum playing in which the snare drum was held with a sling around the neck while marching. In order to accommodate the slanted position of the snare drum while marching, percussionists began to hold the left-hand stick differently from the right. There are two advantages that make the matched grip the preferred grip taught by many beginning-band instructors. Students can compare their left and right hands and make them look the same if they use matched grip, and students can transfer this grip to almost all of the other percussion instruments fairly easily. After the matched grip is established, it is easy to switch students over to a traditional grip at some point later in their development if desired.

Establishing a matched grip is fairly easily accomplished by having your students open their hands so that their palms face the ceiling. From this position, you can simply hand them a pair of sticks and ask them to close their hands around the stick gently. Next have students turn their palms to face the floor while they are holding the sticks. Have students check for the following:

1. *The main balance point for the stick should be the fulcrum created by the thumb and the first joint of the first finger.* The fulcrum is the "tension adjuster" for the stick. We can tighten or loosen the tension by gripping or relaxing at this point. Adjust the tension created by the thumb and first finger to control the bounce of the stick when playing. Holding the stick too high or too low on the shaft will inhibit a relaxed bounce. Most players find holding the stick about one-third from the butt end of the stick, so that about an inch and a half of stick is visible on the end, is about right.

2. *All of the other fingers wrap lightly around the shaft of the stick.* Sometimes the little fingers like to wander off the stick—especially when students begin to perform rolls.

3. *Palms should point directly to the floor.* If you are set up correctly, your sticks should drop directly to the floor if you opened your hands.

4. *Sticks should be in the shape of a pizza slice.* Start with the sticks at a 90° angle. The angle may close in a bit as students get more comfortable playing, but watch that the angle does not get too small or move wider than 90°.

5. *Wrists should be straight.* Move your body closer to and farther from the drum pad to find a position where the wrists are relaxed and straight. Also experiment with the height and angle of the elbows so that the wrists are straight. Have students drop their arms to their sides while holding their sticks and notice their wrist angles. Keep this angle when moving up to playing position.

6. *Forearms should be almost parallel to the floor.* Move closer to and farther from the snare pad and adjust the height of the pad so that your forearms are almost parallel to the floor. Be sure the shoulders are relaxed and that the arms just "hang" in the correct position. This position may be slightly lower than parallel, but avoid holding the forearms too low or above a line parallel to the floor.

7. *Thumb and first finger are close neighbors.* There should be no more than a tiny space between the thumb and first finger along the side of the stick. You should not be able to insert the butt of a stick into this space.

8. *Relax!* Your entire body should be balanced and relaxed. Any tension will spread to other parts of your body and keep you from playing well.

Many playing problems that percussionists encounter in beginning band can be avoided with proper instrument positioning. Begin by standing straight in a relaxed position with the feet shoulder width apart. Adjust the height of the pad or the snare drum so that the arms can hang naturally with the forearms almost parallel with the ground. Some directors instruct their beginners to make a loose fist with their right hand and place it directly underneath their navel and then adjust the height of the pad or the drum so that the top of the drum sits just beneath the bottom of the student's clenched right fist. Teach your percussionists the mechanics of how to adjust the height of their instrument stands. It is easy to pinch fingers in the moving parts or to over-tighten the adjustment screws on many beginning-percussion kits unless you are very careful.

Playing Spots

Understanding the acoustic principles of the drum helps us determine the best playing spots for each of the instruments. All properly tuned drums, including the timpani, bass drum, and snare drum, have similar characteristics when it comes to vibration. The center of a drum vibrates the least, and the edge of the drum vibrates most. Since most of the time we want a compact, strong sound from the snare drum, the default playing position is nearer the center of the drum (fig. 4.1). Playing closer to the edge of the drum is softer, but it is also more resonant and produces more overtones. We can also play on the rim of the drum for special effects or to isolate stickings or timing during practice.

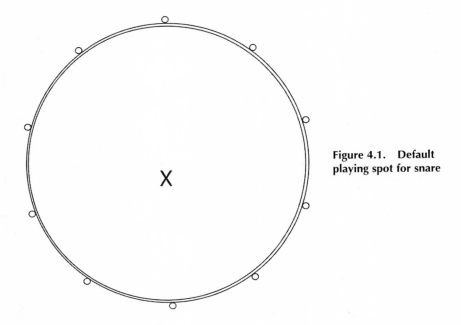

Figure 4.1.   Default playing spot for snare

Five Basic Strokes

Non-percussionists are often intimidated when they look at a chart of the standard rudiments that snare drummers are asked to master. In reality, almost all of these rudiments are made up of five basic kinds of strokes and their combinations. By mastering each of the five basic strokes in isolation before combining or moving on to the other strokes, we can develop strong technical fundamentals in our percussionists. Emphasize to your students that they must learn to execute each of the strokes equally well with both their left and right hands. Since we're developing fine- and gross-motor co-ordination, it is important to move deliberately and slowly (while remaining flexible and relaxed) when mastering these fundamentals. Gradually increase the tempo only as students become comfortable executing each of the strokes and their combinations. Some teachers choose to introduce the basic strokes in a different order from that presented here; you will have to decide the order that works best in your situation. Many teachers have been successful proceeding in the following order:

1. *Rebound stroke.* The default stroke for the percussionist is the rebound stroke (sometimes called the *legato stroke*). The performer allows the stick to bounce back off the drum head while playing. Students should take time to develop ease and speed in both left and right hands using this stroke. Students also need to learn various permutations of rebound strokes using combinations of left- and right-hand stickings.
2. *Diddles.* Diddles are performed by letting the stick bounce two or more times while using a single rebound (legato) stroke. This motion allows students to perform rolls and other important rudiments.
3. *Tap.* This is a light stroke in which the player drops the bead of the stick gently from its beginning position (about one to three inches above the drum head) and allows the stick to bounce back to the starting position.
4. *Upstroke.* This stroke begins with a tap followed by lifting the stick up to about twelve inches above the drum head after it is struck.
5. *Downstroke (accent).* The downstroke is like the rebound stroke without the rebound. Instead of letting the stick bounce back, the performer stops the stick dead after striking the head of the drum.

LEVELS

Percussionists often use a system of stick heights to visualize the mechanics of each stroke and to describe how to perform different dynamics. The different levels are often expressed in terms of inches.

While most teachers don't actually use a ruler to measure these stick heights, the system does give students a relatively familiar reference they can use to monitor the mechanics of their playing.

> 9" – Default *legato stroke* for beginners—very loud, lots of rebound and wrist
> 6" – Mezzo forte—for faster playing
> 3" – Piano—light playing, fastest playing; use the fingers more than the wrist
> 1" – Default *tap stroke*—useful visualization for unaccented notes and taps within various rudiments

Relaxed Single Strokes: Developing the Rebound (Legato) Stroke

Developing a comfortable, efficient rebound stroke sets your students up to play in a relaxed, facile manner. Students should use the wrist of the hand as the primary lever in the rebound stroke rather than the arm. Have the students hold their sticks in normal playing position and then bend their wrists so that the palms are facing straight forward and both sticks are pointed straight to the ceiling. Have them move that hinge back and forth so that they get the feeling of moving their wrist instead of their arm to make the stick move. After the students get the feeling of the wrist movement, start working to get the students to feel the rebound of the stick off the pad or drum head.

1. Begin with the sticks one to three inches above the head of the drum.
2. Lift the right stick about nine inches off the drum head, and then immediately strike the head, and allow the stick to *bounce back* off the drum head to the nine-inch mark. Have your students think about dividing the effort of playing so that the wrist motion delivers 50 percent of the effort, and 50 percent of the motion is a reaction of the bounce off the head. Sometimes it helps to use basketball to illustrate the action of the wrist and the effect of the bounce.
3. Your students can adjust the amount of pressure at the fulcrum made by the thumb and first finger on the stick to control the bounce— loosen the grip to let the stick bounce more; tighten the grip to get more control over the stick.
4. Relax! Any tension in the hands, shoulders, neck, and so forth will make it difficult to play faster and more fluently.
5. Constantly check to be sure that your students are maintaining correct hand position and the proper angle between the sticks (see the "Grip and Playing Position" section above).

Here are some common exercises that help students develop a relaxed rebound stroke. Each of these exercises should be taught by rote first. Introduce the notation only after your students can play each of these exercises easily without thinking about them.

One of the first exercises many beginning percussionists learn is "eight on a hand." Start with eight, relaxed rebound strokes on each hand. Be sure that the nonplaying hand stays in position near the center of the drum head. Remember that you are helping your students develop fine- and gross-motor skills here; begin with a tempo of quarter note = 112. Gradually increase the tempo with a goal of quarter note = 220. As you increase the speed, have your students use less motion from the wrist, use the fingers more, and lower the stick height a bit. You can vary this exercise by playing other numbers of strokes on each hand (7, 12, 3 on a hand). Develop left-hand strength by starting the exercise with the left hand (fig. 4.2).

Figure 4.2.   Eight on a hand

You can also teach your students a *countdown* exercise. Alternate rebound strokes beginning with eight strokes on each hand followed by seven, then six, then five, and so forth. This exercise works the students' hands as well as their brains and helps develop counting skills and the ability to keep their place in musical patterns (fig. 4.3).

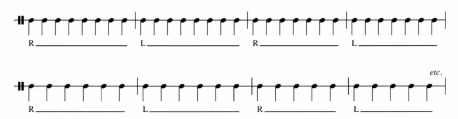

Figure 4.3.   Countdown

Alternating Hands and Single-Stroke Rudiments

After your students can successfully play consecutive rebound strokes in hands separately, you can start to introduce alternating hands. Again, these exercises are taught by rote first. The students focus on the sound of the patterns and how they are executed without the additional distraction of having to decipher the notation. The following exercise is often used to introduce alternating hands. Listen to be sure that the volume (stick height) is the same in both the right and left hands and that each stroke is even. Start slowly, and gradually increase the tempo. Begin this exercise with the left hand as well as the right (fig. 4.4).

Figure 4.4. Dut dut dugga dugga: Single strokes

We can also begin working to keep rapid, consecutive single strokes even. The following exercise employs a recurring *check pattern* of consecutive sixteenth notes (taught by rote at first) to help students keep their hands moving a consistent speed with a good sound. Introduce each new eighth/ sixteenth measure separately, adding one new pattern at a time. Teach the students to recognize each new rhythm as a separate "word" or combination of notes by rote first, and introduce the notation after they have mastered the performance of the entire exercise. As with all of these exercises, start at a deliberate, manageable tempo, and then gradually speed up. Begin this exercise with the left hand as well (fig. 4.5).

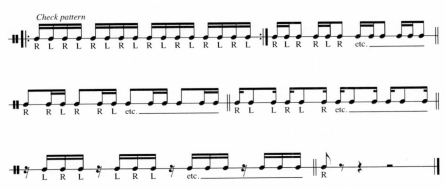

Figure 4.5. Sixteenth note timing

We can also introduce the first step in teaching concepts related to the rudiments of the *paradiddle* family. For now, perform these rudiments using single strokes with a standard rebound stroke. In the next step, we can increase the tempo and introduce the concept of letting the *diddles* of the *paradiddle* rudiments bounce.

Single paradiddle	R L R R and L R L L
Double paradiddle	R L R L R R and L R L R L L
Triple paradiddle	R L R L R L R R and L R L R L R L L
Paradiddle-diddle	R L R R L L and L R L L R R

Bounce Strokes and Diddles

After single strokes have been well established, you can begin to work on allowing the stick to bounce multiple times for each wrist stroke. Begin with a rebound stroke, but instruct students to relax the pressure at the fulcrum so that the stick bounces as many times as possible. The bounces will start slower and gradually speed up as the stick bounces lower and lower. Watch carefully to be sure that students are not moving their arms in a swimming motion as you gradually speed up the tempo.

Some teachers continue developing the multiple bounces until they work into performing closed (buzz) rolls. Other teachers move next to controlling the multiple buzzes so that the stick bounces only twice and proceed with teaching open rolls (two bounces per wrist stroke). Percussionists call the two bounces performed with a single wrist stroke a *diddle*. By using a little bit more pressure with the fulcrum created by the thumb and first finger against the stick, students can use one wrist stroke and allow the stick to bounce exactly twice for each stroke. A good exercise to get that feeling is shown in fig. 4.6.

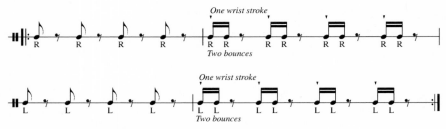

Figure 4.6. Singles and diddles

We can also go back to our *dut dut dugga dugga* exercises and this time use diddles to perform the exercise (fig. 4.7).

Figure 4.7.   Dut dut dugga dugga: Diddles

Notice that the sound of this exercises is the same as the single-stroke version, but now we move our wrists at a constant eighth-note speed and allow the stick to bounce exactly twice on the sixteenth notes. We could also perform this exercise using multiple-bounce (closed) rolls. It is important not to set the tempo for this exercise *too slow* or it will be very difficult for students to play the diddles and rolls.

Accents (Downstrokes) and Taps

The final two strokes we can teach our students are the *accent* and the *tap*. Downstrokes are accented attacks that are performed like a standard rebound stroke, but the performer does not let the stick bounce back off the head. This "dead" stroke begins nine inches above the head of the drum, but then the performer keeps the stick low after impact, allowing the stick to rebound only one to three inches above the drum head. We can isolate the accent stroke and work on placing it on various parts of the beat with the following exercise. Play each bar of the following exercise four times with the right hand, then four times with the left hand (fig. 4.8).

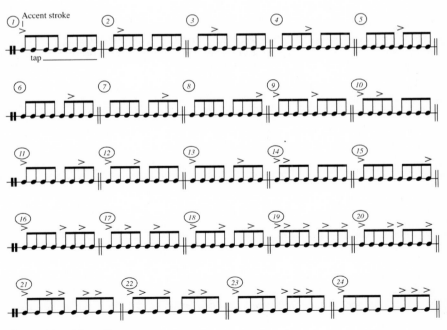

Figure 4.8.   Move it on over

The taps played between each accented note in this exercise are performed by dropping the stick from the default starting position one inch above the drum head, allowing the stick to gently tap it quietly.

Combining Strokes

After we have mastered the execution of each of these strokes individually, we can combine them to play other rudiments, like the flam, which is made up of a downstroke, an upstroke, and a tap. We can combine paradiddles, flams, and accents to begin to gradually master many of the other rudiments.

Rolls

The various roll rudiments are combinations of wrist movements and diddles. It is important to understand the rhythm of the wrist movement (sometimes referred to as the "skeleton" of the roll) and the placement of the diddles or buzzes. In a five-stroke roll, the wrist moves three times (RLR or LRL), and the stick bounces twice on the first two wrist bounces (Rʀ Lʟ or Lʟ Rʀ L).

We can use exercises like the following ones to work on keeping the hands moving the correct speed while moving back and forth between either open or closed rolls. In the following exercise, the wrists continue to move as if they were playing sixteenth notes, but in the second measure, we allow the stick to bounce either twice per wrist movement (for rolls/diddles) or many times (for closed rolls) (fig. 4.9).

Figure 4.9.   **Chicken and a roll**

Another way to gradually introduce various combinations is with a roll timing exercise. Introduce one new measure at a time in the following sequence, and then continue to repeat the check pattern after every new rhythm (fig. 4.10).

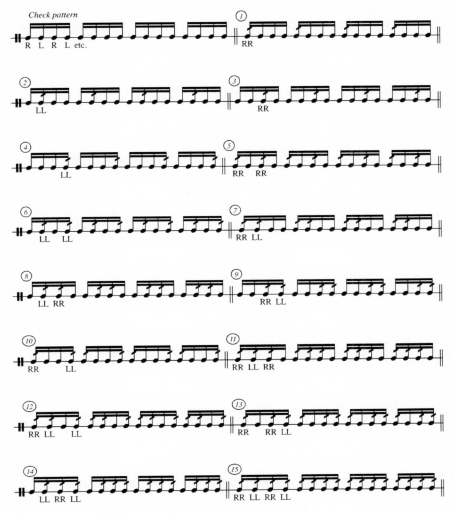

Figure 4.10. Roll timing exercise

Reading Music for Snare Drum

As we mentioned in chapter 2, students learn most efficiently if they move from sound (rote presentation of exercises) to sign (reading the musical notation of what they can already play). After the students begin to associate what they see with what they play, we can begin to help them establish the principles and theory behind what they are reading in order to help them interpret new music. One of the initial reading skills your students should master is that of matching the pattern they hear with a selection of patterns they see. If they can select which pattern is being played from a list of choices, they can begin to decode new music or read patterns based on those they have encountered previously. See chapter 2 for more information on this stage of learning to read music.

Playing through lines from a beginning method book is an excellent way to help your students improve their reading ability. When reading lines from a beginning method book, have your students count and air-drum the music first, then play. Chapter 5 offers some specific recommendations for introducing musical notation to students.

Snare-Specific Method Books

Most of the percussion books that are published as a part of other beginning-band method series are not sequenced very well and do not lead percussionists through a logical progression of skills they will need to advance to the next level of reading and performance. If you have a heterogeneous class of beginners with percussionists mixed with the other instruments, you will most likely need to rewrite and supplement the materials that are provided in those books.

There are a few snare drum—specific methods that many directors have found success with in homogeneous percussion classes. Appendix C compares the scope and sequence of each of the following snare books:

Crockarell, C., and C. Brooks. 2010. *The snare drummer's toolbox*. Nashville, TN: Row-Loff Productions.
Wessels, M. 2002. *A fresh approach to the snare drum*. Prosper, TX: Mark Wessels.
Wylie, K. 2001. *Simple steps to successful snare drumming*. Flower Mound, TX: K. Wylie.

ESTABLISHING FOUNDATIONS
FOR MALLET PERCUSSION PLAYING

In addition to learning snare-drum skills, your beginning-percussion students should also develop skills on the keyboard instruments. Balancing keyboard work with work on the snare drum helps emphasize that you are educating complete percussionists—not just "drummers." Remind your prospective and current students that professional percussionists play all of the percussion instruments—not just snare drum or drum set. Many directors find that selecting prospective percussion students who have prior experience with piano allows them to move quickly when introducing the keyboard instruments.

The Keyboard

While there are many similarities between the keyboard instruments and the technique for playing the snare drum, there are also some notable differences. There are also differences between the skills needed to play the keyboard and those needed to play melodic wind instruments. The keyboards are visual instruments and do not provide as much direct kinesthetic feedback from the keys as might a woodwind or brass instrument.

One way we can help our students learn the visual aspects of the keyboard is to show our students how to draw one. Drawing a keyboard helps students learn the patterns and layout of the various keys and helps you reinforce the names of the keys. It also gives students a way to create a quick visual reference they can use on written tests and examinations. Teach your students the following steps (fig. 4.11):

1. Draw fifteen vertical lines across the upper part of your paper.
2. Draw two horizontal lines—one on the top of the set of lines you drew and the other on the bottom. This will give you all of the "white keys" of the piano keyboard.
3. Now it's time to add the "black keys." Skip the very first line that creates the outside left edge of your piano keyboard. Now draw a small, rectangular box on top of the second vertical line. Color that line in with your pencil to make it dark.
4. Draw another rectangular box on the next line. Color it in. You should have your first set of "black keys."
5. Skip a vertical line and then draw a set of three "black keys" on the next three vertical lines.
6. Skip one more vertical line, and then make one more set of two boxes followed by another set of three boxes to complete your keyboard.

After your students know the musical alphabet, you can begin to teach them how to place the note names on the "white keys" of the keyboard. After they know sharps and flats, they can label the "black keys."

Help your students to visualize the patterns of notes on the keyboard based on the physical layout of the keys rather than by relying on the stamped letters that are found on many beginning-percussion and beginning-keyboard sets. You can cover up the note names printed on the bars with a small piece of electrical tape or gaffer's tape. You can help your students visualize scale patterns by showing them diagrams like the ones found in *The Complete Instrument Reference Guide for Band Directors* by Williams, King, and Logozzo (2001).

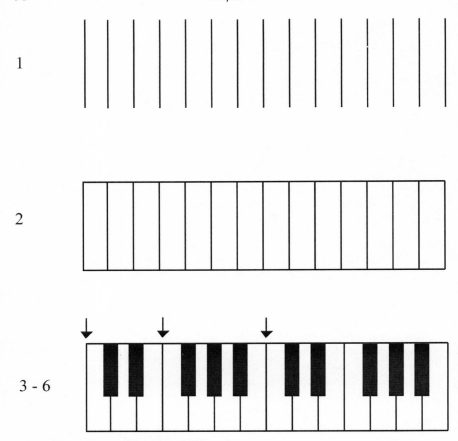

Figure 4.11.   Drawing the piano keyboard

Grip Commonalities

The foundations of a matched snare drum stick can be applied to many of the other percussion instruments including the melodic keyboard instruments. All of the same principles apply to holding a keyboard mallet:

- Create a fulcrum with the thumb and first finger against the shaft of the mallet
- Other fingers (including the little finger!) wrap lightly around the shaft of the mallet
- Palms face the floor
- Wrists straight
- Make a 90° angle (or slightly less) with the sticks (pizza slice)
- The forearms should be almost parallel to the floor

Try to alternate left and right hands whenever possible; avoid playing consecutive notes with the same hand. Some students will try to play every note with their dominant hand. Insist on correct sticking when students play, and make proper sticking a part of your assessment of their performances.

Playing Technique

The mallet instruments differ acoustically from the battery instruments. Each bar on the keyboard instruments has two acoustic nodes—places of little or no vibration—located approximately one-fourth of the length from each end of the bar. The screw or strings that hold the bar into place are usually located at the center of the acoustic node. It is best to avoid this spot by striking the bar in the direct center. This is the spot of greatest resonance on any keyboard bar.

Since we usually want the key of the mallet instrument to vibrate as much as possible, we should allow the head of our mallets to touch the bar of the keyboard instrument for as little time as possible. Use a stroke that is similar to a rebound stroke on the snare drum to lift the head of the mallet off the keyboard as quickly as possible when playing. You might have your students visualize tapping the surface of a hot iron with their finger to test the temperature to get the feeling of the stroke. This will be an important technique to use on all of the instruments on which we want to create free vibrations, such as timpani and bass drum.

When students move to larger percussion instruments, such as the marimba, we need to begin to utilize our feet to keep our bodies in position to play as naturally as possible. The size of the marimba makes it difficult for performers to plant their feet and play fluently the entire width of the keyboard. Use sidesteps to move back and forth in front of the keyboard in order to keep your body centered over the notes you are playing. Avoid crossing your feet so you don't get tripped up.

Building Harmonic Fluency and Technique and Teaching Rote Tunes

As with the other melodic instruments, our keyboard percussion students should be taught first a wide variety of simple tunes by rote. Using solfège, teach your students easy tunes that you'll want them to read later. After students can sing and play these tunes, you can begin to introduce the notation as you would with any other melodic instrument (see chapters 2 and 5 for more information about teaching note reading).

Keyboard players must develop a strong relationship between the visual aspects of their instruments and the aural components of music making. Keyboard instruments are one of the few instruments where the performer can look directly at the instrument as he or she plays. One of the first things you can do to help your students build harmonic fluency is by helping them relate the physical/visual representations of major scales to the sounds they hear and sing. Have your students learn how to construct major scales by teaching them the relationships between whole (W) and half (H) steps in a major scale (fig. 4.12).

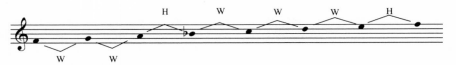

Figure 4.12.   Whole- and half-step intervals of the major scale

Once your students know the relationship between the intervals of the scale, they can figure out the notes of any major scale. You might entice your students to learn these scales by offering a prize for the first student who can figure out and play all twelve major scales for the class. Keyboard players have fewer restrictions as far as range and technique when it comes to applying their knowledge of different keys to their instruments; you can move rote songs into many different keys to help them make connections between various key centers and the functional language they are learning by using solfège in their rote songs.

Keyboard players can gain technical comfort in all the major keys by playing arpeggios and exercises in many different keys. As you continue to help them feel comfortable with these exercises, continuously try to move them from a *visually centered* approach (which is valuable at first) to a *kinesthetic* approach (which is valuable when students begin to read music). The *feel* of D major is different from that of A major.

Reading Music

As we mentioned in chapter 2 and will explore in more depth in chapter 5, we can efficiently use a sound-to-sign philosophy when teaching our keyboard students how to read music; first we learn to sing, then we learn to play what we sing, and then we learn to read what we have already played followed by reading new material. In reality, we often teach three separate streams of concepts at the same time. In one stream, we teach rote tunes; in another, we teach playing technique; and in another, we teach theoretical concepts. Eventually, these three streams converge. The beginning-percussion teacher needs to balance all of these streams in teaching melodic keyboard instruments while at the same time working to develop snare-drumming skills.

When percussion students begin to read music on keyboard instruments, they rely heavily on their peripheral vision. If the students are truly reading music, they will not be able to constantly look down at the keyboard. Many beginning percussionists actually memorize their music for playing tests so that they do not have to use their peripheral vision or look down at the keyboard and back up to the music. Shifting the visual focus from the many lines of written music on the page down to a keyboard and back up again is challenging (see chapter 2 for information on the further complicating factors associated with dyslexia). Teachers can help by teaching our students the kinesthetic feeling of playing in different keys and how to rely on their peripheral vision to help them read the music as they play. Some teachers assess the number of times a student looks down at the keyboard when playing lines for grades and take off points if a student looks down too much. It is important to emphasize that students *not* memorize the music at this point.

One of the first things we can do to help our students utilize their peripheral vision is to position the music stand in the proper spot. The bottom of the music stand should be placed as low as possible near the keyboard. This placement allows the student to keep the music close to the instrument so that shifting the focus back and forth between the keyboard and the printed page is as easy as possible. Several beginning-mallet percussion methods emphasize this peripheral-vision approach to teaching beginners (Eyles 1989; Wessels 2007).

After your students have learned a wide variety of rote tunes, after they have seen those tunes written out in musical notation, and as they begin to read and discriminate between different patterns, your students are ready to read new music. Remind your students that they should not memorize the pieces. You would approach having your students read a new piece of music in a method book just as you would with any other beginning-woodwind or beginning-brass class.

1. Sing the line using solfège or note names (or both).
2. Sing and touch the keys with the back end of the sticks lightly to get the kinesthetic feel of playing the line.
3. Play the line.

Mallet-Specific Method Books

As with snare drum, most of the mallet books found accompanying the full band instructional series of method books are not geared toward the specific development of the mallet percussionist. The mallet parts in these method books are often merely copies of the lines from the oboe book. Several excellent mallet-specific method books have been developed to help your beginning percussionists advance on these instruments:

Eyles, Randy. *Mallet percussion for young beginners*. Ft. Lauderdale, FL: Meredith Music, 1989.
Wessels, Mark. *A fresh approach to mallet percussion*. Prosper, TX: Mark Wessels, 2007.
Whaley, Garwood. *Primary handbook for mallets*. Hal Leonard, 2002.
Wylie, Kennan. *Simple steps to successful mallets and more percussion*. Flower Mound, TX: K. Wylie, 2001.

OTHER IMPORTANT PERCUSSION INSTRUMENTS

The snare drum provides the foundation for most of the other battery instruments of the percussion section. A firm foundation of basic technique on the snare will enable your students to develop their skills to a high level and help them be successful technicians on the other percussion instruments. The melodic keyboards are also integral parts of the beginning curriculum in that they establish melodic fluency and technical proficiency on an important component of the percussion family. There are four common percussion instruments on which you should take time to deliver specific instruction to your beginners: the bass drum, crash cymbals, suspended cymbal, and timpani. Most of these instruments build upon concepts introduced in study of the snare and keyboard, but each of them has peculiarities that are best addressed in the later months of beginning-band instruction.

Bass Drum

Setup and Playing Spot

The ideal setup for a bass drum is to angle the body of the drum slightly so that the player can strike, muffle, and dampen the drum easily. An angled bass drum also allows your students to perform rolls more easily. Have your students use bass drum beaters rather than timpani mallets or gong beaters (fig. 4.13).

Recall that the very center of the drum head is the least resonant spot, so if you want a very dry sound, you would strike the bass drum near the center. Most of the time, you'll want a slightly resonant sound, so the default playing position on the head is slightly below the center. In order to execute rolls, you'll want to move the playing spot closer to the edge where the drum is more resonant. Most players choose a location that is near to the five- and eleven-o'clock positions on the drum head (fig. 4.14).

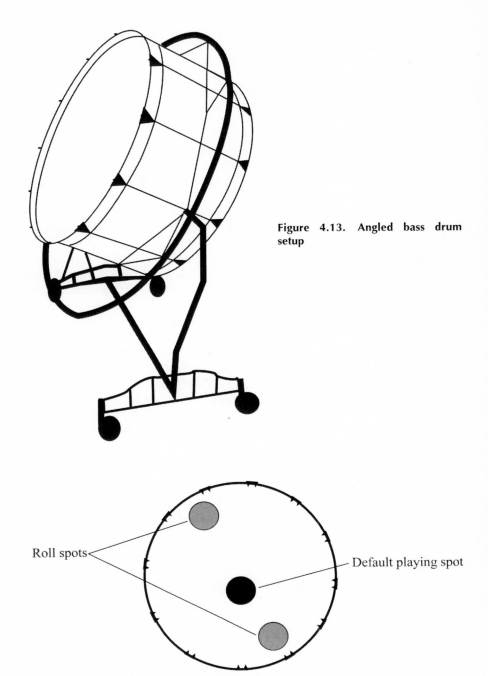

Figure 4.13. Angled bass drum setup

Roll spots

Default playing spot

Figure 4.14. Playing spots for bass drum

Stroke

The hand position for bass drum is exactly the same as the matched grip for the snare drum turned sideways. The palm of the hand faces the head of the drum just as in snare drum playing. While the wrist is the primary hinge in playing the bass drum, there will be some additional arm move-ment—especially at stronger dynamic levels. As with the melodic keyboard instruments, you will need to minimize the amount of time that the bass drum mallet is in contact with the head of the drum so that the instrument vibrates as freely as possible. The stroke for the bass drum is more like an upstroke in that the performer lifts the mallet away from the drum head immediately after striking the head to minimize contact with the head and maximize vibration for a full, characteristic sound.

Bass drum players often choose to muffle the bass drum either mechani-cally or with the fingers. You can muffle the drum mechanically by laying a cloth or hand towel across the head of the drum from the top of the rim or use a few fingers of the non-playing hand to keep contact with the head while playing. For even more muffling power, you might add the forearm of your non-playing arm or even your knee pressed against the head of the drum. Dampening the drum refers to stopping the sound of the bass drum for rests and to create silence. You can dampen the bass drum with your hands, fore-arms, knee, or a combination of these methods. Sometimes another player can help to dampen the sympathetic vibrations from the non-batter head of the bass drum. Many students fail to execute the *rests* properly when playing bass drum parts. Other players dampen the instrument *too* much and fail to let the drum vibrate on longer note values. Be sure that your students are aware of rests in the music and understand how to dampen the sound of the drum to create silence when appropriate. You may even need to edit the bass drum part to match lengths of notes in the wind parts.

Rolls

Select a striking spot closer to the rim of the drum in order to get the head of the bass drum to resonating more freely. Remember that this is the most resonant part of the drum head. Use a matched pair of mallets when playing rolls, and try to strike each beater the same distance from the rim for an even sound. Use even, regular stokes to get the entire head of the bass drum vibrating freely; fast strokes will not allow the bass drum head to vibrate freely.

Crash Cymbals

The weight and instability of the crash cymbals often challenge beginning-band students. It is important to help your students utilize a secure grip and playing technique to help them successfully manipulate and play these instruments.

Grip and Playing Technique

The hands do not go through the straps when gripping the crash cymbals. Instead, grasp the strap from underneath and allow it to cross the first joint of the first finger and rest against the palm of the hand. The other fingers wrap around the strap making a loose fist as if grasping a snare stick. The thumb may rest against the cymbal pad to provide stability by creating pressure between the fingers and the pad. It is often easier to grasp the cymbals if they are resting in a stand or cradle.

For younger players, it is helpful to use the dominant hand to create most of the motion. Keep the non-dominant hand of the crash cymbals steady to provide a steady "target" for the dominant hand. Angle the moving plate slightly so that one edge of the cymbal hits a fraction of a second before the other, creating a "flam," to avoid creating an air pocket between the cymbals. Dampen the sound by pulling the plates of the cymbal into the sockets where the arms meet the torso of the body. Smaller students and females might be more comfortable dampening the sound by pressing the plates of the cymbals into the stomach or hips. Younger students will have more control over the cymbals if they keep the plates closer together while playing.

As with bass drummers, young cymbal players often forget to take note of the rests in the music. Remind your students to closely follow the written notation and match the sounds of the cymbals with what the wind players in the ensemble are playing. Musical notation indicating that players should let the cymbals vibrate often confuses younger percussionists. The term *laisser vibrer* (abbreviated *l.v.*) means to let the instrument vibrate until the sound naturally decays. This can also be indicated with a note "tied" to a rest (fig. 4.15).

Figure 4.15.   *Laisser vibrer* two ways

Suspended Cymbal

The suspended cymbal is played with sticks or mallets using a matched grip. Alternate single strokes on opposite edges of the cymbal (at the three- and nine-o'clock positions) to produce rolls. Dampen the sound by grabbing the cymbal with the hands around the edge of the instrument. As with bass drum and crash cymbals, it is important to observe the rests written in the music. The sound of the suspended cymbal can be changed in several ways. The edge, the shoulder, and the bell of the cymbal produce their own characteristic and distinctive sounds. You can also vary the sound of the suspended cymbal by using different sticks and mallets. The tips of different sticks may be made of different materials and come in a variety of sizes; mallet heads may be soft or hard and made up of varying materials—each giving a different sound.

Timpani

Setting up the instruments, using proper playing technique, and learning how to tune the timpani are important concepts that you can introduce to your beginning-band students after they have mastered a few fundamentals.

Setup

The instruments should be arranged in a wide semicircle with the tuning pedals pointed directly toward the player. The lowest, or biggest, drum should be to the player's left. Younger players often incorrectly assume that the arrangement of the timpani is similar to the arrangement of the tom-toms on a drum set with the higher notes to player's left; the high notes of the timpani are to the player's right. Be sure to point out this important difference. The music stand should be placed just above the drums and directly between the player and the conductor so that the student can see her music, the conductor, and the drums using peripheral vision (fig. 4.16).

Playing Technique

Professional timpani players utilize several different grips when performing, but the easiest way to start beginners is to have them use the same matched grip that they utilize with the snare drum. Be sure that your timpani players are using timpani mallets and not keyboard mallets. Select a playing spot that provides the richest vibration possible—somewhere between two and four inches from the rim depending on the size of the drum. Alternate left and right hands whenever possible, and avoid crossing the arms over each other. Use steady, single strokes for all rolls instead of allowing the sticks to bounce. The speed of the roll depends on two factors—the size of the drum and the tension on the head. The smaller the timpani, the faster the roll can be; the low timpani needs slow, steady hands to create a good-sounding roll. The more tension there is on the head, the faster the

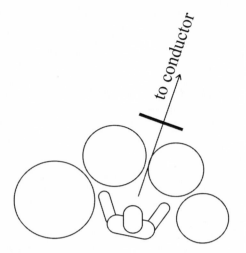

Figure 4.16.   Timpani setup

roll can be. A timpani head cranked up to its highest pitch can be rolled upon very fast, but a loose head needs slow, steady rolls.

Tuning

Tuning the timpani can be challenging, even for advanced percussionists. It is important to know the range of notes that are possible on each timpani. Many references, such as *The Complete Instrument Reference Guide for Band Directors* (Williams, King, and Logozzo 2001), provide practical ranges for each of the different sized drums. Each drum sounds best when tuned in the middle of its range; low notes on each drum sound floppy, and high notes on each drum sound thin. Use a pitch pipe or reference note from a reliable instrument to find the starting pitch (just do not become a distraction by running around in the back of the ensemble getting pitches). Adjust the tuning of the drum by manipulating tension on the drum with the foot pedal while tapping the head of the drum very softly. Some performers prefer to hum the pitch softly into the head while they adjust the tension on the drum; the head will vibrate sympathetically with the humming when the matching pitch is reached. Most performers find that starting below the pitch and then tuning up to the desired level is the easiest way to match pitch.

As you continue to develop your students' aural skills, they will feel more and more comfortable tuning the timpani. After they have successfully tuned the first drum, they can tune the other timpani in relationship to the first. If they have been taught functional solfège while learning rote tunes, they can simply sing the intervals between the two drums using solfège. Here are a few melodies that correspond to the most common intervals used to tune the timpani:

- Perfect fifth: "Twinkle, Twinkle, Little Star"
- Perfect fourth: Wagner "Bridal Chorus" ("Here Comes the Bride")
- Major second: First two notes of a major scale

Other Accessory Percussion

Many of the reference texts listed at the end of this chapter have specific playing techniques for other accessory instruments. Teach your students how to care for, organize, and play each of these instruments. The most common problem most students encounter when performing on these instruments is that they fail to hold them high enough so that the audience can hear them and so that they can make eye contact with the conductor.

Percussion Ensembles

Developing individual skills on the snare drum, the melodic keyboard instruments, the most important secondary percussion instruments, and the accessory instruments in the percussion section are of vital importance. In addition to these viable skills, your beginning-percussion students should learn ensemble skills. The ability to perform independently is of extreme importance for the percussionist as most of the time they are performing individual parts without any help from others playing the same music.

Playing in ensembles also provides some variety in the instructional sequence and helps foster continued interest in studying percussion instruments, particularly after the beginning year when students begin to read band music that may not be quite as challenging as the music they played during their beginner year. By utilizing a wide variety of percussion ensemble literature, you can keep your students playing different percussion instruments, which helps maintain excitement and enthusiasm for the program.

QUESTIONS FOR DISCUSSION

1. Why do you think some percussion students memorize music rather than read music as they are playing? How can you be sure that your percussion students are reading music and not just playing from memory?

2. Do you think classroom management and organization are more or less important for beginning-percussion students? Why do you feel this way?
3. If you've taken a percussion methods class, take out your notes and textbook from that class and compare it to what you've read in this chapter. What similarities and differences do you notice?
4. What do you think will be the most challenging aspect of teaching a young percussion section?

FIELD EXPERIENCE CONNECTIONS

1. What method books do the percussion students in your school use? Why did your cooperating teacher select that particular method book?
2. Do the beginning-percussion students in your school meet as a separate class, or are they combined with other instruments? When are melodic keyboard instruments introduced? How often do they play keyboard instruments?
3. Is there a percussion expert that teaches the beginning-percussion class at your school? If the teacher of the percussion class at your school is not a percussion expert, how has he or she prepared to teach the class?
4. How does your cooperating teacher maintain interest in the percussion section after the beginning year?
5. See if you can help the percussion section in an ensemble improve their playing techniques quietly during rehearsal.

REFERENCES

Colwell, R. J., and M. P. Hewitt. 2011. *The teaching of instrumental music.* 4th ed. Upper Saddle River, NJ: Pearson Education.

Cook, G. D. 2005. *Teaching percussion.* New York: Schirmer.

Crockarell, C., and C. Brooks. 2010. *The snare drummer's toolbox.* Nashville, TN: Row-Loff.

Eyles, Randy. 1989. *Mallet percussion for young beginners.* Ft. Lauderdale, FL: Meredith Music.

Instrumentalist Company. 1995. *Percussion anthology: A compendium of articles from the* Instrumentalist. Evanston, IL: Instrumentalist Company.

Wessels, M. 2007. *A fresh approach to mallet percussion.* Prosper, TX: Mark Wessels.

Wessels, M. 2002. *A fresh approach to the snare drum.* Prosper, TX: Mark Wessels.

Whaley, G. 2002. *Primary handbook for mallets.* Milwaukee: Hal Leonard.

Whaley, G. 2001. *Primary handbook for the snare drum.* Milwaukee: Hal Leonard.

Williams, R., J. King, and D. Logozzo. 2001. *The complete instrument reference guide for band directors.* San Diego, CA: Neil A. Kjos Music.

Wylie, K. 2001. *Simple steps to successful mallets and more percussion*. Flower Mound, TX: K. Wylie.
Wylie, K. 2001. *Simple steps to successful snare drumming*. Flower Mound, TX: K. Wylie.

WEBSITES

Pearl Drum. Academy series instrument information. www.pearldrum.com.
Percussive Arts Society. International drum rudiments. www.pas.org/Learn/Rudiments.aspx.
Vic Firth. Education resource center. www.vicfirth.com/education.
Vic Firth. 40 essential snare drum rudiments. www.vicfirth.com/education/rudiments.php.

5

From Rote to Note: Reading Music

Jason Hughes was wrapping up the fourth month of his first job as band director at Christa McAuliffe Middle School. He was very proud of all the things he'd accomplished with his beginning-band students thus far. Jason felt that his students, for the most part, were playing with good, centered tone qualities and were progressing well technically on their instruments. Each of his beginning-band classes had learned a rich and varied repertoire of rote tunes in major and minor tonalities and in duple and triple meters. Jason was using the techniques that had been introduced to him at the big state university just down the road. His professors there had stressed a "rote-before-note" approach to teaching music. Now, as Jason began to prepare for the final, short week before the Thanksgiving break, Mr. Willis, the head director of the high school and district fine-arts coordinator, wanted to have a conference with him to review his work.

Jason knew and respected Mr. Willis well; the venerable director's ensembles at the high school were legendary. His high-school groups consistently attained honors and accolades in national concert-band festivals, and the marching band was competitive at the national level. Jason was thrilled when he was chosen to be a director at one of the middle schools in Mr. Willis's district—now Jason would have the chance to work with and learn from one of the renowned leaders in the profession.

Jason had to admit that he was a little nervous as he drove into the high-school parking lot for his meeting with Mr. Willis. When Jason entered the roomy office in the high-school band hall, Mr. Willis was hard at work repairing an oboe.

"Come in, Jason!" said Mr. Willis. "I was just finishing up. Please, have a seat."

Jason sat down in the chair across the desk from Mr. Willis. The director, easily old enough to be Jason's grandfather, came around the desk to sit in the chair next to the young director.

"Jason," Mr. Willis began, "I wanted to talk to you a little bit about your beginning-band classes. To be honest, from what I hear, they are just not progressing at the pace we need them to be."

Jason felt as if he had been kicked in the stomach. This was not what the young teacher expected to hear.

"Mr. Willis," Jason stammered, "I'm totally shocked and surprised. I really feel like my kids are doing great. They mostly all have decent sounds, they're picking up on a lot of the tunes we're learning, and they're really enthusiastic about playing."

"Well that may be true, Jason, but from what I hear, they haven't learned to read music at all yet. And we're more than halfway through the semester!"

"Well that's not completely true," replied Jason. "We started reading some of the lines from the first few pages of our beginning-band method book just a few weeks ago. In addition to that, most of my kids can read the socks off the rhythm flashcards that we use in class. And you should hear them sing!"

"Jason, you mean to tell me that it's almost Thanksgiving, and you're only beginning to read out of the beginning-band book? In years past, the students at McAuliffe Middle School have already finished book 1 by the winter break! I don't care if they can sing or not; if they're not reading music, they're not going to be ready to perform at the level we need them to play when they move up to the high school."

Jason thought for a minute about what he should say next. He really enjoyed his job at the middle school, and he admired and respected Mr. Willis a great deal. Maybe his professors at the university were wrong; maybe his students would move quicker if he pushed them to read music earlier. After all, learning from the beginner book alone worked just fine for Jason when he was a beginner. . . .

If you are like most instrumentalists, and you were taught using a notation-based system of instruction, then you may be a bit intimidated or confused by a rote-to-note approach to teaching beginning-band students. You may be convinced by the argument that music may be learned as we learn a language, but you may also have reservations about that approach if you've never experienced this type of instruction before. Perhaps you can see the advantages of beginning with aural-based instruction, but like Mr. Willis in the story above, you are afraid that your students will never learn to move beyond rote learning to develop the valuable skills of reading music. A notation-based system of learning music does produce some results, and it is rewarding for teachers and students to move through many lines out of a beginner-band book. The problem with a notation-based system is that students will often associate the written music with a mechanical response of pressing down a button or a key rather than associating the notation with a musical sound. Many notation-based students become "button pushers" who have trouble associating note names, notation, musical sound, and harmonic function with each other.

It is also true that, if we only teach our students by rote, our students will not learn to read music and will be unable to learn new music in any other way. If students only learn to play the tunes that we introduce to them by ear, they will never develop the reading skills necessary to become independent musicians. Leaving out the theoretical and practical knowledge of reading music would be akin to leaving out reading and grammar in our study of language. It would be unacceptable for teachers in our elementary schools to teach their students new vocabulary and new stories exclusively through imitation or storytelling and fail to teach students how to read or to understand the principles of grammar.

The reality is that we are not faced with an either/or choice in selecting an approach to teaching young instrumentalists. The most efficient method of teaching musicians involves a *combination* of note reading and rote teaching in which we can teach plenty of music by ear, associate those tunes to their written symbols, and then help our students develop a theoretical understanding of how the notation and sound relate to each other so that they can develop the musical literacy to read, write, and improvise music that is both new and familiar. This chapter will pull together several of the ideas presented earlier in the text and illustrate how to make the transition from rote-based learning to notation-based reading and then move on to solidify students' theoretical understanding. After our students can play by ear, interpret the notation of those songs, and recognize the familiar patterns, they are ready to move on to developing an understanding of the theoretical underpinnings of what they have performed.

QUICK REVIEW: MUSIC AS A LANGUAGE

Chapter 2 details the ways that learning music might be compared to learning a language. In language acquisition, we first learn to speak by imitating the people in our surroundings. Next we learn how to read words with which we are already familiar. Our speaking vocabularies are much further ahead of our ability to read words at this point, so the sentences we read may seem very simple compared to the sentences we are speaking. In this stage of language acquisition, we learn the letters of the alphabet and the sounds they make as well as the sounds of various combinations of letters. We learn to recognize combinations of letters as words and develop a wide vocabulary of words that we can interpret at sight. As we are building our speaking and reading skills, we also began to learn to write. We write each letter, and we combine those letters into words and eventually combine those words into paragraphs. Eventually, we build great structures of ideas and meanings that we associate with various words. The word "frosty" has many connotations, including cold weather, a cold reception from a former friend, or even the name of a popular snowman.

Learning music can be approached in the same way. We first learn to play our instruments by imitating the people who play for us. At this stage, we absorb elements of tone quality, intonation, pulse, articulation, and melody from the performers who teach us how to play. In music acquisition, we do this by learning many songs by rote. After we know numerous songs, we next learn to recognize these songs by observing their musical notation. We also learn various rhythmic and melodic patterns and how they go together to make up new musical "words." We can also begin now to combine our knowledge of the notation of these familiar songs with the recognition of familiar rhythmic and melodic patterns in order to read new music. After we hear and read many different musical tunes, we began to create structure and develop theoretical underpinnings that allow us to understand overt and sublime musical elements. We begin to learn about style as well as key signatures. For instance, we learn about the differences between jazz and classical articulation. We learn the definition for enharmonic notes and about harmony. The progression of sound to sign to theory is directly related to the way we learn language.

In many ways, a notation-based classroom is structured in exactly the opposite sequence. Consider the theory-to-sign-to-sound method illustrated by the following sequence of events:

1. Students are taught the names of the lines and spaces on a staff (theory)
2. Students learn that a whole note *always* gets four beats (theory)

3. Students shown a whole note on the second line and told that the name of the note is G and that it is *always* fingered "open" (sign)
4. Students are then asked to play the first note—don't forget . . . pat your foot so that you hold the note four counts! (sound)

The remainder of this chapter illustrates how we can link the concepts of teaching by rote (see chapter 2) and introducing great sounds on each of the instruments (chapters 3 and 4) with the skills and knowledge necessary to read melodic and rhythmic patterns and to develop reading skills with our beginning-band students.

MOVING FROM SOUND TO SIGN: ASSOCIATING NOTATION TO SOUND

The critical link between playing and reading music occurs when students begin to make connections with what the music sounds like with the ways in which we can notate that sound. In this intermediate step, the teacher reveals the notation for the rote tunes along with melodic and rhythmic patterns derived from those tunes. The teacher may choose to introduce concepts related to the staff, note values, and so forth, but one of the primary purposes of this stage of learning is merely to establish the relationship of musical symbol to musical sound using material that the students have already been performing. The teacher should resist the urge to provide more information than is absolutely necessary at this stage. Don't bog down on theoretical concepts; remember that more in-depth theoretical knowledge is best introduced after students have gained more skill in reading and is based on what students have already played. Give the students what they really *need* to know at this stage.

So how do you know if the students are actually reading the music at this stage? Remember that the students can already play the pieces or patterns on which you are working, so associating the musical notation to what they are playing may be easier for them than you may first imagine. Initially, you will just want your students to play through the music and experience the ways that the sounds they play are notated. After they develop only a little bit of skill, you can begin to test their discrimination skills. Let's take one of the examples we used earlier, "Hot Cross Buns," as an example (see figure 2.1). If we have been using an aural-based approach, the students have already been taught the tune by rote and have been playing it for a while, so they are quite familiar with the tune. As they are beginning to read the song for the first time using musical notation, you might want to quiz their discrimination skills by playing the fifth measure and asking them to point to the music and indicate which of the measures you played. Is it possible that you might have played any other measure in that tune? Why or why not? Now go back and play measure 1 and ask your students to find that measure in the music. Could you also have been playing a different measure? After you've read through several tunes, you might display on the board in front of the class the notation for a song they have already read. Ask the students to audiate the music silently for a few seconds, and then have them raise their hand if they can identify which piece is on the board. As the students continue to read tunes that they have already played by ear, we can begin to introduce skills in reading rhythmic and melodic patterns. This reading ability will allow them to accomplish these tasks more quickly and proficiently. The next two sections discuss ways to teach rhythmic and melodic reading.

DEVELOPING RHYTHMIC READING SKILLS

To briefly recap the progression we followed so far, we have taught our students to play many tunes by ear, and we have introduced the notation for those tunes in a very general way. Now we can take those tunes to introduce various rhythmic and melodic concepts. Think of the rhythms our students would need to know to play the "Hot Cross Buns" example above. The rhythms in that tune include whole notes, half notes, and quarter notes if we choose to notate that melody in common time. (It is entirely possible to notate that tune in other meters, and we should introduce those concepts at some point as well!) Now we can pull from that tune the rhythmic concepts of whole notes, half notes, and quarter notes and develop some simple rhythmic patterns that we could drill with our students. We might make flashcards, electronic rhythm exercises, or write these rhythms on the board. Some combinations we might come up with include those shown in fig. 5.1.

Figure 5.1. "Hot Cross Buns" rhythms

In addition to pulling rhythms from the tunes students already know and after students understand the concept of rhythmic notation in various meters, we can introduce new rhythms that students will need to be able to read later. Teachers should present these new patterns by rote at first and then introduce the notation as before. After students have learned what these individual patterns sound and look like, you can begin to test their memory, reading, and writing ability using each of these patterns. As students gain skill, you move from a rote-based, teacher-centered approach when introducing each new rhythmic pattern to a notation-based, student-centered approach. Each new step below, adapted from Feldman and Contzius (2011), might be viewed a new "layer" of skill that you might gradually add for each new set of rhythms. You would not want to do all of these steps each time; the outline below is presented here to show a progression from rote/teacher-based instruction to note/student-based performance.

Establish pulse and meter. Get students' large muscles moving by having the class tap their heels on the ground.

Level 1: Model the new rhythmic pattern aurally using a call-and-response technique without notation (sound).
   a. Teacher models rhythm chanting a neutral syllable ("doo" or "bum"); class echoes.
   b. Teacher models rhythm chanting with counting-system syllables ("one, two, three-te, four"); class echoes.
   c. Teacher plays rhythm; class echoes playing instruments.
   d. Teacher models rhythm using a neutral syllable; class echoes using counting-system syllables.

Level 2: Teacher introduces the notation for the new rhythm (symbol).
   a. Teacher models rhythm using counting-system syllables while showing the notation to the class; class echoes.
   b. Teacher models rhythm while showing the notation; class echoes playing instruments.
   c. Teacher shows the music; class chants using counting-system syllables.
   d. Teacher shows the music; class plays rhythm on instruments.
   e. Teacher shows several different rhythms from collection the students have already chanted and played; students chant using counting-system syllables or play the correct rhythmic pattern on instruments.

Level 3: Students write what they hear using new musical notation. Teacher plays a rhythm, students write what they hear.

COUNTING SYSTEMS

There are many different systems in use for counting beats and subdivisions. Which one is best? Some counting systems use the same syllable for different divisions of the beat and can be somewhat confusing. For instance, some systems name the second subdivision of the beat as "1 ta te ta," so a rhythm like the following would be counted "1 ta ta" (fig. 5.2).

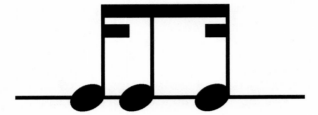

Figure 5.2. Sixteenth-eighth-sixteenth

It would be more precise to use a system that used a unique syllable for each subdivision such as "1 ti te ta" so that the same rhythm would be vocalized as "1ti ta."

It turns out that one system is not necessarily any better than any other system *as long as a system is used consistently.* Hopefully, teachers can agree on a counting system that students can use from kindergarten until they graduate from high school—or at least throughout their band experience.

Three common areas present particular problems when introducing rhythms: feeling subdivisions of two notes on a beat, feeling four notes on a beat, and dotted-note rhythms. Getting large-muscle groups involved in feeling the pulse and subdivisions are particularly helpful in teaching all of these concepts. Here is one way that you can help your students get the *feel* of subdividing the beat into two or more parts:

1. *Establish pulse and meter.* Get students' large muscles moving to the pulse of the music by having the class tap their heels to the ground. Be sure that each student keeps the heel movement steady. Have a reliable, external beat source, such as a metronome, during these exercises. Remember we are developing gross-motor skills here, so you'll want to keep the tempo slow and the movements very deliberate, almost mechanical.
2. *Establish downbeat feel by clapping the hands each time the heels touch the floor.* Be sure students stay with the metronome!
3. *Establish the upbeat feel by clapping the hands each time the heels come up.* Watch the students' feet to be sure that they are opposite of the hands. This may take some practice for some of your students. Right now it is permissible (even desirable) to have your students move their heads and bodies to help them get the feel of the subdivision.
4. *Introduce the sound of the complete eighth-note subdivision.* Instruct half the class to continue clapping the upbeats while the other half of the class claps the downbeats. Check the students' feet to be sure they

are staying with the metronome. Switch groups so that each student reviews clapping upbeats and downbeats independently.

5. *Imitate the sound of the eighth-note subdivision by having everyone clap on both the upbeat and the downbeat.* Check the feet to be sure they are staying with the metronome and not patting on the subdivisions of the beat in double time. This may take some practice.

6. *Introduce the concept of subdividing more than one note on each beat.* Students can play two notes on each upbeat and downbeat (sixteenth notes) or even four notes on each half of the beat (thirty-second notes!).

Learning these melodic patterns in isolation is similar to the concept of learning various words in a language by sight. When students see the letters *d-o-g*, they think of the word "dog" rather than the individual letters. When musicians see a combination of tones, such as the ones in the example above, they do not necessarily see each individual note, but rather, they interpret the whole combination of notes as a harmonic "word."

Musicians do the same things with patterns of notes that readers do when they interpret text. There are four common combinations of sixteenth notes that should be learned as basic "words" in our rhythmic vocabulary. You can help your students read and feel these patterns by pointing out the relationship of the sixteenth notes to the downbeats and upbeats in each pattern. For example, the second pattern below is executed by feeling two notes on the downbeat (like we performed in the exercise above) followed by a single note on the upbeat (fig. 5.3).

Figure 5.3. Common sixteenth-note patterns

Practice each of these patterns individually at first. When the students are comfortable performing entire measures of the same rhythm (as notated above), have your students perform sets of rhythms that change patterns on each beat. For example, have your students play pattern one on beat one, followed by pattern two on beat two, and so forth as shown in the second line of the example above.

The third challenging rhythmic concept is the dotted note. You can approach this concept by using ties. A tie is a curved line on the staff that connects two notes of the same pitch. A dotted note is the same length as the original note tied to a note that is half as long as the original note. Introduce the theoretical concept of the tied note after you've played some tunes that have dotted notes in them so that students understand how the sounds of dotted notes match the notation. For example, a dotted half note would get all of the counts of a half note (2) plus half that number of counts (1) for a total of three counts (fig. 5.4).

Figure 5.4.   Dotted half note addition with ties

We can use the same concept to demonstrate dotted quarter notes and dotted eighth notes.

Directors can use technology to help produce and display rhythmic patterns to their classes. Many directors use presentation software like Microsoft PowerPoint to create and project slides with one- or two-bar rhythms written out. There are several websites that feature pre-prepared PowerPoint rhythmic notation shows. Software such as SmartMusic can be of particular assistance in developing rhythm exercises and assessing student improvement. Some websites such as RhythmBee offer special exercises tailored to beginning-band students. A listing of the websites for these resources is at the end of this chapter.

DEVELOPING PITCH READING SKILLS

In the same way that we can use familiar rote tunes to help students begin to read rhythms, we can also learn the concepts of reading pitch. In addition to the intermediate step of showing the students the notation of the rote songs and exercises they already know, we can also begin to show students the notation of various melodic patterns that they have used in these rote songs and exercises. These patterns are first introduced aurally, without notation, just as we did with the rhythmic concepts outlined above. Identify the patterns that are used in the rote tunes that you've taught your students. Most of these patterns will be made up of simple diatonic steps, skips, and occasionally leaps. Let's look at some of the patterns in the folk tune "Lightly Row" (fig. 5.5).

You will notice that the melody is made up of skips of a third, steps up a diatonic pentascale in the key of C major, and a leap of a perfect fifth. You can pull at least four melodic patterns that you could introduce to your students based on tonic and dominant harmonies (fig. 5.6).

Figure 5.5. "Lightly Row"

Figure 5.6. Melodic patterns from "Lightly Row"

Here is one way that you could introduce these patterns to your students using a sound-to-symbol approach:

1. *Teacher tonicizes in the key of the piece.* Play the I–V7–I chord progression to help establish pitch and to give a tonal context to what the class will sing.
2. *Teacher sings a melodic pattern using a neutral syllable (such as "bum" or "doo"); students echo pattern.* The rhythm of the pattern is not important.
3. *Teacher sings the melodic pattern using solfège; students echo the pattern.* If you are in a homogeneous class, you can also sing note names. Heterogeneous classes may take turns singing note names to avoid confusion of using different letter names for each note.
4. *Teacher reveals the notation of the pattern and sings; students echo.*

After several tonal patterns have been learned in this way, you can begin to mix the patterns and quiz your students on their reading abilities. Show your students the pattern, then ask them to audiate the pattern, and then have them sign the pattern on your signal. After they master recognizing several patterns, have your students write out these same familiar patterns as you sing or model them.

As always, only provide enough theoretical information as is absolutely necessary to perform the pattern. You can fill in the theoretical information after students become more comfortable reading and performing familiar songs and patterns. The theoretical foundations will help your students read and interpret new, unfamiliar music. This approach is an *emergent* method of teaching how to read; concepts are introduced after students have played some piece that contains the concept (a particular rhythm or interval) and after the students have encountered the notation in some way through performance.

INTRODUCING THEORETICAL CONCEPTS

Introducing theoretical concepts only after students have played and read familiar musical lines helps your students learn how to read unfamiliar music and sets them on the path to becoming independent readers. Present concepts only as the need emerges. If you can get by without "labeling" a concept—if you can play or read a piece without the theoretical knowledge—wait to introduce the concept. This does *not* mean that you completely eliminate teaching music theory from your classes! By waiting to introduce a term or a concept until after the student has performed a musical piece that exemplifies the term or concept, the definition or image that you attach to that term or concept will be more significant since you can draw upon the student's experience to make the meaning more clear. In other words, the student experiences a concept by playing it, then the student reads the musical concept, and finally the student labels the concept.

Play→Read→Label

When you introduce the theory behind playing and reading music, you will need to solidify these concepts in a multitude of ways for aural, visual, and kinesthetic learners. Insist that each of your students keeps notes and regularly uses a notebook to organize these materials in band class. Students should record very specific definitions for each of the terms that you introduce in the classroom. Give great thought when developing and adapting definitions so that your explanations are clear, concise, and easily understood by beginning-band students. For instance, the *Oxford Dictionary of Music* defines embouchure in this way:

> In brass and some woodwind playing, the mode of application of the lips, or their relation to the mouthpiece.[1]

This is a fine definition for a developed musician, but a more appropriate definition for a sixth-grade beginner might be something like:

> The way we form our face to produce a sound.

Written notes help visual learners, but these types of students also benefit from diagrams and visual notes written on the board or projected onto a screen in the classroom. Take the time to write out each definition so that your students can see your verbiage. If you can draw a diagram or a picture of the concept, that may help your visual learners as well. For example, you might draw a picture of what the direction of the airstream in the mouthpiece might look like when moving from high notes to low notes on the trombone.

Play and sing examples of each of your definitions whenever possible to help your aural learners. If you are working to explain that notes get higher when you move up the staff, reflect that concept with your voice. Have your students move or rearrange the physical elements of your classroom to help the kinesthetic learners. If your classroom has risers, you might talk about step-wise motion versus skips by moving (carefully!) between the risers. Introduce each musical concept in as many different ways as you can to help as many different types of students as possible. Remember that, if you first play and read tunes that feature the concepts you wish to introduce, the students have already experienced these ideas through performance and have seen the concept represented in written notation, so the act of labeling these experiences will be more meaningful.

COMMON THEORETICAL CONCEPTS

Here are some common musical concepts expressed in terms that may be more understandable for young students. The definitions may not be universally accurate in all situations or applicable to advanced musicians, but the concepts are solid for beginners. You may need to modify them for your own students, but remember to keep the wording appropriate for the age and experience level of the students.

Musical alphabet: A, B, C, D, E, F, G. Be sure that your students can recite the alphabet both forward and backward. Point out that the musical alphabet does not have a beginning or an ending. You might introduce this concept by showing students a board or screen filled with the musical alphabet repeated over and over.

Staff: Five lines and four spaces that tell you which notes of the musical alphabet to play. Number the lines and spaces from the bottom to the top (fig. 5.7).

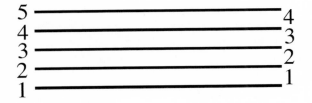

Figure 5.7. Staff: Lines and spaces numbered

Treble clef (G clef): Tells us which notes of the musical alphabet go with the lines and spaces. Use the following procedure to draw a treble clef:
1. Start just above the staff and draw a vertical line down to just beneath the staff.
2. Draw a half-heart shape to the right from the top of the vertical line to the fourth line on the staff.
3. Continue this line down to the left and curl around the second line on the staff.
4. Add a little flair to the bottom of your treble clef to finish it off!
   The treble clef is called the "G clef" because it circles around the second line G. We can label the rest of the notes in the staff if we remember that we go forward in the musical alphabet when we go up on the staff and backward in the musical alphabet if we go down (fig. 5.8).

Figure 5.8.   Treble clef note names and numbers

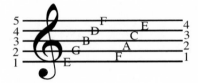

Bass clef (F clef): Tells us which notes of the musical alphabet go with the lines and spaces. Use the following procedure to draw a bass clef:
1. Draw a dot on the fourth line of the staff.
2. Draw a half-heart shape to the right from the dot on the fourth line back to the first space.
3. Draw two dots in the spaces above and below the fourth line.
   The bass clef is called the "F clef" because the three dots we made are all centered on the fourth line F. We can label the rest of the notes in the staff if we remember that we go forward in the musical alphabet when we go up on the staff and backward in the musical alphabet if we go down (fig. 5.9).

Treble clef lines and spaces: We can pull apart the musical alphabet on the staff and name just the lines—E G B D F—or just the spaces—F A C E. You might choose to give your students mnemonic devices to learn the names of the lines and spaces ("Every Good Boy Does Fine").

Bass clef lines and spaces: We can pull apart the musical alphabet on the staff and name just the lines—G B D F A—or just the spaces—A

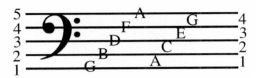

Figure 5.9.   Bass clef note names and numbers

C E G. You might choose to give your students mnemonic devices to learn the names of the lines and spaces ("Good Boys Do Fine Always"; "All Cows Eat Grass").

Ledger lines: Short lines above or below the staff that extend the staff.

Bar lines: Vertical lines on the staff that divide the staff into measures; these lines tell us when to start counting over again.

Measure: The space between the bar lines.

Double bar: Indicates the end of a section of music.

Time signature: Two numbers on the staff that tell us the value of the notes.

Top number of a time signature: Tells us how many beats are in a measure; each number represents one beat.

Bottom number of a time signature: The bottom number is not a number—it is a symbol for a note value. The bottom number tells us what kind of note gets one beat.

Bottom number chart: Use the following chart to help you figure out what kind of note gets one beat:

1 = whole note
2 = half note
4 = quarter note
8 = eighth note
16 = sixteenth note

Time signature sentence: Fill in the blanks to help you understand each time signature:

"There are _____ beats in each measure, and the _____ note gets one beat."

Breath mark: Looks like a comma. You must breathe when you see a breath mark unless you are told otherwise. Shorten the note before the breath mark.

Fermata: Musical time stops; hold the note longer than its original value or until the director signals you to stop.

Repeat sign: Repeat the music between the repeat signs.

First and second endings: Play through the first ending once only. Jump to the second ending the second time through the music.

Fine: The end of the music; stop playing.

Da capo (DC) al fine: Go back to the beginning, and repeat to the fine.

Dal segno (DS) al fine: Go back to the sign and repeat to the fine.

Slur: A curved line connecting two or more notes of different pitch; tongue the first note only.

Tie: A curved line connecting two notes of the same pitch; tongue the first note only.

Interval: The musical distance between two notes.

Half step: The smallest interval in Western music.

Whole step: Two half steps.

Sharp (♯): Raises a note one half-step.

Flat (♭): Lowers a note one half-step.

Natural (♮): Cancels out a sharp or a flat.

Accidentals: A flat, natural, or sharp sign that is not in the key signature.

Accidental rule: Accidentals last an entire measure unless canceled out by another accidental.

Key signature: Tells you what sharps or flats to play.

Order of flats: The flats on the staff appear in the following order: B♭ E♭ A♭ D♭ G♭ C♭ F♭.

Order of sharps: The sharps on the staff appear in the following order: F♯ C♯ G♯ D♯ A♯ E♯ B♯. (Notice that the order of sharps and the order of flats are mirror images of each other.)

Solo: One person plays.

Soli: One group plays.

Tutti: Everyone plays.

Unison: Everyone plays the same musical line.

Melody: The tune of a piece of music.

Consonance: Two or more notes that sound pleasing to the ear when played together.

Dissonance: Two or more notes that clash when played together.

Accompaniment: A musical part that supports the melody.

OTHER IMPORTANT CONCEPTS AND SKILLS

Drawing a Piano Keyboard

See figure 4.11 for detailed instructions on drawing a piano keyboard. Being able to draw a keyboard gives students a visual way to understand concepts such as intervals, note names, and so forth. Students can draw a keyboard to help them figure out answers on quizzes and exams.

Key Signatures

Key signatures are directly related to scales. Key signatures not only in-dicate what sharps or flats to play, but also they can indicate which note is tonic. Teach your students how to build scales and how to figure out how to determine the major key and scale that are implied by the key signatures.

Intervals of a scale: The pattern of whole and half steps in a major scale is:

Whole Whole Half Whole Whole Whole Half

W   W   H   W   W   W   H

If your students can draw a keyboard and understand whole and half steps, they can figure out the notes in any major scale.

Key signature rules: You can figure out which scale a key signature is based on by following two rules (*note the exception for the key of F major below*):

1. *Flat keys:*
   a. Find the last flat using the order of flats.
   b. Go back one flat using the order of flats.
   c. That note is the name of the tonic (*do*) of the scale for this major key.
2. *Sharp keys:*
   a. Find the last sharp.
   b. Find the note one half-step above the last sharp.
   c. That note is the name of the tonic (*do*) of the scale for this major key.

Important key signatures to memorize: Two key signatures do not follow the other key signature rules and should be memorized:

Key of C major: No sharps or flats
Key of F major: One flat—B♭

FINAL THOUGHTS

In a perfect world, we would teach our students great playing fundamentals through a wide variety of tunes taught by rote, then learn how to read those tunes, and then learn the principles that would allow us to continue to develop our reading skills. As we discussed in chapter 2, the reality is that many teachers move their students along in three separate streams—skill development, rote tunes, and theoretical knowledge. At some point, all of these streams converge, and hopefully we can progress with musically liter-ate students who can perform well on their instruments and are proficient readers. It is up to the teacher to carefully balance each of these skills and present the materials in a carefully thought-out sequence to maximize student learning. In the next chapter, we'll take a look at some of the music and materials we might use to help our students progress along this path.

QUESTIONS FOR DISCUSSION

1. What would you say to Mr. Willis if you were Jason Hughes in the opening story of this chapter? Would you defend your position? How? Why is it sometimes difficult to defend a position that might be in conflict with a more experienced teacher?
2. Find a simple tune, and pull out melodic and rhythmic patterns used in the song. Teach these patterns to a group of students using the approaches presented in this chapter.
3. Examine one of the first few pages from a beginning-band method book. Make a note of all of the theoretical concepts a student would need to know to read the music on that page. Can you list them all? What concepts do the students need to know before they *play* these lines by rote? What concepts would they need to know before they *read* these lines? Are there any concepts that students would not really need to know yet? Why or why not?
4. Will computer notation take the place of printed manuscript? Can a modern musician get by without knowing how to draw a treble clef? Do modern math students need to know how to do long division? Why or why not?

FIELD EXPERIENCE CONNECTIONS

1. Ask your cooperating teacher if the classes study music theory. How are new theory concepts introduced to the beginner classes? How are students assessed on their knowledge?
2. Look at the beginning-band method book your cooperating teacher uses. How are new theoretical concepts introduced in the book?
3. What opportunities does your cooperating teacher provide for students to practice their notation skills?

REFERENCES

Feldman, E., and A. Contzius. 2011. *Instrumental music education: Teaching with the musical and practical in harmony.* New York: Routledge.
Kohut, D. L. 1996. *Instrumental music pedagogy.* Champaign, IL: Stipes.

Mixon, K. 2011. *Reaching and teaching all instrumental music students.* Lanham, MD: Rowman and Littlefield Education.

WEBSITES

RhythmBee. www.rhythmbee.com.
SlideShare. Rhythm flash cards in 4/4 by Erin Contrady. www.slideshare.net/econtrady/rhythm-flashcards-in-4.
SmartMusic. www.smartmusic.com.
Soundpiper. Music and literacy activities. Rhythm flash cards. www.soundpiper.com/activities2.html.

NOTES

1. *Oxford Music Online,* s.v. "Embouchure," http://www.oxfordmusiconline.com.

6

Music and Materials
for Young Bands

Selecting music and materials for beginning band students is an important part of developing musical literacy skills. In keeping with the sound-to-sign-to-theory philosophy, one should only introduce written materials after solid foundations of playing and tone quality have been established through rote tunes and other isolated tone and executive-skill exercises have been introduced. The previous chapter presented ways in which you can help students link their ability to play by ear to the important skill of reading music. This chapter discusses selecting an appropriate method book, developing supplementary materials of your own, as well as selecting appropriate beginner-level solos and ensembles. Working with a beginning-band method book is not as easy as opening the cover and working your way sequentially through the lines in the book. You will need to be able to identify pedagogical issues that are presented in each line and develop an ability to sequence those materials and problems in order to best help your students progress.

There are many factors that go into your decision as to which beginning-band method book and supplementary materials you might choose to use. If you have a solid philosophy of music education—if you have a clear idea of why music should be taught, what kind of music is valuable, and why music should be taught in public schools—you may have an easier time selecting an appropriate method book (see chapter 12 for more information on developing a philosophy of music education). The scheduling of classes at your campus may also influence your decision; if you have homogeneous classes, you can tailor your method book selection to each individual class. If you have heterogeneous classes, then you will need to find a method book that balances the needs of each of the instruments in the classroom. It also helps to have curricular goals for your beginning-band classes. If you have a clear vision of the specific skills your students should be able to do at the end of the year, finding method books and materials that match those goals is much easier (see chapter 12 for more information on setting curricular goals for your students).

There is no such thing as the perfect method book. What works in one situation may not work in another, and what one teacher finds viable may be insignificant to another. Authors of method books realize that there are compromises that must be made in order to sell method books and balance the pedagogical concerns of each of the instruments. Some of the compromises stem from the fact that most method books are still designed to be used with a notation-based system of instruction. The selection of starting notes for instruments is often a compromise. Beginning with concert B♭, C, and D are popular choices that work well for clarinets, saxophones, and trumpets—the most popular beginning-band instruments. These three notes are not as technically comfortable for flutes and trombones: the flutes are forced to cross the break almost immediately using these notes, and the trombones must wrestle with sixth-position C right away.

Appendix D provides a detailed comparison of the concepts and skills introduced in some of the most widely available method books. As technical advances continue to appear, we will undoubtedly see more and more electronic resources to help our students learn to read.

SEQUENCING MATERIALS

Much of the materials contained in method books and many of the supplementary materials that you will develop are intended to introduce specific musical concepts. These concepts may be technical, theoretical, or musical. A particular line from a method book may be used to introduce a new note or some technical skill, such as skipping between two new notes. Another line might be used to introduce the concept of key signatures. Perhaps the main purpose of an exercise that you have developed is to work on dynamics or balance. The important thing to remember is that you are not merely playing a line of music because it comes up next sequentially in the method book or because one of your fellow teachers used a particular exercise, you are selecting activities to address a certain concept or fundamental skill.

The publishers of beginning-band method books take great care and time to consider the sequence of the materials in their books. Nevertheless, you often need to adjust the sequence or introduce supplementary materials or activities as you move through a typical beginning-band method book. As you select lines from the book, ask yourself a few questions:

1. *What is the main purpose of this line? What concept is being introduced or reinforced with this line?* Often the title of the line or the explanatory text in the book will give you clues. The teacher's edition of the method book may also contain insight into the purpose of the material.
2. *Have the students encountered this concept before?* Is the concept presented in a line of music a new concept or a reinforcement of something the students have seen before?
3. *Is this line introducing more than one new concept at a time?* If so, you will need to break up the concepts and introduce them separately before you ask your students to perform them simultaneously.
4. *Have we played this concept before?* If the students have not *experienced* the concept through performance, they should do so before they are required to read music that features the concept. For example, if the students have not heard and played a *glissando* on trombone, they should not read music with *glissandi*.
5. *Is this line the best way to introduce this concept?* Might there be a better way, utilizing the sound-to-sign-to-theory approach, to introduce the concept addressed in the line? Could you introduce this concept aurally before requiring your students to read music containing this concept?
6. *Is there an appropriate way to expand upon the concept introduced in the line?* For instance, if we're learning about subdividing the beat into two parts in common time, might we also be able to introduce subdividing the beat into two parts in cut time or 4/8 time in a subsequent lesson?

All of these questions drive your decisions when sequencing materials. You'll often have to develop supplementary materials or move things around as you move through a method book, but as long as you have planned carefully, your students will progress smoothly.

SPOTTING PEDAGOGICAL ISSUES IN METHOD-BOOK TUNES

So how do you know what pedagogical concepts are introduced in a beginning-band method line? How do you know what makes a line easy or difficult? How do you help students solve common problems encountered in each of these lines? Some of these answers are fairly obvious; we're learning a new note or a new rhythm of some type, or we're introducing a concept such as *theme and variations*. Many method-book publishers highlight these new concepts graphically so that they will be easy to identify.

Some issues that make lines difficult for beginners are less easily identified:

1. *Intervals.* In general, skips are more difficult than steps, and leaps
   are more difficult than skips—especially for brass instruments when
   moving between or skipping across harmonics. Remember that your
   students should be able to sing these intervals before they play them
   and that they should play these intervals before they read them.
2. *Long notes.* Many students fail to hold long notes out full value. This
   is often caused by students losing track of the pulse or beat or by
   developing an inaccurate concept of the duration of the notes. For example, a dotted half note in common time receives three entire beats,
   but many students think they should stop the note when they have
   mentally counted to three. In reality, they should hold the note out
   until they reach count four. Some directors use the analogy of movie
   times: If a movie lasts three hours and starts at one o'clock, then the
   movie gets out at four o'clock. Your students can practice the feeling of
   sustaining notes full value by holding their hands together to indicate
   the length of the longer notes when clapping and counting. In our
   dotted-half-note example above, the students would hold their hands
   together three entire beats.
3. *Rests.* Students often fail think counts during the rests. Remind your
   students that "rests" are not really about relaxing; rests are indications
   of musical silence. Be sure that students know how many counts each
   rest receives. Students sometimes run into problems if they have long
   notes that precede rests; if they do not hold out the long notes full
   value, they will begin their rests too early. Counting rests that follow
   eighth notes is sometimes difficult for young students—help your
   students feel and keep track of the pulse on the rests that follow the
   last eighth note. Your students can practice showing rests when they
   clap and count rhythms by holding their opened hands out to their
   sides to indicate the rests.
4. *Ties.* Tied notes often throw students off because they often indicate
   rhythms that do not align with the strong beats of the measure. Take
   the ties out to practice, and be sure that your students understand
   where the downbeats are in each part of the measure.
5. *Instrument-specific pedagogy.* It helps to be familiar with the specific
   pedagogical issues that each of the instruments might encounter in
   a particular line. Sometimes these instrument-specific pedagogical issues are indicated in the method book, but you may need to consult
   other experts or references to understand the issues introduced in a
   new line. Pay careful attention to lines that call upon the woodwind
   instruments to cross the break between harmonics (while clarinet

is the most famous in this regard, all woodwinds have a "break" between the registers). Consider issues involving range and crossing harmonics in the brass. Instruments may have specific executive-skills issues that may need to be addressed (flicking in the bassoons or moving between sixth and first positions for trombones). Look carefully at the individual fingerings and their combinations for each instrument on each new line of music.

Despite your best preparation and planning, your students will encounter problems when playing through various lines of music. If they could play each line perfectly, they would not need to work through the music with you. When your students have trouble with a particular line of music, try to determine the primary cause of the problem. The *cause* of the problem will influence your *choice of technique* for addressing the issues encountered in the line. The performance problems may be caused by a breakdown in the aural concept that the student has, a rhythmic issue, an executive-skills challenge, or a misconception of the musical style of the piece. Isolating the problem area is the most efficient way to address the errors.

Aural-Skills Issues

Wrong notes in an exercise may be caused by an incorrect aural concept of how the music should sound. If the student cannot clearly conceptualize or audiate how the music should sound, he or she may have a difficult time reproducing the music through the instrument. In general, if a student can sing a line of music, he or she will be more likely to be able to play it. Let's say that your students are having trouble with the minor-seventh leap in the third and eleventh bars of the Mexican folk song "Chiapanecas" (fig. 6.1).

Figure 6.1. "Chiapanecas"

You might choose to isolate this leap in two ways: (1) perform the two notes involved in the leap in isolation, and (2) take away the rhythmic component of the music. Sing the notes first using solfège (*ti, la*) or the note names (A, G), then sing and finger, then play these pitches slowly and deliberately. *When working on aural-skills issues, isolate the pitches by removing the rhythm from the equation.* Next you might zoom out a bit and sing the notes immediately before and after the pair of notes you sang and played before (*do, ti, la, sol*) or (B♭, A, G, F). In each step, as you break down this music, be sure to (1) sing, (2) sing and finger, and then (3) play. (Some teachers have their brass players buzz the intervals on their mouthpieces after singing and before playing on the assembled instrument.) Finally, the students can put the collection of notes back into an even broader context by performing the entire piece as written.

Rhythm-Skills Issues

Students must be able to feel the rhythm of the piece and understand what that feeling looks like when it is notated. Continuing with the "Chiapanecas" example, let's say that your students are having trouble playing bars 3 and 4 with accurate rhythms (there are those pesky rests again!). Isolate the rhythm in two ways: first remove the playing requirement entirely by clapping and counting the rhythm, and then remove the note-reading issues by playing the rhythm on a single pitch. Clap and count the two measures with rests in isolation first; then clap and count the entire piece. Next, play the rhythm of the two measures on one pitch (the tonic note is usually a good choice) followed by performing the rhythm of the entire piece on one pitch. *When working on rhythm-skills issues, isolate the rhythm by removing the pitches from the equation.* Finally, the students can put the collection of rhythms back into a larger context by performing the entire piece as written.

Executive-Skills Issues

Often, note mistakes and rhythmic errors are caused not by a misunderstanding of how to read the music but by an inability to manipulate the fingers or hands to execute the technique involved in playing the line. Imagine that your trombone students are having trouble playing the fifth and sixth bars of "Chiapanecas." The students can sing and count the line, but they are still not playing the skips between second-position A, sixth-position C, and third-position E♭ smoothly. Review the sound of the combination of the notes by singing first; then isolate the executive skills involved in those measures by singing and fingering the notes. Remove the rhythms of the line, and finger through each note slowly. As when addressing aural-skills issues, it is most efficient to (1) sing, (2) sing and finger, and then (3) play.

Another technique that helps isolate the executive-skill issues is to add one note at a time. Begin by playing the first note (A), then add the second note (A, C), then play three notes consecutively (A, C, E♭), and so forth. Begin by playing each note without a specific rhythmic value, and then begin playing the notes in a slow rhythm, gradually working up to the performance tempo. *When working on executive-skills issues, isolate the technical skills by removing the rhythm from the equation.* Finally, the students can put the measures back into context by performing the entire piece as written.

Stylistic Issues

Sometimes your students will need help performing stylistic or interpretive aspects of the lines of music. Beginners should be given a steady diet of legato, connected playing as they begin to develop their skills on performing their instruments. Avoid introducing any other note lengths until all of your students can play a wide variety of tunes by rote and using notation using a beautiful legato sound. Eventually, you will want to introduce your students to notes of different lengths and shapes. *The most efficient way to communicate style to your students is through modeling.* If a picture is worth a thousand words, a musical model is worth a million. Words are a poor substitute for modeling when it comes to musical style. Instead of talking through the ways an accented quarter note should be performed, model that sound for your students. Model style by playing the passage on one note and asking students to echo your performance. Follow this up with singing, moving, and diagramming the style for your students. *When working on stylistic issues, isolate the style by modeling and by removing the note changes from the equation.* The best model is one demonstrated using the same instrument that the students are playing. If you cannot model well on their instrument, use an instrument with which you feel comfortable.

REHEARSING METHOD-BOOK TUNES

As you can see, reading lines from a beginning method book during beginning-band classes is a *part* of your daily routine for these classes. Ideally, you will introduce important executive-skill, rhythmic, and aural concepts before playing exercises or rote tunes by ear. Reading lines from the beginning-band method book then becomes a *part* of what you do each day to reinforce concepts that you have already introduced rather than being the primary method in which you present skills and ideas to your students. Here is one approach to reading new lines from the method book:

1. *Isolate the key concept in the line.* For instance, if there is a new note or rhythm in the piece, review the necessary skills out of context before you launch into reading the music.
2. *Use a whole/part/whole approach to presenting materials.* Present the entire piece; then work on any individual combinations of notes or

concepts that need more work; then put your work back into context with a final performance of the entire piece.

3. *Sing, sing and finger, and then play.* Singing without playing isolates and allows you to check for aural and rhythmic understanding and helps you monitor style as well. Singing and fingering helps match the sounds of the piece with the executive skills of moving the fingers and slides. Some teachers like to have their brass players buzz on mouthpieces after they sing the line.

BEGINNING SOLOS AND ENSEMBLES

Working on solos and ensembles is a valuable part of developing solid playing fundamentals. How you handle performance and contest experiences, selecting solos or ensembles for students, and organizing rehearsal experiences are important factors that contribute to the success of a solo and ensemble experience. If carefully crafted, solos and ensembles can help develop confidence and playing skills far beyond what students may be able to develop playing in a concert band setting. Balance, blend, tone quality, and independent musicianship skills can each be honed through solo and ensemble playing.

Selecting an appropriate solo or ensemble for your students can be a challenging task. Carefully consider the ranges and key signatures as well as the rhythmic and metrical challenges of the work. Solos and ensembles tend to be more exposed since there is usually only one person playing each part; choose music that is technically a bit easier than what you might choose otherwise. Fatigue is often a factor, particularly for young brass players, and can negatively impact a solo and ensemble performance. Be wary of solos or ensembles that are very long or contain few opportunities for students to rest mentally and physically. Some ensembles are not equally balanced in the difficulty of the various parts. Feel free to rearrange written parts so that each performer takes turns playing the more difficult or interesting parts of the ensemble.

Rehearsing solos and ensembles takes careful planning and coordination. If you assign the same ensemble or solo to each of the members of your class, you can rehearse these pieces during class time, but the students will still need opportunities to practice in small-ensemble settings or as individual, solo performers. If you have the space, you can send students to practice rooms or have the students break up into small groups throughout the classroom. Multiple solos and ensembles rehearsing at once may sound chaotic, but this allows you to work with individuals and groups and to monitor student behavior.

There are many options when it comes to accompanying solos. Playing with a capable accompanist helps students develop the skills of maintaining a steady beat and playing with accurate intonation. Some directors choose to have students perform solos unaccompanied. Other directors utilize electronic accompaniments, such as a recorded version of the piano part or with interactive accompaniment software such as SmartMusic. This software allows the performer to adjust the tempo and can be calibrated to follow the student's tempo fluctuations. Be sure to arrange for amplification if using computer or recorded accompaniment, and be sure to train your students how to "play" the accompaniments during performances.

Working up a solo or an ensemble is an exciting way to introduce students to the thrill of public performance. A well-organized recital of solos and ensembles can be an effective way to showcase your students' progress. Students can also be selected to play solos or ensembles between band performances at a concert. Many directors choose to host a solo and ensemble festival with professional judges to adjudicate performances.

The music teacher is one of the few professional educators in the school that gets to completely design the curriculum for his or her students. This design includes selecting the "textbooks" and "workbooks" for the class. Selecting an appropriate beginning-band method, choosing great solo and ensemble literature, and being able to make decisions about how to teach music using these materials is an important part of what music teachers do. By carefully selecting, designing, and utilizing music and materials for your students, you can help your students transition from great rote-tune players to literate musicians who can read and write music.

QUESTIONS FOR DISCUSSION

1. Take a look at some student books from a beginning-band method series. What factors make the book appealing visually? What factors make the book appealing pedagogically? What would you like to see more of in the book? What would you take away?
2. Select a line from a beginning-band method book. See if you can list one or two main purposes for the line. What does this line teach or reinforce? Has this concept been used or introduced previously in the book? Is the new concept reviewed or expanded upon later on in the book?
3. Teach the line you selected to a group of students. Record your teaching episode, and watch the recording at least once. What went well during your lesson? What could you have done differently? What did you notice on the recording that you did not hear or see "live" during the teaching episode?

FIELD EXPERIENCE CONNECTIONS

1. Ask your cooperating teacher if you can look through the school's collection of solo and ensemble literature for your primary instrument. Do you recognize any of the pieces? Do you recognize any of the composers or arrangers? What do you think about the difficulty of the solo or ensemble parts?
2. Ask your cooperating teacher what factors she considers when selecting a beginning-band method book. What aspects does she like about the current book she uses? What would she change? How does she supplement the material presented in the book?
3. As you listen to a group of students rehearse (beginners or more advanced students), do you find that they make counting errors or note errors more often? If they make counting errors, what types of errors are most common? If they miss notes, do you think it is because of an aural-skills problem, an executive-skills problem, or both?

REFERENCES

Bullock, J., and A. Maiello. 1996. *Belwin 21st century band method.* Miami: Belwin-Mills.

Feldstein, S., and L. Clark. 2001. *The Yamaha advantage.* Paoli, PA: PlayinTime.

Lautzenheiser, T., J. Higgins, C. Menghini, P. Lavender, T. C. Rhodes, and D. Bierschenk. 1999. *Essential elements 2000.* with DVD. Milwaukee: Hal Leonard.

O'Reilly, J., and M. Williams. 1997. *Accent on achievement.* Los Angeles: Alfred Music.

Paschall, S. S. 2006. A review of beginning band method books for inclusion of comprehensive musicianship and adherence to the national standards for music education. Master's thesis, Bowling Green State University.

Pearson, B. 2004. *Standard of excellence.* San Diego: Neil A. Kjos Music.

Pearson, B., and R. Nowlin. 2011. *Teaching band with excellence.* San Diego: Neil A. Kjos Music.

Pearson, B., and R. Nowlin. 2010. *Tradition of excellence.* San Diego: Neil A. Kjos Music.

Sheldon, D. A., B. Balmages, T. Loest, and R. Sheldon. 2010. *Measures of success: A comprehensive band method.* Fort Lauderdale, FL: FJH Music.

Sheldon, R., P. Boonshaft, D. Black, and B. Phillips. 2010. *Sound innovations for concert band.* Los Angeles: Alfred Music.

Smith, R. W., S. L. Smith, M. Story, G. E. Markham, R. C. Crain, L. J. Gammon, and J. Campbell. 2003. *Band expressions.* Los Angeles: Alfred Music.

Sueta, E. 1974. *Ed Sueta band method.* Bloomfield, NJ: Macie.

WEBSITE

SmartMusic. www.smartmusic.com.

III

MOVING BEYOND THE BASICS

7

Advanced Instrumental Pedagogy

CAUTION: DO NOT ADVANCE BEYOND THIS POINT!

This chapter introduces some of the first advanced techniques that your students will encounter as they continue to develop on their instruments. Students should work to develop their tone quality, range, flexibility, and technical proficiency to help make them ready to play more advanced and challenging literature. Students should be able to play simple tunes with a nice, relaxed tone quality in the "beginner" range of their instruments before moving on to more advanced skills and techniques. Closely monitor your students as they begin to expand their range and technical skill to be sure that they maintain the fundamentals of great tone quality, posture, and hand position. Spend a little time each day working to develop these advanced techniques, and be prepared to leap back to exercises that concentrate on the simplest fundamentals of playing at the first sign of inefficient or strained playing. Do not sacrifice beautiful, efficient playing for "advancement" in technique or range; a trumpet player who can play a three-octave G scale with poor tone quality is not a well-rounded musician. Anytime you see your students stressing, straining, or contorting their bodies or faces to accomplish any exercise, have your students stop, relax, shake things out, and play something that everyone in the class can play easily to refocus the students on correct fundamentals of playing. Let's take a look at some of the first advanced techniques your students are likely to encounter and some ways that you can help your students develop those techniques in efficient ways.

FLUTE

Tone Quality

The best way to develop tone quality in the flute section is to engage in daily long-tone exercises. As the name implies, long tones are simply exercises made up of slow, connected, long notes that allow the performer to concentrate on producing a smooth, steady, rich tone throughout the range of the instrument. At first, the flute section can perform these long tones using a straight tone and then add vibrato as those skills are developed. Since long tones are viable on each instrument, we will take a little time here to discuss some ways to approach these exercises to build tone quality and embouchure strength.

One important, overriding principle of long-tone exercises is to start with a great sounding, easy-to-produce note and then match that sound to surrounding notes. Begin with an easy note in the middle of the range that everyone in the class can play with a beautiful tone. Next move downward or upward in small intervals. Concentrate on matching the tone quality and vibrancy of the initial note with every other note. On every instrument, the further a performer moves away from the original note, the more difficult it is to match the sound of the first note. This is often caused by differences in the resistance of the instrument created by differing lengths of tubing used to play different pitches on the instrument; a short tube is generally less resistant than a longer tube (fig. 7.1).

Figure 7.1.   Generic long tone exercises

As the section begins to match notes that are close together, they can begin to work to match wider intervals. This is the approach used by great teachers of almost every instrument, including Marcel Moyse on the flute and Emory Remington on trombone. Remington's long-tone exercises[1] can be easily applied starting on any pitch that your students can play with a great tone quality (fig. 7.2).

Figure 7.2.   Remington exercise

Some of the best of Marcel Moyse's exercises from the *De la Sonorité* method have been expanded upon and adapted for beginning to advanced students by Trevor Wye. See the list of publications at the end of this chapter for more information.

Flexibility and Range

Flute players move between registers by manipulating the size and shape of the embouchure and by changing the direction of the air moving into the instrument. Moving smoothly and purposefully between registers is an important skill that students must learn. Some students try to move between registers by blowing more or less air, but that method often results in problems with intonation and tone quality. Rather than changing the *amount* of air, students should learn to control the *focus* and *direction* of the air by manipulating the following three variables:

1. *The size and shape of the aperture.* The opening created by the lips in the flute embouchure is called the aperture. As flute players move between registers, they change the size and shape of the aperture. Lower notes have a larger, football-shaped aperture, middle-register notes have a smaller football-shaped aperture, and high register notes are even smaller and more round. Help your students notice these small changes by having them practice in front of a mirror often (fig. 7.3).

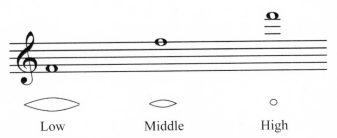

Low   Middle   High

Figure 7.3. Flute aperture shape for various registers

2. *The direction of the airstream.* Flute players aim their airstream down into the headjoint for low-register notes. As notes move higher, flute players direct their airstream higher as well. These direction changes are small and gradual; don't let your beginners exaggerate these small adjustments. A product called the Pneumo Pro developed by Blocki Flute Method helps give students feedback as to where they are ac-

tually aiming their air. See the listing at the end of this chapter for contact information.

3. *Lip placement.* As flute players move to the higher register, they bring their lips slightly forward (toward the music stand) to help focus the airstream. Again, these adjustments are very small and should not be exaggerated by your students.

Players can begin to work on flexibility and playing in different registers by isolating this skill on the headjoint. This is also a good exercise to use when introducing the different octaves of the flute. Instruct the students to remove their headjoint and close the open end with the palm of their right hand as they did when first learning how to play on their "small instruments." Have the students experiment moving between the high note and the low note produced by the headjoint by manipulating aperture size, air direction, and lip placement as described above. Students should move between the high and low note purposefully and not randomly. Be sure that your students are slurring between the high and low notes rather than using their tongue to help in the register change.

After your students can perform register slurs on their headjoints alone, they are ready to move on to playing octave slurs on the complete instrument. Have your students focus on matching tone quality and volume between octaves in the middle range of their instrument first. Start slowly, working to match pitch, vibrancy, and tone quality between octaves, and then gradually increase the tempo to develop flexibility (fig. 7.4).

Figure 7.4.   Octave slurs for flute

Another great way to work on flexibility is by playing harmonics. Finger a low note in the first octave of the flute, and change aperture shape, air direction, and lip focus to move to higher notes in the harmonic series without changing fingerings. Start very slowly with this exercise—perhaps with only the first two notes of the harmonic series—and gradually expand range after students can perform the slur without tightening up or forcing the sound (fig. 7.5).

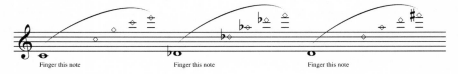

Figure 7.5.   Flute harmonics

Chromatic Fingerings and Trills

Students should be introduced to chromatic fingerings and trill fingerings as they are encountered as a part of their normal development and advancement. Ideally, students should be exposed to these new fingerings by rote before they encounter them in written music. If you can show the students a new fingering by using a rote song or an echo game before they encounter the fingering in the written music, they will be more likely to remember the fingering and understand why the new fingering may be useful. Students often balk at alternate fingerings because they are challenging and awkward at first. Help them work through these initial apprehensions by gradually working these techniques into their daily routines to help them feel more comfortable with the skills. Perhaps the first alternate fingerings your students will need to know will be the three ways to finger B♭ (fig. 7.6).

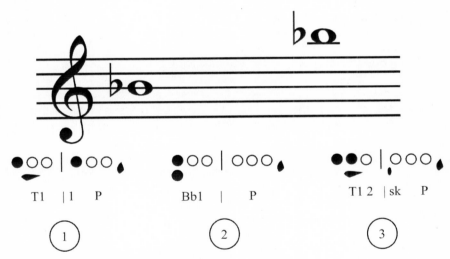

Figure 7.6.   Finger flute B♭ fingerings

1. *One and one B♭.* There is some disagreement among flute teachers as to which is the standard fingering for B♭. Most beginning-band fingering charts list the "one and one" B♭ as the standard fingering. This fingering provides support for the young player by adding a finger in the right hand to help hold the instrument and keeps the fingers of the right hand in a natural playing position. This fingering should always be used when playing chromatically between B and B♭.
2. *Thumb B♭.* Some teachers contend that thumb B♭ should be used as the default fingering since it is used when playing diatonically in most flat key signatures. Playing B♭ with the thumb simplifies the technique by

allowing the player to move fewer fingers and by isolating the movement in one hand.

3. *Side B♭*. This fingering for B♭ is only used for trills or fast, chromatic passages since the tone quality and intonation is not as desirable as the other two standard fingerings.

Your flutes will also need to know alternate fingerings for trills. Consult a good fingering guide, such as Williams, King, and Logozzo's (2001) *The Complete Instrument Reference Guide for Band Directors* or the *Woodwind Fingering Guide* online. Remind your students that they should always trill upward diatonically from the written pitch unless otherwise indicated.

FINGERING PRINCIPLES FOR WOODWINDS

When making decisions between two or more alternate fingerings for woodwinds, you will need to consider the fingering for the note before and after the note in question. The alternate fingerings presented throughout this chapter utilize the following principles:

1. *Keep technique in the same hand when possible.* If you can keep the fingers of the same hand moving rather than moving from hand to hand, chose that note (the exception being the pinky keys).
2. *Avoid sliding fingers of the same hand between notes.*
3. *Move as few fingers as possible.* Keep as many fingers in place as you can.
4. *Alternate pinkies.* Avoid using pinky fingers of the same hand consecutively.

Have a system of identifying the fingers of each hand: 1 = index finger, 2 = middle finger, 3 = ring ringer. The "pinkie" refers to the little finger of each hand. The thumb is also used on each woodwind instrument. List the fingers in the left hand first followed by the fingers in the right hand. For example, you could describe the fingering for first-line E on saxophone as "1 2 3 | 1 2." The fingering for top-line F# on flute would be thumb "1 2 3 | 3 pinky." Give each key used in chromatic fingerings a specific name, and stick with that name. For example, the A-flat one ledger line above the treble clef on flute is fingered "thumb 1 2 3 + A♭/G# key." Insist that your students are very specific and use these principles when they name fingerings for you to avoid confusion and to solidify knowledge.

Vibrato

Vibrato is a basic component of a standard flute sound. Introduce vibrato after your flute students can produce a relaxed, full tone across a wide range of basic notes. Flute vibrato is a variation in the amount of air going through the instrument. While there is some pitch variation when using vibrato, most flute performers conceive of vibrato as a variation in the strength of the air column. Vibrato takes a lot of air, so some students resist playing with it even after they've developed the skill because it takes some extra effort.

Introduce vibrato by having your students go through an exercise that isolates the physical processes used in producing vibrato in an exaggerated way. Instruct your students to play a note using a breath attack using the syllable "hee" or "hoo." Start by playing quarter notes in common time at sixty beats per minute using the "hee" or "hoo" breath attack on each note. Gradually increase the tempo, and then switch to eighth notes and triplets. At first, ask your students to keep the notes separated and deliberate, but gradually lengthen and connect the notes until they make a natural-sounding vibrato. After they can play individual notes using a connected vibrato, apply the same technique to long tones and other warm-up exercises.

OBOE

Chromatic Fingerings

Introduce chromatic fingerings and other alternate fingerings whenever students need them to successfully accomplish the technical requirements of the music. Help your students work through initial apprehensions by gradually working these skills into their daily routines and helping them feel more comfortable with new technique. The two most common alternate fingerings for oboe are those for F and G♯/A♭.

There are two ways to finger F on oboe (fig. 7.7):

1. *Standard F fingering.* Default fingering used in most playing.
2. *Forked F.* Used when moving from a note where the third finger of the right hand is used immediately before or after F. (For instance, when moving between F and D, between F and E♭, or between F and D♭.) Introduce this fingering when learning the E♭ scale or the D♭ arpeggio.

The other common alternate fingerings your young oboe students may encounter are the two fingerings for G♯/A♭ (fig. 7.8).

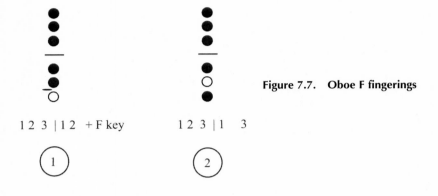

Figure 7.7.   Oboe F fingerings

1 2 3 | 1 2 + F key   1 2 3 | 1   3

(1)   (2)

1. *Standard G♯/A♭ fingering.*
2. *Alternate G♯/A♭ key.* Use this key for fast passages involving this note. You can hold down the alternate G♯/A♭ key and not affect other notes in the passage.

Consult a good fingering guide such as Williams, King, and Logozzo's (2001) *Complete Instrument Reference Guide for Band Directors* or the Woodwind Fingering Guide online for trill fingerings and other alternate fingering options.

Reed Adjustments

Ideally, you will want your students to learn how to make and adjust their own reeds under the supervision of an expert teacher. If you have the

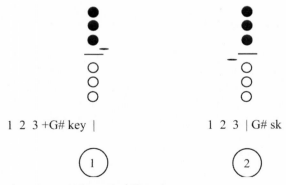

1 2 3 +G# key | 1 2 3 | G# sk

(1)   (2)

Figure 7.8.   Oboe G♯/A♭ fingerings

skills and materials available, you should instruct your students on making minor adjustments to their reeds using a reed knife (at home!) or sandpaper along with a mandrel and plaque. A great guide to reed adjustment for younger students is Robinson's (2001) *Embryonic Oboist*. An oboe reed should have a slightly elongated football shape when properly adjusted and soaked (see figure 3.4). Even if your students do not master the techniques of using a knife or sandpaper, they should still understand basic manual adjustments of their reeds:

1. *Reed too open.* Produces a wild, raucous sound that is often flat in pitch. Gently squeeze the top and bottom of the reed with the thumb and first finger just above the string. Be careful to make this adjustment after the reed is thoroughly soaked, and be gentle so that you do not crack the reed.
2. *Reed too closed.* Produces a thin, hard-to-blow sound that is often sharp in pitch. Gently squeeze the sides of the reed just below the tip. Again, be sure that the reed has been thoroughly soaked.

Vibrato

Vibrato is a standard component of the oboe sound. After a characteristic straight tone can be produced in the two main registers of the instrument, introduce vibrato as described in the flute section above. Some teachers teach jaw vibrato to their students, but the diaphragmatic vibrato utilized in flute playing is the more standard approach. See the explanation of vibrato in the bassoon section below for more information on teaching jaw vibrato.

BASSOON

Naming the Keys

Bassoon players are saddled with having to utilize more keys than any other woodwind instrument. To avoid confusion and to be very specific with instruction, it is important to use proper terminology when referring to all of the various keys. Rather than asking your students to press down "this key" or "that little silver key over there," refer to each key by its standard name (fig. 7.9).

Half-Hole

Half-hole technique involves venting the hole beneath the first finger of the left hand in order to help three notes in the middle register of the

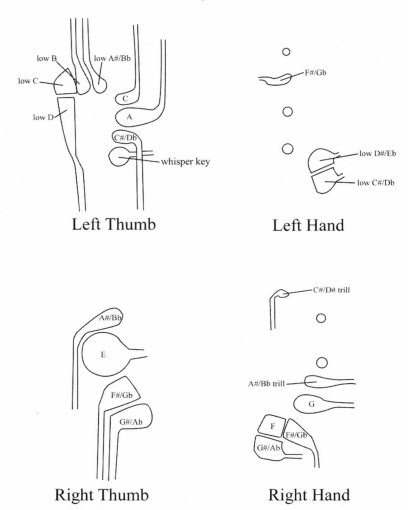

Figure 7.9.   **Bassoon key names**

bassoon speak. Roll the first finger down onto its side (instead of lifting or sliding the finger) to open the hole. Insist that your students use this technique from the very first day, and insist that they continue to use this fingering every time they play these notes. Use half-hole on the notes shown in fig. 7.10.

Figure 7.10.   Half-hole notes for bassoon

Flicking

Use the left-hand thumb to quickly tap, or flick, the A or C key to help midrange notes speak on the bassoon. This technique is especially helpful when moving from low-register notes to higher-register notes.[2] Octave slurs utilizing these notes are a great way to practice flicking. For instance, practice long-tone exercises moving from first-space C up to the C above the bass clef. Insist that your students use the flicking technique each time they play these notes to develop the habit. Flick specific keys to help specific notes speak (fig. 7.11).

Figure 7.11.   Bassoon flick keys

Chromatic Fingerings

The two most common alternate fingerings for bassoon are those for F♯/G♭ and G♯/A♭. There are two ways to finger F♯/G♭ on the bassoon. Choose the fingering that will allow you to avoid sliding thumbs in the same hand to move between notes (fig. 7.12).

1. *Left-thumb F♯/G♭*
2. *Right-thumb F♯G♭*

For example, if you were moving between a B♭ (using the left thumb on the B♭ key) and a G♭, you would want to choose fingering number 2 to avoid sliding your thumb between the B♭ key and the F♯/G♭ key in the left hand.

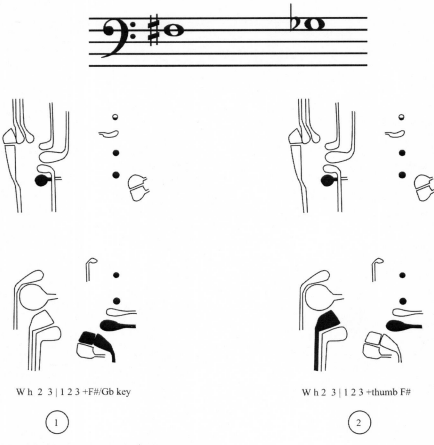

Figure 7.12.   Bassoon F♯/G♭ fingerings

There are also two ways to finger G♯/A♭. These two options give you an alternative to avoid sliding pinky fingers of the same hand between keys (fig. 7.13).

1. *Right pinky G♯/A♭*
2. *Right thumb G♯/A♭*

For example, if you were moving from low F below the staff (using the right-hand pinky) to A♭, you would want to choose fingering number 2 above to avoid sliding pinkies between notes.

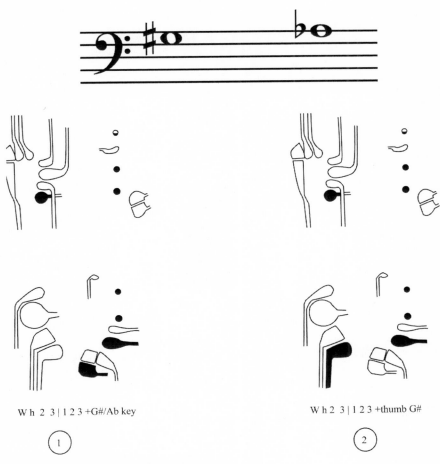

W h 2 3 | 1 2 3 +G#/Ab key   W h 2 3 | 1 2 3 +thumb G#

     ①   ②

Figure 7.13. Bassoon G♯/A♭ fingerings

Reed Adjustments

As with oboe students, you will want your young bassoonists to learn how to make and adjust their own reeds under the supervision of an expert teacher. There are two primary methods bassoonists use to adjust reeds. The first method involves using a reed knife to scrape and shape the bassoon reed. Using a knife to adjust reeds is best left for work at home or with a private-lesson instructor. The other method used to adjust bassoon reeds is by adjusting the first and second wires of the bassoon reed using a pair of needle-nose pliers (fig. 7.14).

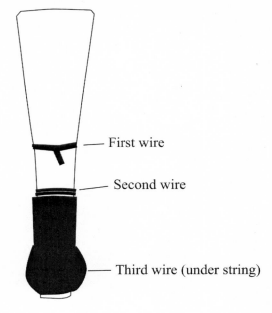

Figure 7.14.   Bassoon reed wires

First wire

Second wire

Third wire (under string)

1. *Reed too open.* Hard to play, buzzy, hollow sound, generally sharp in pitch.
   a. Squeeze the first wire from top and bottom (this may actually raise the pitch!).
   b. Squeeze the second wire from the sides.
2. *Reed too closed.* Thin sound, soft reed, bright sound, generally flat in pitch.
   a. Squeeze the first wire from the sides.
   b. Squeeze the second wire from the top and bottom (this may actually lower the pitch!).

Be sure to make these adjustments carefully and gradually and only after the reed is thoroughly soaked. Feel free to experiment; unlike working with a knife or sandpaper, each of these adjustments can usually be easily undone.

Vibrato

Unlike the flute and oboe, most bassoon teachers advocate a jaw vibrato. As with all instruments, introduce vibrato only after a relaxed, vibrant straight tone is produced in the middle range of the instrument. Start by bending the pitch down using the jaw alone, and then make the movement rhythmic by moving the jaw using a "yah, yah, yah" kind of movement. Introduce vibrato using the same types of exercises outlined in the flute section above (starting very slowly with isolated single notes and then move to eighth notes and triplets) only using the jaw as the primary vibrato mechanism. Vibrato is an important part of the fundamental sound of the bassoon, so have students work toward using vibrato all the time when playing.

CLARINET

Register Key Exercises

The lowest two registers of the clarinet (the chalumeau and the clarion registers) should be mastered in isolation first before being combined. After notes in these two registers are comfortably produced, you can expand the range into the altissimo register. Many clarinet teachers advocate the use of *voicing* to help their students move between registers. Voicing involves moving the tongue to different positions depending on the register being played using specific vowel sounds. The low register is voiced with an "ooh" sound, the middle register is voiced with an "ahh" sound, and the higher register uses an "eee" sound. Register-key slurs are an excellent way to drill these voicing changes (fig. 7.15).

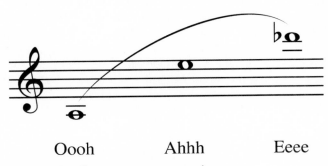

Oooh   Ahhh   Eeee

FIGURE 7.15.   CLARINET REGISTER SLUR ON A

Finger the first note in the lower octave, and then add the register key for the second note. The final high note is added by venting the first finger of the left hand using the same half-hole technique that bassoonists use. Clarinet players should practice register slurs daily to help develop embouchure strength and great tone quality across each register.

Be sure that your students understand and can read the note names when they complete register slurs. Remember that the clarinet over-blows only the odd harmonics (not octaves like the other woodwinds), so the low A in the example above is fingered the same way as the third-space E with the addition of the register key. Some students mistakenly conceptualize the clarion register as an identical extension of the note names from the chalumeau register. These students think they are playing "high G" when playing fourth-line D since it is fingered the same way as G below the staff. Sing note names when fingering through register key exercises—whether playing them by rote or using printed music—to help solidify the note names. Have your students sing note names when fingering through two-octave scales to help develop note-reading skills in each register.

Crossing the Break

While each instrument has a "break" between registers, the breaks between the chalumeau, clarion, and altissimo registers of the clarinet often present problems for advancing beginning-band students. You can smooth the transition between the registers by keeping a few principles in mind.

1. *Develop facility in the chalumeau and clarion registers independently before trying to bridge the gap between registers.* Be sure that students can play songs and exercises in each register with a clear sound and with a great tone quality before making the move across the break. Students should be able to play down to a low E below the staff in the chalumeau register and a third-line B in the clarion register without any extra squeaks or stuffy sounds. Be consistent with correct finger placement—especially those fingers that are *not* in use for each note. The fingers must remain close to the keys to make crossing the break easier (fig. 7.16).

Figure 7.16.   Clarinet tunes in two registers

2. *Cross the break by moving from the clarion register to the throat tones.* Moving down from a written third-space C or third-line B to a third-line B or a second-space A helps students to keep correct hand position more easily than trying to move the opposite direction. The fingers of the left and right hand need to be in place—close to the keys—in order for the notes in the higher register to come out (fig. 7.17).

Figure 7.17. Crossing the break

3. *Keep the right hand down when possible.* Keep the fingers of the right hand down on the following notes to help ease the transition between registers when possible. Adding the fingers of the right hand also improves resonance and intonation on these notoriously thin (and often sharp) notes (fig. 7.18).

Figure 7.18. Right hand down

Pinky Keys

Just as the bassoonist must contend with many thumb keys, the clarinet player must deal with what seems like an overwhelming number of pinky keys. As with the bassoon, be consistent in naming each of the pinky keys rather than referring to the "top key" or "that key over there." The clarinet has left- and right-hand options for three of the notes activated by the pinkies (fig. 7.19)

Work carefully in each register to help your young students understand that they can play most of the notes activated by the pinky keys in either the left or right hand (fig. 7.20).

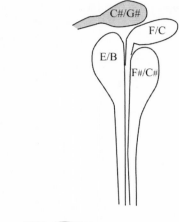

Figure 7.19.   Clarinet pinky key names

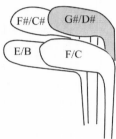

As with all of the woodwind instruments, the guidelines for deciding which pinky key to use include trying to alternate pinkies when possible, moving as few fingers simultaneously as possible, and keeping technique in the same hand. For instance, if you had a fourth-space E♭ followed by a third-space C, you would need to play the C with the left-hand (nonstandard) pinky. If you were playing an arpeggio in the key of A major, you would want to try to keep the technique in the right hand—even though the standard fingering for C♯ is in the left hand (fig. 7.21).

As with the other woodwind instruments, these different fingerings will feel awkward and *more* difficult for students at first, but with consistent work and careful guidance, students will soon learn to appreciate the increased facility that these alternate fingerings provide.

Technique

In addition to the choices of alternate pinky keys to help technical passages, there are three common alternate fingerings that the advanced begin-

Making Intelligent Fingering Choices

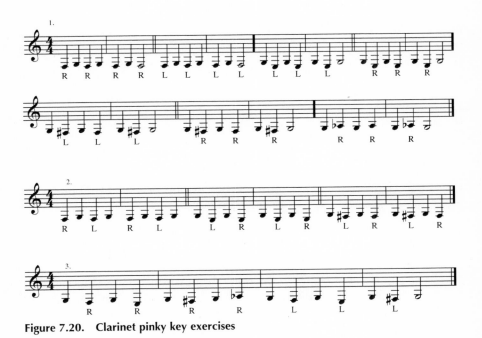

Figure 7.20.   Clarinet pinky key exercises

ner should know. The two ways to finger B in the chalumeau register (or F♯ in the clarion register) are shown in fig. 7.22.

1. *B/F♯* – The standard fingering for B in the chalumeau register or F♯ in the clarion register.
2. *Chromatic B/F♯* – Adding the chromatic B♮/F♯ key with the third finger of the right hand keeps students from flip-flopping the first and second fingers of the right hand in chromatic passages. Adding the B/F♯

Figure 7.21.   Clarinet pinky key choices

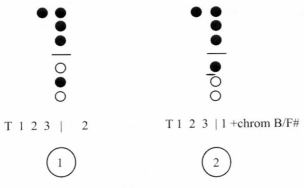

Figure 7.22.   Clarinet B/F♯ fingerings

key requires moving just one finger as opposed to flip-flopping the first and second fingers of the right hand.

The three ways to finger E♭ in the chalumeau register (B♭ in the clarion register) are shown in fig. 7.23.

1. *Side E♭/B♭* – The standard fingering for most diatonic passages.
2. *Chromatic E♭/B♭* – Adding the E♭/B♭ key with the third finger of the left hand keeps the technique in the left hand for chromatic passages.
3. *One and one E♭/B♭* – Useful for playing arpeggios from B♭ below the staff or top-line F. This keeps the technique in the same hand and moves the fewest fingers possible.

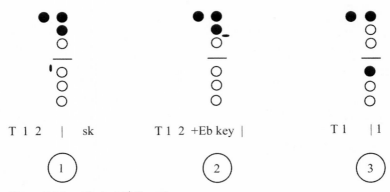

Figure 7.23.   Clarinet E♭ fingerings

The third most common alternate fingering beginners should know is for first-space F♯ (fig. 7.24).

1. *F♯* – Standard fingering for most diatonic passages.
2. *Chromatic F♯* – Use this fingering for chromatic passages to avoid flipping between the thumb and first finger in the left hand.

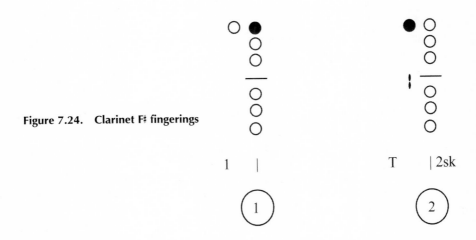

Figure 7.24. Clarinet F♯ fingerings

SAXOPHONE

Tone and Flexibility

One of the best ways to develop tone and flexibility on the saxophone is through slurred long-tone exercises in octaves. Slur from high notes to low notes starting in the second octave. If the instrument (particularly the octave key mechanism) is working properly, students should not have to force the lower notes to respond. Some saxophone teachers advocate voicing similar to the technique used in clarinet playing. These teachers advocate an "ahh" sound in the second octave, switching to an "ooh" sound in the lower octave (fig. 7.25).

Figure 7.25. Saxophone slurs

Practice these slurs slowly, with a metronome, and without vibrato. Work to even out the sound so that the tone quality and volume of the notes in each octave match.

Chromatic Fingerings

Since all the woodwind instruments are based on the same fingering system, many alternate fingerings for the woodwinds share similar characteristics. Chromatic F♯ for saxophone is almost identical to the chromatic B fingering for clarinet (see figure 7.22). A great resource for exercises addressing each of these, as well as other alternate fingerings, is Larry Teal's (1963) *Art of Saxophone Playing*.

As with the flute and clarinet, saxophone players can play B♭ three ways (fig. 7.26)

1. *Side B♭* – Many saxophone professionals consider this an "alternate" fingering, but many band directors teach this as the default fingering for most playing. Young alto saxophone players generally do not encounter a written B♭ (concert D♭) for some time in their music, so keeping the technique simple by keeping the first finger of the left hand in place for B♭ makes a lot of sense. Adding the side B♭ key is an easy addition for young saxophone students.
2. *Bis B♭* – Many saxophone professionals consider this the "standard" fingering for B♭ since it keeps the technique in the flat keys in the left hand. *Bis* (pronounced "beess") is French for "alternate."
3. *One and one B♭* – Useful for arpeggios involving the right hand.

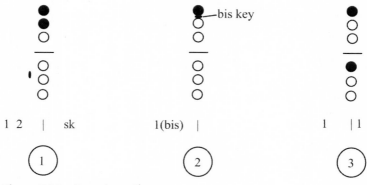

Figure 7.26.   Saxophone B♭

Vibrato

Most saxophone teachers advocate a jaw vibrato. Develop this technique as you would on the bassoon using a "yah, yah, yah" movement of the jaw to bend the pitch. Start slowly in an exaggerated way, and then move to a more fluid, connected vibrato. Vibrato is a standard component of classical saxophone playing, but its use is not universally standard in concert band or jazz band. Lyrical, solo work often incorporates vibrato, but playing a march or a unison line as a part of the jazz saxophone section would use little or no vibrato.

Woodwind Technique

Your woodwind students should learn major scales in all twelve keys through an intermediate range for their instruments (fig. 7.27).

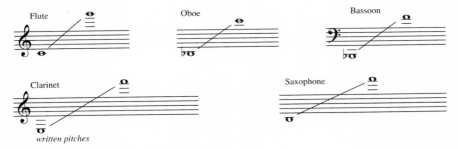

Figure 7.27. Intermediate range for woodwinds

In order to accomplish this, your woodwind students will need to develop both range (see the flexibility and range section above) and the executive skill involved with moving their fingers. Teach scales slowly, and ask students to move their fingers very deliberately to help them develop muscle memory involved in the executive skills utilized in playing each scale. Begin with five-note mini-scales in each key signature within the ranges in which your woodwind section can play comfortably. After your students can play each mini-scale, work on different intervals within the scales to help your students develop fluency in each key. When your students can play various exercises and mini-scales, you can combine separate mini-scales to create each major scale. When your students can play a one-octave scale in a particular key, introduce scales in thirds and arpeggios. After your students become comfortable with one-octave scales, scales in thirds, and arpeggios in the middle register, you can begin to introduce the higher or lower octave to the scale. Learning technique is a gradual process and should not be rushed. Be certain that your students continue to play with a relaxed, full tone, eliminating all tension in the hands, fingers, neck, and body.

BRASS

Building Range and Endurance through Tone Quality Exercises

Range and endurance can be developed by focusing on producing a rich, clear tone in the middle register and then working to expand that great sound to other registers. Some teachers suggest buzzing the mouthpiece as a part of the daily routine for brass players. Buzzing can help develop flexibility and reinforces pitch placement and accuracy. Other teachers feel that buzzing is not as "authentic" as playing the entire length of the tubing of the instrument because of the relative lack of resistance that is felt when buzzing on the mouthpiece alone. Brass players can add resistance to the mouthpiece by closing part of the opening at the end of the shank of the mouthpiece with the little finger, but that hand position is sometimes awkward for younger students. Mechanical devices, such as the BERP, help provide some resistance. This device clamps on to the lead pipe to help simulate a normal playing position.

Long tones help build endurance and a focused, centered tone. Donald Hunsberger's (1980) arrangements of Emory Remington's *Warm-Up Studies* are a valuable addition to the literature and can be adapted to the other instruments.Remember that you should help your students (especially low-brass students) develop their lower range as well as expanding upward (see figure 7.2).

Flexibility

Brass players can work to develop flexibility in their embouchures by moving from register to register using lip slurs. Start in a comfortable register, and then add notes in the harmonic series one note at a time. When

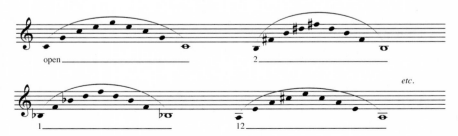

Figure 7.28.   Lip slurs: Harmonic series

students are able to produce the notes with a clear, vibrant tone quality, add another note in the harmonic series. Play lip slurs using each slide position or valve combination (fig. 7.28).

Most brass players find ascending slurs more difficult than descending slurs. Be certain to check that your students are not tonguing notes during slurs in an effort to get the notes to respond.

There are three variables that brass players manipulate to move between registers:

1. *Air speed*. As brass players move from lower to higher notes, the speed of the air gets faster and colder. As brass players move from higher to lower registers, the speed of the air gets slower and warmer.
2. *Air direction*. Brass players direct the air lower into the cup of the mouthpiece to reach higher registers and higher into the shank of the mouthpiece for lower notes.
3. *Vowel sounds*. Brass performers can think of different vowel sounds to play in different registers. Some teachers advocate an "ooh" sound for the low register, an "ahh" vowel shape for the middle register, and using an "eee" syllable for the higher register.

In addition to these three common methods for changing registers, some teachers advocate methods that are more controversial. Some teachers suggest that students should consciously adjust the aperture in the lips by making the opening smaller for higher notes. Other teachers believe that this method leads to increased tension in the embouchure. Another controversial method of changing registers is to curl the lips slightly inward when moving to higher registers. It should be remembered that different visualizations work for different students. If something works for your students and does not produce tension or degrade the sound quality, that method could be added to the teacher's tool kit.

Technique

Brass players can work on the same scales, arpeggios, and technical exercises that woodwind players undertake. The technical exercises of Herbert L. Clarke and the material in the My First Arban series for brass instruments are excellent resources for developing technique on brass.

Brass players should learn to use alternate fingerings to aid facility and tuning. Teach your students the harmonic series as the basis for alternate fingerings so they understand how they are derived (fig. 7.29).

For example, you might recommend that your trumpet players play fourth-space E (typically a flat note) with the first and second valves instead of the standard "open" fingering. Perhaps you might help your trombone

Figure 7.29.   Overlapping harmonic series fingering chart

students tackle tough technical passages by suggesting alternate slide positions (fig. 7.30).

Students playing four-valve tuba and euphonium should be taught to use the fourth valve as soon as possible. The fourth valve serves as a substitute fingering for the first-and-third valve combination and offers a more in-tune option of playing notes fingered this way. For example, a BB tuba player would want to use the fourth valve to play the C below the bass clef staff instead of the (usually sharp) first-and-third-valve combination.

Figure 7.30.   Alternate fingerings for facility

More fluid: 4   5   6   5   4   5   6   5
Awkward: 4   1   3   2   4   1   3   2

Double Tonguing

Double tonguing involves using two different parts of the tongue to articulate rapid passages. In addition to using the front part of the tongue as in normal articulation ("too" syllable), the player can use the middle part of the tongue ("koo" syllable). Rapidly alternating between these two areas of the tongue allows the performer to quickly increase tongue speed. Most teachers begin teaching the concept of double tonguing by first introducing each syllable separately and then combining the syllables for a true double tongue (fig. 7.31).

T T T T T T T T
K K K K K K K K
T K T K T K T K

Figure 7.31.   Double tonguing syllables

Most students will fail to use enough air when beginning to double tongue; insist on a fast airstream when working on articulation. It often helps students to visualize their tongue as a flag that requires a very strong breeze (their air) to make it "flap" rapidly. Each student will need to determine the speed at which he or she will need to switch from single tonguing to double tonguing. Trying to double tongue at too *slow* a tempo will sound heavy and awkward. Students should continue to work on single-tongue speed to help bridge the gap between rapid single and double tonguing. After students can play isolated exercises on one note, apply this skill to exercises they already know, such as the Remington series (fig. 7.32).

Figure 7.32.   Remington double tongued

Vibrato

Most brass teachers advocate a jaw vibrato for their students. As with all instruments, introduce vibrato only after a great, relaxed straight tone can be produced in the middle range of the instrument. Start by bending the pitch down using the jaw alone, and then make the movement rhythmic by moving the jaw using a "yah, yah, yah" kind of movement. Introduce vibrato by starting very slowly with isolated single notes, and then move to slow eighth notes and triplets. Gradually work to make the vibrato faster to make a natural sound.

Mutes

Students should be exposed to proper playing technique utilizing mutes as soon as the music they play requires these accessories. The most common mute used in literature for middle-school bands is the straight mute for the trumpet and trombone section. Straight mutes can be made of metal or fiber, and each has a distinctive sound. It may be worth the investment to purchase a set of mutes for your students to borrow during the school year. Eventually, you will want your advanced students to purchase a straight mute of their own. Most straight mutes have three or more corks that help the mute rest safely in the bell of the instrument. Give the mute a very slight twist to seat the corks in the bell to help the mute stay in place. Some brass players blow a quick blast of warm air into the bell to help form a layer of condensation on the cold bell to help the mute stick in place. Remind your students to be careful when picking up or replacing their mutes on the ground during performances and practice. Consider purchasing a few carpet squares for your brass sections so that they have a soft surface on which they can set their mutes during performances.

It is also important to check the effects of the straight mute on the intonation of the instruments. Most straight mutes will cause brass players to sound sharp. Start by tuning the instrument regularly, and then go through the same tuning procedure with the mute inserted. Students should notice how far they need to adjust their tuning slides when playing with the mute. Be sure to remind students to readjust their tuning slide after they remove the mute. Young students can be instructed to mark "pull out" and "push in" on their music to help them remember to make the proper adjustments until this action becomes a part of their normal routine when changing from open to muted and back again.

Occasionally, composers of young band music will write parts for muted French horn. It is important to understand the difference between muted horn and stopped horn. Advanced students and professionals perform stopped notes on horn by completely closing the opening in the bell of the instrument with the right hand. Many young players find this technique difficult because of the size of their hands. Each major mute manufacturer makes mechanical "stop mutes" that feature corked ends that are inserted into the opening of the bell and produce the same sound as stopped horn more easily for younger players. Stopped horn lowers the pitch of the horn one half-step. For example, a stopped note fingered as a first-space F on the horn will sound like a first-line E.

DEALING WITH ORTHODONTIC BRACES

More and more students are facing the challenges of playing wind instruments while wearing orthodontic braces. Brass players are especially challenged when it comes to making playing adjustments whenever braces are added to or removed from the teeth. Each student and situation is different, and some students have an easier time than others when it comes to making these adjustments, but all students will have to endure some type of acclimation period whenever braces are added, adjusted, or removed. One of the best pieces of advice you can give your students is to take things slowly. The students are, in essence, having to relearn how their embouchures work. Shorten practice sessions to help the embouchure muscles readjust. Have your students play in the middle range of the instrument at a softer dynamic level. Some teachers advise their students to switch to a mouthpiece with a wider, smoother rim. Some performers use orthodontic wax or putty over their teeth, but other players find these products messy. There are several commercially produced guards that fit over the braces that can help cushion the lips such as Morgan Bumpers and Braceguard. The students and teachers will need to remain patient and work slowly to help students move though these challenging times.

REFERENCES

Flute

Clardy, M. K. 1993. *Flute fundamentals: The building blocks of technique.* Valley Forge, PA: European American Music.
McCaskill, M., and D. Gilliam. 1983. *The flutist's companion.* Pacific, MO: Mel Bay.
Moyse, M. 1934. *De la sonorité.* Paris: Luduc.
Soldan, R., and J. Mellersh. 1993. *Illustrated flute playing.* London: Minstead.
Wye, T. 2003. *Beginner's book for the flute.* Parts 1 and 2. London: Novello.
Wye, T. 2004. *Practice book for the flute.* Vol. 1, *Tone.* London: Novello.
Wye, T. 1988. *Proper flute playing.* London: Novello.

Oboe

Robinson, W. T., III. 2001. *The embryonic oboist: An illustrated guide for beginning oboe players.* Huntsville, AL: Ligature.

Bassoon

Polonchak, R. M. 1982. *Primary handbook for bassoon.* Galesville, MD: Meredith Music.
Spencer, W. 1969. *The art of bassoon playing.* Evanston, IL: Summy-Birchard.
Weissenborn, J. 1995. *Practical method for the bassoon.* New York: Carl Fischer.

Clarinet

Baermann, C. 2011. *Complete method for clarinet.* Parts 1 and 2. Charleston, SC: Nabu.
Brymer, J. 2001. *Clarinet.* Yehudi Menuhin Music Guides. London: Kahn and Averill.
Endresen, R. M. 1991. *Supplementary studies: Clarinet.* Chicago: Rubank.
Hite, D. L. 1994. *Melodious and progressive studies for clarinet.* San Antonio: Southern Music.
Hovey, N. W. 1985. *First book of practical studies for clarinet.* Los Angeles: Alfred Music.
Ridenour, T. 2002. *The educator's guide to the clarinet.* Denton, TX: T. Ridenour.
Thurston, F. 1985. *Clarinet technique.* New York: Oxford University Press.

Saxophone

Teal, L. 1963. *The art of saxophone playing.* Miami: Summy-Birchard.

Trumpet

Arban, J. B., E. F. Goldman, W. M. Smith, and C. Gordon. 2005. *Arban's complete conservatory method for trumpet.* Platinum ed. New York: Carl Fischer.
Clarke, H. L. 1970. *Technical studies for the cornet.* New York: Carl Fischer.
Foster, R. E. 2001. *My first Arban: Trumpet.* New York: Carl Fischer.
Hickman, D. R. 2006. *Trumpet pedagogy: A compendium of modern teaching techniques.* Chandler, AZ: Hickman Music Editions.
Lillya, C. 2000. *Method for trumpet and cornet.* New York: Carl Fischer.

Horn

Farkas, P. 1956. *The art of French horn playing.* Evanston, IL: Summy-Birchard.
Foster, R. E. 2001. *My first Arban: Horn.* New York: Carl Fischer.

Trombone

Arban, J. B., J. Alessi, and B. Bowman. 2000. *Complete method for trombone and euphonium.* Maple City, MI: Encore Music.
Foster, R. E. 2001. *My first Arban: Trombone.* New York: Carl Fischer.
Kleinhammer, E. 1996. *The art of trombone playing.* Evanston, IL: Summy-Birchard.
Wick, D. 1971. *Trombone technique.* London: Oxford University Press.

Euphonium

Arban, J. B., J. Alessi, B. Bowman. 2000. *Complete method for trombone and euphonium.* Maple City, MI: Encore Music.
Bowman, B. L. 1985. *Practical hints on playing the baritone.* Los Angeles: Alfred Music.

Tuba

Foster, R. E. 2001. *My first Arban: Tuba.* New York: Carl Fischer.
Getchell, R. G., and N. L. Hovey. 1985. *First book of practical studies for tuba.* Los Angeles: Alfred Music.
Little, L. 1985. *The embouchure builder.* Los Angeles: Alfred Music.
Phillips, H., and W. Winkle. 1992. *The art of tuba and euphonium.* Miami: Summy-Birchard.

Brass

Amis, K. 2006. *The brass player's cookbook: Creative recipes for a successful performance.* Galesville, MD: Meredith Music.

Bailey, W., P. Miles, A. Seibert, and W. Stanley. 2006. *Teaching brass: A resource manual*. New York: McGraw-Hill.

Bellamah, J. L. 1983. *A survey of modern brass teaching philosophies*. San Antonio: Southern Music.

Colson, J., J. Stoneback, and R. Stoneback. 1998. *Braces and brass*. San Antonio: RBC.

Farkas, P. 1989. *The art of brass playing*. Evanston, IL: Summy-Birchard.

Hunsberger, D. 1980. *The Remington warm-up studies*. North Greece, NY: Accura Music.

Hunt, N. J., and D. Bachelder. 2001. *Guide to teaching brass*. New York: William C. Brown.

Johnson, K. 1981. *The art of trumpet playing*. Ames: Iowa State University Press.

Whitner, S. 2007. *A complete guide to brass instruments and technique*. Belmont, CA: Thompson Higher Education.

Other Books

Colwell, R. J., and M. P. Hewitt. 2010. *The teaching of instrumental music*. New York: Prentice Hall.

Williams, R., J. King, and D. Logozzo. 2001. *The complete instrument reference guide for band directors*. San Diego: Neil A. Kjos Music.

WEBSITES

2reed.net. Double-reed making and adjusting. www.2reed.net/reed.html.

Blocki Flute Method. www.blockiflute.com.

Braceguard. www.braceguard.com.

Flute Talk. www.theinstrumentalist.com/magazine-flutetalk.

International Double Reed Society. www.idrs.org.

International Horn Society. www.hornsociety.org.

International Trumpet Guild. www.trumpetguild.org.

International Tuba Euphonium Association. www.iteaonline.org.

Morgan Bumper. www.morganbumper.com.

Musical Enterprises. BERP mouthpiece buzzing aid. www.berp.com.

National Flute Association. www.nfaonline.org.

Saxophone Journal. www.dornpub.com/saxophonejournal.html.

Tube-Euph.com. www.dwerden.com.

Woodwind Fingering Guide. www.wfg.woodwind.org.

YouTube. Bassoon basics: flicking. www.youtube.com/watch?v=8y3018ep-Xs.

NOTES

1. Hunsberger, D. (1980). *The Remington warm-up studies*. Accura Music.

2. A good video demonstration of flicking technique can be viewed at http://www.youtube.com/watch?v=8y3018ep-Xs.

Good rehearsal technique
Dumb down; teach good
ens

- mel, tech
- Full band counter mel, etc
  sectional rehearsal vs
- Teach music
  - symbols marking
  - divisi?
- Rehearsal
  - warmup, routine (pg 180)
    etc where sit,
- Good warmup? stuff

Rehearsing and Performing with Young Ensembles

Kaylee's beginning band was having a horrible rehearsal—worse than she had ever imagined. After forty-five minutes of practice, the students were becoming restless and agitated. The rehearsal had been scheduled for after-school hours, and Kaylee had forgotten to request air-conditioning for the band room; now the temperature and humidity were becoming quite unbearable for both her and her students. The band hall was not designed to hold the more than one hundred students in the beginner band, but somehow Kaylee managed to cram them into the small room for this important rehearsal. The flute players did not have room to sit properly, and the trombone players kept clanging their slides into the music stands or into the backs of the chairs in front of them.

Kaylee was beginning to lose her voice, but she continued to try to shout over the constant murmuring of the students in the ensemble. The students' musical performance was not at the level she hoped it could be, but Kaylee knew she would have to end the rehearsal in a few minutes. Already several parents had gathered at the doorway to collect their children. Some of the parents looked amused as they watched their children rehearse, but others seemed annoyed at the fact that they had to make another trip to deliver their children to yet another extracurricular activity. Kaylee planned to end rehearsal with some final instructions regarding procedures for the big concert. She raised both of her hands and yelled, "Quiet!" She waited what seemed like an entire minute for the students to stop talking and to focus attention on her.

> When the students were finally silent, Kaylee began her announcements using a quiet voice. "Now, when you arrive at the high school tomorrow night . . ."
>
> Suddenly, one of the percussion students bumped into a large suspended cymbal, knocking it to the floor with a tremendous crash. The class screamed and laughed and was immediately out of control again. . . .

No matter how you have your beginning-band classes divided, you will probably want to provide them with some type of full-band experience. Performing for an audience, with all of the instruments represented in a full ensemble, gives students a feeling of professionalism. When students perform as a part of a large ensemble, they engage in activities that more closely resemble those of a professional musician. Knowing what you're going to teach in the full-band rehearsals, planning and organizing your presentation of that information, and organizing your performances can make or break these important rehearsals.

You may have your beginning-band classes divided in a variety of ways depending on the size of your beginning-band class, the makeup and expertise of your instructional staff, and the scheduling and facility concerns of your campus (see chapter 13 for more information). If you have heterogeneous band classes with a complete instrumentation that meets every school day, then you may not have to make significant adjustments in your teaching style or procedure, and you may not have to arrange for any special rehearsals outside of the normal school day. There will, however, be a significant shift in focus as you begin to prepare for concerts, contests, or festival performances.

If you teach homogeneous classes or smaller classes made up of one or two similar instruments, then preparing for full-band performances can be a big switch from your normal rehearsal plans. One of the advantages of teaching homogeneous classes is that you can take the time to go over all of the intricacies of each individual instrument part much as you would during a sectional rehearsal for your more advanced groups. The challenge that students in homogeneous classes will face is that they may not be aware of the other parts of the ensemble. You will need to help your students understand how their parts fit within the rest of the ensemble. What do the other parts sound like? When does each section have the melody? When are our musical lines serving in supporting roles? Playing a recording of the music when the other parts are not present may help students understand how their parts contribute to the whole group.

If the individual sections of your band meet in separate classes during the school day, you will want to plan for a full-band rehearsal before the big concert. This rehearsal is a special and exciting event for students and teachers alike. If this practice session is carefully planned and coordinated, it can be one of the most exciting events of the school year for the students. One of the first decisions you'll need to make is when to schedule your rehearsal. You may choose to have your rehearsal during the school day. This is convenient for the students and band directors since the students are already on campus. Many principals and teachers are concerned with losing valuable instructional time when band students are pulled from academic classes. If you've developed a good relationship with your principal and if your principal recognizes the special nature of this rehearsal, it is sometimes possible to make arrangements to hold a full-ensemble practice session during the school day. Be sure that you communicate with the other teachers on your campus to inform them well in advance of this rehearsal. Teachers will need to make special arrangements for changing instruction on band-rehearsal day if large numbers of their students are in band. Some music teachers offer to excuse students from individual band class so that they can complete make-up work or to catch up on instruction they may miss during this rehearsal.

If arrangements cannot be made to have your full-band rehearsal during the school day, you may be able to hold this special rehearsal either before or after school. Again, be sure to have this activity approved by your principal before scheduling this event, and make arrangements with your facilities administration for heat or air-conditioning in your rehearsal space. Communicate any special procedures for picking up and dropping off students with parents and guardians well in advance of the big event. You may need to make special arrangements for students who ride the bus or walk to and from school if your rehearsal is before or after school. Check to see that your room is large enough for all of the students and their equipment, and see that you have adequate chairs and stands for all of your students. You may need to have students bring folding music stands from home, or you may need to borrow chairs from another classroom. Careful thought related to the logistics of this rehearsal will help you accomplish your musical goals.

INTRODUCING FULL-BAND MUSIC

As accomplished musicians, it is sometimes difficult for us to remember all of the musical skills we take for granted when we read a piece of ensemble music. You will need to teach students how their printed parts work in relationship to the full ensemble and how to mark their parts in order to help the rehearsal and performance run smoothly and musically. Let students know that marking their music is a lot like performing a crossword puzzle or completing a complicated math problem; sometimes we will need to change our minds or make different markings, so students should only use a pencil when making marks on their music.

There are several markings that you would want your students to add to their parts immediately when receiving their music. The first thing you should have your students add is their name so that their music can be returned to them if misplaced. Next, have each student number each measure. To save valuable rehearsal time, have your students write measure numbers in the middle of each bar above the staff using very small numbers.

Students should also utilize some type of musical shorthand to help them remember important musical concepts. Here are some important rehearsal shorthand marks your students should learn (fig. 8.1):

Breath marks – indicate a light break or breath between notes. Shorten the note before the breath mark.
Accidentals – mark repeated accidental notes or notes in a measure. Remember the accidental rule: an accidental lasts one entire measure unless cancelled out by another accidental.
Pitch tendencies – Place an up arrow above notes that sound flat to remind you to lip them up; place a down arrow above notes that sound sharp to remind you to lip them down.
Sustain arrows – Draw long, horizontal arrows to remind you to hold long notes out full value.
Eyeglasses – Draw eyeglasses in places where you really need to watch the conductor carefully.
Beat marks – Add vertical lines to help you remember where the beats are in difficult measures.
Circle practice places – Circle passages that require special work at home.

There are a few other aspects of reading parts that may cause your beginning-band students some confusion. Help your students understand how to read *divisi* parts written on the same staff. Let your students know that more performers should play the bottom *divisi* part since these parts are generally more difficult to hear. Reading and counting multiple-measure rests often gives young students a challenge. Sometimes students forget the time signature as they are keeping track of rests. Let your young players know that it is helpful to count rests on their fingers to keep their place. If your students do not have individual measures numbered, then they will need to learn how to count measures before and after rehearsal letters. If the director asks the band to start at the fifth measure *after* rehearsal letter *K*, then the students will need to count measure *K* as the first measure. If

Marking Your Music

Always use a *pencil!* Be very neat!

Number each measure!

It is better to have a short pencil than a long memory

Figure 8.1.   Rehearsal markings

the director asks students to start four bars *before K,* then students do not include measure *K* in their count. Finding rehearsal spots in the music during
rehearsal can be confusing for some young students, so it's a good idea to
practice this skill by having your students physically touch the music with
their index finger while you stand behind the students to be certain they
are in the correct spot. After students gain some skill in counting measures,
check their understanding by asking students to see if their neighbors are
pointing at the same measure. While these procedures may seem simplistic,
they help reinforce the skills needed to read and perform from ensemble
parts during rehearsals and performances.

PLANNING FOR INSTRUCTION

After arrangements have been made for the logistics of the full-band rehearsal and after students understand how to read and rehearse their individual parts, you'll need to consider planning for the rehearsal of the music
itself. In addition to considering how you'll actually rehearse the literature
you will perform, think about the routines and procedures your students
will follow before, during, and after rehearsal. Students will need to know
exactly where to sit during the big ensemble rehearsal. Create a seating
chart on the board that everyone can see, or make name tags that can be
placed on the chairs or stands in the rehearsal space. If you're teaching a
homogeneous class, you may even go over this seating chart during class
time, before the big rehearsal, in order to help your students know where
they should sit.

In addition to knowing *where* to sit, your students should know *how* they
are expected to sit in the larger rehearsal. If you have already set up clear
rehearsal procedures during students' normal band class, then it will be
easy to transfer those expectations of behavior to the full-band rehearsal.
Ensemble discipline is particularly important if your full ensemble is very
large. Physical space may be at a premium, and even the slightest noise or
conversation can quickly become distracting. Remind students that talking,
even whispering, can be very distracting and disruptive in a large group.
You can demonstrate how loud a large group making even a little sound
can become by having your students quietly rub their music back and forth
against their music stand; even a tiny noise can be very loud when a large
number of people engage in that activity.

Students need to know exactly what they should do as they enter the rehearsal space. If you are rehearsing in your regular classroom, then students
should already have a clear idea of what they should do when they enter the
room. While they should know where to put their cases, where to put their
materials, and so forth, students may need reminders when the excitement
of the full-band rehearsal kicks in. If you're rehearsing in an unfamiliar

rehearsal location, then you'll need to make it clear where student should put backpacks, cases, supplies, and so forth before rehearsal begins. Remind students that, just as in regular band class, they should not play their instruments unless instructed to do so. The full-band rehearsal can be an exciting time for students; help students channel their excitement in a way that will be most productive for a successful performance.

"Warm-Up" Activities

Warm-up activities are designed to physically stimulate the lips and fingers, to mentally awaken the performers by activating their brains in a positive way, and to develop individual and ensemble performance skills. While some of these activities occur during the beginning of the class during "warm-up" time, you are not restricted to performing these exercises only during the first part of the class. If an activity is more relevant to a particular song that you plan to rehearse at the end of the class, feel free to include that "warm-up" activity with the part of the rehearsal that relates directly to your instruction on that specific piece. There are three types of warm-up activities that are typically utilized during ensemble rehearsals:

1. *Daily drill.* Activities that are a part of your everyday routine to activate and develop the lips, fingers, and mind. Long tones and lip slurs are two examples of elements that might be part of the daily drill. A consistent regimen of daily drill can help students develop a routine that helps them mentally and physically prepare for class. Be sure to keep your students' minds engaged during daily drill so that they do not mentally "check out" during these exercises. Give them a clear focus *each time* they play, and give them clear feedback on their performance in relationship to your instructions.
2. *Cyclical exercises.* Exercises designed to keep technical skill "under the fingers" for the ensemble. For example, you may choose to work through a cycle of different scales, or you may choose to run a particular set of related rhythmic exercises over a period of time.
3. *Ad hoc exercises.* Special exercises that address specific issues that arise in the literature you are performing. For instance, you may choose to develop an exercise that features a few of the rhythms found in a particular piece, or you may choose to play a chorale in the key of a certain piece.

A Sound-to-Sign-to-Theory Approach to Ensemble Fundamentals

Ensemble fundamentals can be viewed as an extension of the fundamentals our students work to develop on each of the individual instruments (see chapters 3 and 4). Recall that the most efficient way to introduce the fundamentals of playing an instrument is to use a sound-to-sign-to-theory model: students hear a concept demonstrated, then perform that concept, and then see musical notation that illustrates that concept. You can introduce the fundamentals of ensemble playing in the same way by first introducing exercises by rote, then allowing students to view the musical notation when necessary. Working on ensemble fundamentals without musical notation allows your students to focus their full attention on the sounds they are producing and playing techniques involved in making those sounds.

Ideally, you could teach all of your ensemble fundamental exercises without using music at first, and then introduce the music when the requirements of the music became more complicated. For instance, your brass players may be able to play lip slurs chromatically fairly easily without using music, but your woodwinds may benefit from seeing the notation. As you get to know the ability level of your particular ensemble, you'll be able to make these decisions more effectively.

So what types of warm-up activities can we perform if our ensembles don't have printed music? Without using musical notation, you can start working on block notes (as presented in chapter 3) to develop the ensemble's ability to breathe together, start notes together, sustain the sound with equal energy throughout the note, and then release together. Start with a comfortable note that is easy to play for all of the instruments, such as a concert F. Some directors instruct their alto saxophones and horns to play a concert C instead of a concert F. This would put the alto saxophones on their written A (rather than a concert F, which is a notoriously sharp note for the instrument) and the horns on a written G (an easier range for most players). To help match section volume and to check individual sections on their beginnings, middles, and ends of notes, you can play an "F around the Room" exercise where each section of the band plays concert F individually. Most directors play this exercise starting with low instruments, moving to high instruments. By isolating the sections, directors can hear each instrument group much more easily, and students can assess if their section is matching the energy, tone quality, volume, and pitch of the other sections.

Rehearsing Literature

The whole-part-whole approach of introducing rote tunes and method-book lines to students can be applied to teaching band literature as well. If possible, start with a run-through of the entire piece (or a fairly large chunk of music) before diving into the details. After running a larger portion of the tune, zoom in to smaller sections to work on individual issues that need attention. During the "zoom in" stage of rehearsal, isolate one or two important elements to address in greater detail. By concentrating on just a couple of the most important items, you keep yourself from bogging down and losing your students' attention and enthusiasm. After zooming in to work on small details, follow up with a run-through of larger chunks of music or even the entire piece to complete the whole-part-whole process. Great rehearsals often include many of these "zoom in–zoom out" cycles throughout the rehearsal. We play a large chunk, then isolate one or two elements, and then zoom out to play that chunk again to assess our progress.

Effective Teaching Cycles

When great teachers zoom in to rehearse individual issues in the music, they often employ successful techniques utilizing effective teaching cycles. Effective teaching cycles as have three parts:

1. *Set.* Tell your students what you want them to do.
2. *Follow through.* Have your students do what you ask them to do.
3. *Response.* Give your students specific feedback on how they did.

As a simple example of the teaching cycle, consider a director whose trombone section is playing an accompaniment part louder than the melodic line at letter E in a particular piece. The director might ask the trombone section to play softer at letter E (*set*). Then the director would have the ensemble play at letter E to give the trombone section a chance to make the necessary adjustments (*follow through*). After the run-through of the section of music at letter E, the director would give the section feedback as to whether or not the students had made an improvement in the balance (*response*).

A subtler example can illustrate a different approach to the same trombone balance problem that still uses effective teaching cycles. The director might ask the ensemble to play again at letter E and ask the trombone section if they can hear the melodic line in the flutes and trumpets while they are playing (*set*). The director then has the ensemble play at letter E (*follow through*). Finally, the director asks the section again if they could hear the melody and gives the students feedback on their improvement (*response*).

One of the most common mistakes teachers make in utilizing effective teaching cycles is that they fail to allow their students a chance to fix the problems that they point out. The director may be giving out correct information, but if the students do not have the opportunity to try to make the correction or to improve their performance, then there is no way to tell if any learning has taken place or if the director's instruction has actually improved the students' performance. The second most common breakdown in the teaching cycle is that teachers either fail to give their students feedback or they give feedback that is not specific enough to reinforce learning (responses such as "good" are not specific). If a director chooses to stop and rehearse something in the music, they should consider it a prime teaching opportunity for the entire ensemble, ensuring that the teaching cycles are complete for greatest effectiveness.

Isolating Concepts

When working on individual performance problems, eliminate as many distractions as you can in order to focus students' attention on the elements that are giving them trouble. For example, if students are having trouble with a rhythm in a particular measure, isolate the rhythm by playing the rhythm on one note to remove the note changes. Removing the note changes allows the students to concentrate their efforts only on the rhythm at hand; they do not have to worry about moving their fingers or adjusting their embouchures. Here are some ways to isolate common issues (see chapter 5 for an in-depth presentation of these issues):

Rhythmic problems. Remove the note changes, and play the rhythm on a single note. Choose a note that makes sense musically and is in a comfortable range. The first note of a passage or the tonic note of the key are often good choices.

Aural-skills problems. If students are missing notes because they cannot hear the correct intervals, then isolate the passage by removing the rhythm and having students sing or buzz each pitch.

Executive-skills problems. If the students are missing notes because they cannot manipulate their fingers, remove the rhythm of the passage, and have the students finger through the notes without playing. Start with two notes, and then gradually add more notes to complete the difficult passage. After students can sing and finger through the passage successfully, have them play this segment on their instruments.

Style mistakes. If the students are playing note lengths or note shapes incorrectly, isolate the style by eliminating the pitches and having students echo a performer who models the correct style. Have students echo by singing the rhythm of the passage or by playing the rhythm on their instruments (or both) on a single pitch so that they can focus on matching the sound and style of the model. Choose a note that makes sense musically and is in a good range.

WHAT ARE WE TEACHING HERE ANYWAY?

It is easy to get wrapped up in teaching notes and rhythms of a piece. Sometimes we get so involved in the *technical* aspects of the piece that we forget about why we are teaching music in the first place; we forget why we chose to be musicians ourselves! More than likely, you did not choose to become a musician solely on the basis of mastering the technical aspects of playing your instrument. You probably had some type of experience where you were moved by music in a special way, or perhaps you had an inspirational teacher who really connected with you personally and musically.

In order to be an inspirational teacher, you need to move beyond teaching just notes and rhythms. Technical proficiency is important, but it is not an end in itself. Hopefully you will have a desire to achieve a high degree of technical success so that you can teach your students something *about* music. The authors of the GIA Publications Teaching Music through Performance series use a Comprehensive Musicianship through Performance (CMP) philosophy that emphasizes this concept of teaching *about* music *with* music. Patricia O'Toole (2003) describes the CMP approach to teaching music exceptionally well in her book *Shaping Sound Musicians.*

The notes and rhythms are very important, but don't let those details distract you from connecting your students to the musical aspects of the pieces they are performing. Help your students develop their knowledge and attitudes toward music as well as their technical development. By doing this, you will increase student enthusiasm for being in your groups and help them develop as musically literate and intelligent musicians.

PERFORMING WITH YOUNG ENSEMBLES

Part of your job as a professional educator is to help students and their families understand how performances work. Allowing your students to feel the excitement of performing onstage (or on the gym floor or in the school's cafeteria) allows them to experience the same kind of excitement that you probably have as a performer and allows students to participate in the same kinds of activities in which professional musicians around the world engage. Students will need to know very explicitly what your expectations are regarding procedures and behavior. It is not a bad idea to walk students through every step of the concert and give them checklists for what to bring, what to wear, where to go, and so forth. Share this information with your students' families as well.

Students will need to know what they should wear to the concert. If your ensemble uses a formal or informal uniform, then be sure that students understand exactly what they will need to wear as a part of that uniform. Remind your students that additions to the uniform are not appropriate as they may distract from the rest of the group. For example, large earrings or noisy jewelry are distracting and should be left at home. If your ensemble does not have a specific uniform, then instruct your students as to the types of clothes they should wear. Help your students understand what is appropriate for a concert. Most groups look very classy in a simple collared dress shirt with dark pants and dark shoes. Let your students' families know far in advance of the concert what they are expected to wear so that they can prepare. Think ahead as to what you will do if a student arrives dressed incorrectly. Will there be a grade consequence? Will you provide an extra shirt or tie?

Be sure that students understand the pre-concert procedures. Where should your students report? What time should they arrive? Where should they store their instrument cases? What music will they need? Hopefully you have established a basic warm-up routine with your students so that, once your ensemble starts playing, your students will fall into their basic routine. See the "'Warm-Up' Activities" section earlier in this chapter for some ideas.

Review the procedures for how students should act during the concert. Remind your students that performance time is not the time to wave to their friends or families in the audience or to pump their fists into the air like rock stars. Many directors like to have a clear procedure for moving between instrument positions based on signals from the conductor. For instance, you might have students sit in rest position until the conductor steps onto the podium. When the conductor steps onto the podium, the students move to ready position. When the conductor raises her hands to start a piece, your students move to play position. While a strict procedure such as this may seem rigid, allowing your students to fall into a familiar framework of activities allows them to relax and focus their concentration in a distracting atmosphere.

Remind students to be classy and professional and to remain relatively still when they are *not* playing—especially during rests or between songs. It is a good idea to have your students stand at the end of their portion of the concert. Parents will want to see their children onstage, and it is often difficult to see students seated in the back rows. Many directors like to have their ensembles stand up at the end of the concert one row at a time, starting with the performers in the back row. This way the audience members can see each of the performers onstage. You will need to practice standing up at the end of the last piece with your students several times, and you might want students to write in the words "stand up" on the last bar of their music as a reminder. Finally, be sure that your students are clear as to what they should do to exit the stage in an orderly and safe manner. Which direction should they exit the stage? Where should they go after their performance? Should they put their instruments away or should they take them to their seats to watch another portion of the concert? Thinking through every step in the concert day is a lot of work, but attention to detail will be rewarded with a smoother performance.

Be prepared to educate audiences on proper, respectful concert behavior. Some families may have never been to a "formal" concert. Links to the National Association for Music Education's guidelines for students is provided at the end of this chapter. Consider printing these recommendations on the last page of programs or taking a few minutes at the beginning of each concert to go over the most important aspects of audience behavior. Remind the audience that concert etiquette is a matter of respect for the efforts of the students onstage; the audience should not do anything that might distract from the performance or make the students' jobs onstage any more difficult.

TRAVELING WITH YOUNG ENSEMBLES

Many directors consider traveling with young bands a horrifying thought, but there are some good reasons to take your group on the road early in their musical lives. Travel with any group requires careful planning, but taking young band students on their first road trip can be particularly challenging from a logistics point of view. Anytime you take your students out of school during the week or away from home on a weekend, you should have a clear educational goal in mind. If your trip does not advance your students' musical lives, if your trip does not teach them some aspect of music performance, if it does not reflect an aspect of your philosophy of music education, then you may wish to postpone that travel opportunity to another time. Some directors take their students to concerts or contests sponsored by a theme park as a reward for a great year. Some directors plan outings to malls or nursing homes to help students engage in some community service activities. Whatever performance venue you choose, your students will more than likely enjoy loading up their instruments and equipment and taking their show on the road.

With careful planning and some advance work, traveling with a young ensemble does not have to be a scary thing. Of course, you will need to secure the permission of your campus principal (and perhaps even a district-wide administrator) before moving forward with travel plans. Start this process early, as it often takes many weeks—and sometimes even months—to get permission to travel. After you have gained permission to make the trip, secure transportation for the instruments and students. Keep in mind that thirty students with instruments take up a lot more room on a bus than thirty students without instruments. You may need to arrange for a separate equipment truck depending on the number of busses and drivers that are available.

Students' safety is the most important aspect of traveling. Provide adequate supervision for your students throughout the trip. Ask early for parent volunteers to serve as chaperones on your trip. A conservative guideline for chaperones is to have one parent for every fifteen students on the trip in addition to your band staff. You may wish to have more chaperones depending on your students and the expectations of your school district; consult with your principal before you make final arrangements for chaperones. Take attendance each time you depart from a location to ensure that all students are accounted for. Be sure that your students understand the expectations for their behavior and safety before leaving school. Students should abide by the school district's code of student conduct at all times and should understand that school discipline procedures apply even on a trip away from campus. Students should always stay in groups at each stop on the trip. You may wish to establish a check-in procedure if your stay at a particular location is more than a few hours.

Think carefully though the procedures of the entire day to develop an itinerary for your trip. Remember that school busses travel slowly, so build in some extra travel time if that is your mode of transportation. Be sure to plan for meals if your trip extends across a traditional mealtime. If your school receives federal support for free and reduced lunch, you may be required to provide money or meals for your students. Check with your principal for more information. Large groups move much more slowly than individuals; a walk that might take you five minutes may take a group of students as much as twice as long. If your group splits up during the day, build in some gathering time to check that all of the students are accounted for before your departure time. See the sample itinerary in appendix E for some ideas.

Be prepared for any mishaps during your trip. Each student should have an up-to-date health form on file with you that includes parent permission to medically treat and transport the student in the event of an emergency. List any medications or allergies on the health form, and be sure that current insurance information is listed. There is a sample health form at the end of the sample handbook located in appendix A. It is a good idea to have the phone number of the person in charge of your transportation in the event of a mechanical emergency or if your transportation does not arrive as planned. You might ask to have contact information for a campus administrator as well in case of emergency. Finally, be sure to have contact information for each of your students' parents or guardians.

Planning all of the details of full-ensemble rehearsals for your young groups can be a time-consuming task. Taking the time to carefully think through all of the details of where, when, how, and what you want your students to rehearse will pay off in a smoother educational experience for everyone involved.

QUESTIONS FOR DISCUSSION

1. What are some things Kaylee might have done differently in the scenario presented at the beginning of this chapter? What makes you think this?
2. Develop an itinerary for a trip to a nearby amusement park. Be sure to include departure times, mealtimes, arrival times, and any other events or information that you feel might be important.
3. Write a letter to a principal justifying why students should be allowed to miss an academic class to rehearse for an upcoming concert.

FIELD EXPERIENCE CONNECTIONS

1. What types of performance opportunities do the students at your cooperating teacher's school have? Does everyone participate in the same performing activities? Why or why not?
2. What types of arrangements does your cooperating teacher have to make to reserve a performance date for one of her ensembles?
3. What types of warm-up activities are used in the ensembles and beginning-band classes at your school? How are they alike? How are they different? Is the same routine used each day? Why or why not?
4. Make a note of the teaching cycles that your cooperating teacher uses. Are they complete? Why or why not?

REFERENCES

Butts, C. M. 1981. *Troubleshooting the high school band.* West Nyack, NY: Parker.

Colwell, R. J., and M. P. Hewitt. 2011. *The teaching of instrumental music.* Boston: Prentice Hall.

Cooper, L. G. 2004. *Teaching band and orchestra.* Chicago: GIA.

Lehr, M. R. 1998. *Getting started with elementary-level band.* Reston, VA: Music Educators National Conference.

Miles, R., and T. Dvorak, eds. 2001. *Teaching music through performance in beginning band.* Chicago: GIA.

Miles, R., and T. Dvorak, eds. 2008. *Teaching music through performance in beginning band.* Vol. 2. Chicago: GIA.

O'Toole, P. 2003. *Shaping sound musicians.* Chicago: GIA.

Yarbrough, C., and H. E. Price. 1989. Sequential patterns of instruction in music. *Journal of Research in Music Education* 37 (3), 179–187.

WEBSITES

GIA Publications Teaching Music Series. www.giamusic.com/music_education/teaching_music.cfm

MENC: National Association for Music Education. Concert etiquette tips:
  For students: www.menc.org/documents/mf/students.pdf
  For adults: www.menc.org/documents/mf/parents.pdf
  For teachers: www.menc.org/resources/view/concert-etiquette-tips-from-menc-s-teacher-success-kit

9

Getting Help

Mike was thoroughly enjoying his new job as the band director at Fillmore County Middle School, but he couldn't believe how tired he was at the end of the first full week of classes. Like many young directors, he had envisioned himself spending countless hours on the conductor's podium leading his ensemble through exciting musical works and quickly and effortlessly rehearsing many different tunes just as he had seen his high-school and college directors do during his time as a student musician. It wasn't leading the classes or conducting rehearsals that was making him so tired. Mike was totally shocked by the number of extra-musical issues that easily occupied the majority of his day: setting up chairs and stands, entering student information into his computer database, filling out reports and budget requests for the school district, submitting attendance and lesson plans to his administrators, working on the programs for the first-week assembly, contacting the local music store to order supplies, writing the band newsletter, updating the band's website . . . The list just seemed to go on and on! As Mike left the band hall on Friday evening at the end of his first full week of classes, he was energized and excited about his new job, but in the back of his mind he wondered, "Can I stay energized and enthusiastic dealing with all of this extra stuff?"

Teaching instrumental music is a tremendously rewarding and fulfilling experience, but there are a lot of moving parts involved in keeping a successful program running smoothly and efficiently. Ideally, most music teachers would like to spend their time primarily studying musical scores and then delivering effective lessons and performances. In reality, there are a great many extra-musical responsibilities that occupy most teachers' time. In addition, there is a wealth of musical and pedagogical knowledge and skills that are required to be a successful teacher, and many teachers find that they need additional help and assistance in teaching the many concepts on each of the assorted instruments found in the band. As you continue to grow and develop as a music teacher—and hopefully you will never stop improving as a professional educator—you will have the opportunity to reach out and improve the skills that you have as well as solidify any gaps in your knowledge. Teachers can get help with all of the extra-musical tasks that fill their days from students, their families, and the many professionals that are a part of our lives. Successful teachers understand that they can't know all the information known to mankind, and they can't do everything for themselves. In addition, every time directors fail to allow others to complete a task by doing that task themselves, they deny other people the experience and the pride of ownership in the successful completion of the activity and the satisfaction of contributing to the success of the organization as a whole. This chapter presents some ideas for getting help from a wide variety of personal and professional sources. Tap into these resources so that you can fill in the gaps in your knowledge and increase the efficiency with which you invest your time.

HELP FROM STUDENTS

It is sometimes difficult for band directors to relinquish control over even the smallest aspect of the music program. Many directors adhere to the old adage, "If you want something done right, you have to do it yourself." The trouble is, most people rarely have the time and energy to do all of the things necessary to allow them to be as effective as they can be as an educator while still balancing their own personal lives and health. Students love to help with tasks in the music room, and they enjoy having responsibility and accountability for completing a job. So what can students do to help? Basically anything that does not require a director's expertise as a professional music educator can potentially be a task that may be delegated to a student. Students can write announcements on the board in the classroom, update the band website, set up chairs and stands for rehearsals, or even organize and perform light cleaning and maintenance of the music room and equipment. Before you start off on your next task, ask yourself the following question: "Do I really need a music degree to complete this task?" If the answer is no, then you might consider delegating the task to a trusted, well-trained student.

Students may serve as either formal or informal leaders and assistants. Regardless of the structure of your student leadership program, students will need careful training on each task you expect them to complete. These students should be shown, in great detail, exactly how they should go about completing each task. The students should understand why their task is important, and they should be helped to visualize the finished job. We can now transform the old adage mentioned earlier to something like, "If you want something done right, *show them exactly how you want things done.*" Students will make mistakes, but as teachers we should support them and use these mistakes as learning opportunities. Students can complete many tasks surrounding your music program; other jobs are best left to parent volunteers.

PARENT VOLUNTEERS

Parents and other adult family members can be valuable assistants who can take care of these tasks that may not require a professional's expertise. Parents, older brothers and sisters, aunts and uncles, and grandparents can be superior helpers given sufficient instruction and guidance. Of course, as we mentioned in chapter 8, you will want to enlist adult helpers to serve as chaperones when traveling with your students. Adults can also serve as monitors at concerts and contests. Parents can also help with the many chores and administrative tasks related to keeping the band functioning smoothly.

Some of these tasks include bookkeeping jobs, such as collecting money during fund-raising events or filling out budget and purchasing paperwork that may be required by the school district. Be certain to check with school-district officials as to the proper procedures and guidelines for how adult helpers should be trained and monitored as they complete these tasks. Have safeguards and auditing procedures in place anytime money is involved so that the music staff or the adult helpers are not put in the uncomfortable position of having to explain any discrepancies in any of the accounts with which they work. Adult family members can also help in less formal, but still vitally important, ways by completing tasks such as repairing broken equipment, building storage equipment and accessories, organizing uniforms, copying music, sorting fund-raiser orders, and so forth.

Some directors like to formalize the organization of adult family members into music booster organizations. The formation of a booster group has many advantages as long as everyone involved understands that the primary purpose of the organization is to support the directors and the students enrolled in band classes. Some booster groups become troublesome when they fail to recognize their function within the overall structure of the school music program. The National Association for Music Education has excellent information for booster organizations on their website and in their *Music Booster Manual*.

Most booster organizations follow standard guidelines, such as those found in *Robert's Rules of Order*, when setting up their constitution and bylaws. These documents outline the purpose of the organization and information about officers and their duties, how officers are selected, membership requirements, meetings, committees, and the finances of the group. The school principal and the band directors should be members of the booster organization and retain copies of all documents pertaining to the structure of the group.

Booster organizations can be of particular value raising funds for the group as well as organizing other adults to help support the various activities. The band director and the principal should give advance approval for any fund-raising effort by the booster organization. Ideally, any money raised through fund-raising should benefit the entire organization (not just one ensemble or select students within the organization) and should supplement, as opposed to replace, funding from the school district. A formal booster organization can help assign volunteers to organize various events, including event publicity, communications, chaperones, and so forth.

PRIVATE INSTRUCTORS

Professional performers serving as private instructors and consultants on the various instruments of the band can serve as valuable resources for your ensembles and beginning-instrument classes. These specialists can provide supplemental, individualized instruction to students as well as assist in the instruction of various sections within the band. In their consultation roles, these professionals can also provide the music staff formal and informal advice for each instrument. Check with your building principal or an experienced music colleague in the school system to see what policies and procedures govern contracting with individual private-lesson teachers; some schools do not allow private instructors to operate within the school day. If they are allowed, private instructors can be invaluable resources when they are selected carefully, conduct their jobs professionally, and are actively involved in the development of the students within the instrumental music program.

Selecting and interviewing potential private-lesson instructors is an important step in ensuring the success of the program. Start by reviewing the school district's policies regarding hiring and screening individuals to work on campus. Most school districts have strict guidelines for completion of criminal-background checks for all personnel who work directly with school children. Even if the school district does not require background checks on individuals you hire as private instructors, it is a good idea to get some type of screening report to avoid hiring people with histories of inappropriate or unethical behavior involving minors or finances. If the school district will be paying private-lesson teachers directly, then these individuals will most likely be required to complete a packet of paperwork to set up the payment process. If students will pay the teachers directly, then the music staff should set up a system to keep track of payments and lessons.

Many directors ask that potential private-lesson instructors submit résumés and complete some type of performance audition. Evaluating each applicant's teaching experience and performance ability is an important part of the hiring process. Hopefully, the private instructor can provide professional references from former employers who can speak to his or her ability, professionalism, and work history. An interview is not only a time for the director to review and evaluate the potential job candidate, but also it is a time in which the job candidate can decide if he or she would want to work in a particular place. Directors should be up front with instructors regarding payment information (how much and how frequently they are paid, how they are paid, and so forth), time commitments asked of the applicant, space availability, and the number of potential students. Most private instructors working at schools make a living by teaching at several different locations each week, so directors should be forthcoming about the details of the position so that they can make informed decisions about the job.

WHO PAYS FOR LESSONS?

So who should pay for private lessons provided by music professionals from the community? The answer depends on several factors including the traditions and economy of the community in which the school is located. Some communities have a tradition of supporting private lessons at schools with individual family contributions; each month or week, families pay for a certain number of private lessons for their children. Other communities rely on fund-raising to raise money for scholarships to offset a portion, or sometimes all, of the expense of paying a private teacher. Other schools are able to provide lessons as a budget item utilizing funds from local or state sources. If you teach at a public school, it is important to realize the spirit of public education is to provide any family free access to each of the opportunities that any other students have available to them. A student should never be denied access to private instruction solely on the inability of the individual's family to contribute money to the lesson program. If the "service" of private lessons is provided to any student, then it should be available to every other student regardless of their ability to pay. This means that, in some cases, you will need to work out payment plans or perhaps service opportunities to help students "work off" their debt to the program. It may mean that you will need to organize fund-raising efforts to help build up a pool of funds that can be used to pay for lessons.

The director of the music program needs to make the expectations for both the students and the teachers very clear—preferably in writing utilizing some type of contract between the private instructor and the student—so that everyone involved in the lesson program understands the tasks and behaviors that are expected. Students should be expected to attend their lessons regularly and prepare for lessons diligently. Expectations for the private instructors should be clearly spelled out in a formal contract that is signed by both the music director and the private teacher prior to beginning instruction each year. This agreement should spell out expectations for the teacher's attendance, including starting and ending lessons punctually. The contract should address how teachers are to keep track of lessons and, if applicable, how they should document student payments for lessons. Private teachers should be asked to prepare thoughtfully for each lesson based on the individual students' needs and should be reasonable in requiring extra materials, such as reeds, music, and other equipment. The private instructors should coordinate with and reinforce the instruction of the classroom instructor as far as the types of material they are working on in lessons. The private teacher and the director should also communicate regularly when performance or behavior problems arise. Directors should make every effort to communicate important calendar events that might impact scheduling of lessons, including music contest dates and state-mandated testing days.

Emphasize that the expectation for behavior of the private-lesson instructor is the same as any music staff member—that of total professionalism. This means that the private instructor should support the music program at the school by supporting the instruction of the director, other members of the music staff, the students, and all school policies. The private-lesson instructor should abide by the upmost standards of professionalism in dress, grooming, language, and behavior. Directors should also encourage private instructors to obtain professional liability insurance. This type of insurance is available through professional teacher associations, such as the Music Teachers National Association, the National Association of Music Teachers, or through many statewide music educators' associations or teachers unions.

There are several structural and procedural issues that need to be addressed before a private-lesson program is implemented. Many of these areas should be addressed in the student and teacher contracts that are signed each year before lessons begin.

1. *Who keeps track of student payments?* In some music programs, representatives from the individual schools collect student payments on behalf of the school district and then distribute the funds to individual teachers on a regular basis. For each period of employment, usually one month, a single check is prepared for each private instructor to compensate him or her for the lessons he or she has taught in the preceding month. The payments are based on comparing two documents—the record of student payments to the school and the record of lessons provided by the teacher. Teachers must submit documentation each month, signed by both the instructor and the student, showing that the lessons have occurred as agreed before the instructors' checks are finalized. One problem with this arrangement is the potential for a time lag between when a student submits payment, when an instructor submits his or her time card, and the time it takes to process this information in order to prepare checks for distribution to the instructors. This system also requires teachers to be efficient in documenting each lesson carefully and in submitting their paperwork in a timely manner.

   Other schools allow students to pay instructors directly, either monthly or by the lesson. This arrangement has the potential to keep checks flowing to teachers if the students' families make regular payments as agreed. Again, it is important for teachers to record payments carefully so that any disagreements between payments received and number of lessons delivered can be resolved more easily.

2. *Where do lessons happen?* Are there sufficient facilities to host private-lesson instructors on campus? Will they teach in the music room? Are there practice rooms available? Are there other classrooms that may be available?

3. *When do lessons occur?* Most private lessons are scheduled on a weekly basis. There are many different options depending on school-district policies regarding "outside contractors," such as private-lesson instructors working on campus during the school day. You may be able to hold lessons during the school day during band classes, during lunch, or after or before school (lessons should not be held during other academic classes). Keep in mind that there should always be adequate supervision during lesson times; directors should not count on private-lesson teachers to meet with students unless a music faculty member is

in the building. Some directors have found that private lessons held in the summer months are particularly helpful for younger students.

4. *What fees and payments are involved?* Check with neighboring directors to get an idea of the fee that private-lesson teachers in your area charge for lessons. Each private-lesson teacher on your campus should be paid the same hourly rate as any other teacher. Some school districts require that a portion of the fee charged to provide lessons on school premises go toward offsetting some of the expense of providing heat, air-conditioning, lighting, custodial services, and so forth.

After all of the hiring, planning, and organization of the private-lesson program has been done, it is time to match students with instructors. Private-lesson instructors will want to be active in recruiting potential students. The band directors' endorsement of individual teachers means a lot to students and their families, but a letter or flyer from the teacher, along with a short recruitment performance during class, goes a long way in attracting potential students. Middle-school students are most interested in the personality of the teacher, so they are attracted to someone who appears to be personable and friendly. More advanced students are more concerned with the teacher's playing and teaching ability. These students will more likely be attracted to flashy playing or by being exposed to some helpful advice during a section rehearsal or master class. They may also be influenced by the success of their peers who study privately with a particular teacher. Parents and students should understand that students will not be penalized for choosing to not participate in a private-instruction program, but they should also understand that students who do participate have the potential to progress faster than those who do not.

Private instructors can be a valuable addition to your instructional team, so it is important to help make their experience a positive one so that they continue to work well within your system. If possible, provide a consistent room or space for lesson teachers. The instructors and the students will feel more comfortable knowing they have a regular meeting spot that meets their needs. Provide materials and equipment the teachers need to be successful. If directors ask a private instructor to help with a sectional, then they should provide them with a score in advance. If there is access to a photocopier or other instructional technology, be sure that the private instructors have access and know how to use those tools so that they can provide materials and instruction to their students. Directors may wish to introduce private instructors to campus administrators and to other teachers so that the private teachers feel like they are a part of the instructional team on campus. Include private-lesson teachers' names in printed programs for concerts and on the music website when possible.

MENTORS

Both experienced and new teachers can benefit from seeking the advice of experienced mentor teachers. Mentors may be assigned by school-district personnel, selected from a formal mentor program, or selected informally based on a director's needs and desires. Mentors assigned by school principals generally tend to be experienced, nonmusic instructors. These teachers can be valuable resources to new teachers for information related to campus and district policies and procedures. These campus mentors can help new teachers understand the basics of classroom management and other fundamental organizational issues.

While nonmusic mentors assigned by campus principals may be beneficial to a certain extent, music teachers often derive the greatest benefit from mentors who are music teachers themselves. In some cases, particularly at smaller schools, the music teacher is the only fine-arts expert in the school, which can make them feel isolated and alone in their work. Because of the specialized nature of their classes, music teachers at the secondary level can benefit from a voice of experience when it comes to the particulars of classroom management in larger classes, contest entry procedures, selecting appropriate music, and dealing with various pedagogical issues related to instrumental music instruction.

So where does one find a music-teacher mentor? Selecting a mentor can be as easy as contacting a respected director in the area. Some states and school districts offer formal mentor programs that help match teachers who are new to the profession or new to the area with veteran music teachers who serve as advisors or mentors. While it is usually best to try to find a mentor who teaches the same grade level and in a similar community, advice from a seasoned teacher can be of use to almost any new teacher. Some teachers have the benefit of working on a staff with more than one teacher assigned to a particular campus. This arrangement allows the other music teachers on campus to serve as consultants to each other. In addition, many teachers find it helpful to hold informal meetings with their peers in neighboring schools to compare notes about the various issues (often nonmusical!) that occupy their time. A weekly or monthly meeting of the music-teacher minds at the local pizza restaurant can be therapeutic as well as informative.

There are several ways mentors, advisors, or consultants can interact with a protégé. One of the best ways mentors can help is to make regular site visits to campus to both observe classes and to discuss various issues related to the job. It is important to not let these sessions feel like an "evaluation" of the protégé's teaching; these sessions should be more informal and strive to point out the director's strengths as well as recommend ways to improve what is going on in the classroom and behind the scenes. If regular site visits are not easily arranged, consider sending your mentor a video recording of a lesson or two, or take advantage of the latest teleconferencing technology. Another valuable way to exchange ideas is to arrange for the less-experienced teacher to visit the mentor-teacher's campus to watch him or her teach. Colleen Conway and Thomas Hodgman's (2006) *Handbook for the Beginning Music Teacher* contains more ideas regarding arranging and developing mentor relationships.

OTHER MUSIC PROFESSIONALS

Directors can also seek to tap the rich resources that can be found in the representatives who work for local music and instrument stores. These professionals are often great points of contact who can provide information on the best and most popular new music products and materials. Working with local music retailers also helps support the local economy. The success of school music programs is deeply intertwined with the success of the local music stores; without great local music stores, local bands and orchestras struggle, and without active local music groups, local music stores have difficulty maintaining profitability. If a community has more than one reputable music store, directors should try to spread purchases among the competing stores by patronizing each company. Spending time to get to know local music representatives can give directors valuable insight into new products and services that will help students.

CONTINUING YOUR DEVELOPMENT

By continuing to develop your knowledge and skills as a professional music educator, you learn to help yourself by filling in the gaps in your knowledge. Great teachers never stop learning and improving. Seeking out opportunities to continue your professional development allows you to become a more effective teacher. Hopefully your school district provides relevant teacher in-service opportunities throughout the school year. Having expert teachers in the music field visit the music teachers in your school district is a great way to bring in other ideas and possible solutions to pedagogical and organizational issues that may arise from time to time. Some school districts allow music teachers to visit other exemplary programs as a part of the regular teacher in-service program.

Another way to gather new ideas and teaching techniques is to visit clinics and conventions provided by many of the state and national music educators' associations. These events often feature presentations by experts in various music-education topics as well as concerts, performances, and master classes featuring great ensembles and performing groups. Many college and universities as well as some instrument companies, such as the Conn-Selmer Corporation, host summer camps and workshops for directors. Many of these workshops can be taken for graduate-school credit.

Keeping up to date by subscribing to publications geared toward music teachers and patronizing pedagogical websites are great ways to fill in the gaps in your knowledge and to pick up on new ideas and teaching techniques. Two of the most popular national publications include the *Instrumentalist* and *School Band and Orchestra* magazine. Many statewide and national music educators' and bandmasters' associations produce monthly or quarterly publications that often feature practical tips for music educators. Membership in the National Association for Music Education includes a subscription to *Music Educators Journal* and *Teaching Music* magazines. Many instrumental guilds and professional societies produce publications geared to the specific needs of their memberships. A list of the websites for many professional instrumental societies is listed at the end of chapter 7.

QUESTIONS FOR DISCUSSION

1. How do you plan to balance work, family, self, and other important aspects in your life as a professional educator? How can you stay connected and active in each of these areas? Do you think a balance is important for a new teacher? Do you think balance is more or less important for experienced teachers? Explain your answers.
2. What are the most important criteria you would use to select a private instructor for a beginning-band student? Would those criteria change if you were hiring a teacher for more advanced students?
3. Does your state music educators' or bandmasters' association provide some type of mentor program for new teachers? How does one sign up to be a part of this program? What might prevent a person from joining these programs?

FIELD EXPERIENCE CONNECTIONS

1. Ask your cooperating teacher if she makes a conscious effort to balance the commitments of work, family, and social life. What are the challenges in balancing these three areas?

2. How are student helpers utilized at your school? Who organizes them?
3. Are parents involved in helping with activities at the school? Is there a formal booster organization?
4. Are private-lesson teachers active in the school? When do they teach lessons? How are they paid? Who keeps track of the payments?

REFERENCES

Conway, C. M., ed. 2006. *Great beginnings for music teachers: Mentoring and supporting new teachers*. Reston, VA: MENC: National Association for Music Education.

Conway, C. M., and T. H. Hodgman. 2006. *Handbook for the beginning music teacher*. Chicago: GIA.

MENC: National Association for Music Education. 1989. *Music booster manual*. Reston, VA: MENC: National Association for Music Education.

Roberts, Henry M., and Daniel H. Honemann, Thomas J. Balch, Daniel E. Seabold, and Shmuel Gerber. 2011. *Robert's Rules of Order Newly Revised*, 11th Ed. Boston, MA: Da Capo Press.

WEBSITES

Conn-Selmer Institute. www.csinstitute.org.

MENC: National Association for Music Education publications. www.menc.org/resources/view/nafme-journals.

Music Teachers National Association. www.mtna.org.

School Band and Orchestra. www.sbomagazine.com.

The Instrumentalist. www.theinstrumentalist.com.

Wiki Band Director. www.wikibanddirector.com.

IV

PLANNING, MANAGEMENT, AND ASSESSMENT

10

Recruiting and Retaining Students and Their Families

Monica's last class of the day—her first day as the assistant band director at Smith Middle School—was filing in quietly. The class was supposed to be made up of about thirty-five beginning-brass students, but if her previous classes were any example, she was bound to find at least a few woodwind and percussion students who had been placed in the wrong class. Some of the students who showed up this morning in her first-period beginning-woodwind class showed up with brass instruments, and several of the students had not even signed up for band class at all! By the time this last class rolled around, Monica had decided that she would take attendance by asking each student to tell her what instrument he or she intended to play.

Monica was worried about the instrumentation in the other band classes as well. Mr. Nguyen, the head band director, taught the advanced band. The students in that class were mostly eighth graders, and the ensemble had a fairly well-balanced instrumentation. In contrast, Monica was assigned to teach the second band made up of a single tuba player, eleven percussionists, eight saxophone players, and a handful of other instruments.

Monica began to call roll in her last-period class. "Alexander Acuña?"

"Here!" answered a short, young boy with very thin lips. "I play the trombone."

Monica quickly sized up Alexander's physical features. She thought to herself, "Alexander definitely does *not* have a trombone face. I hope he can reach seventh position with those short arms. Who placed these kids on these instruments?" She let out an audible sigh.

Monica moved on and called the next name. "Amanda Borch?"

A young girl dressed immaculately for the first day of school answered with enthusiasm, "Present! I am going to be a flute player! We have one at home that belonged to my aunt!"

"Do you realize that a flute is a woodwind instrument?" asked Monica.

"Yes," began Amanda. "Isn't this band class?"

"Amanda, this is the *brass* class; it is for brass players only. The woodwinds class meets first period. We'll have to change your schedule."

Amanda was clearly disappointed. "But I *love* my first-period teacher! I'll just die if you move me! Please, Miss!"

Monica quickly moved on. "Let's talk about it at the end of class—just you and me."

Monica continued double-checking the attendance roster and found, as in the first-period class, most of her students had all chosen one of the more popular instruments. In first period, eighteen of the thirty students had chosen saxophone. Several students in each of her classes were in the wrong section or did not even intend to join band. Monica knew that unless she got on top of recruiting and placement of students in her band classes in a more organized way, she'd never get the bands playing the way she knew they could.

Recruiting students in sufficient numbers to support a strong program is an important task for instrumental music teachers. Recruiting is an ongoing task for most successful teachers. Part of recruiting students is building a positive image for your program. Every time your group performs for an audience, each time one of your students is successful, every time you are out in public, you are creating a positive image for your program. Having a successful program is one of the best ways of recruiting students. People naturally want to be a part of something that is rewarding and fun, and how you frame your students' accomplishments can increase the number of students and families who wish to join your groups.

Communication skills are vitally important in every aspect of recruiting. Ensemble directors can be cheerleaders and ambassadors for community arts programs and should develop clear lines of communication with the teachers, administrators, parents, and students who are involved in their programs throughout the year. These lines of communication can be even more valuable during the recruitment process. Developing a well-thought-out recruiting plan is a team effort involving many different people who are often located on many different campuses.

Gathering data on students in order to help them make the right decisions about which instruments they might choose to study is another important piece of the recruiting puzzle. By matching a student's potential for success with the appropriate instrument, directors position students to have a more enjoyable experience learning about music through study of a band instrument. By clearly communicating a carefully crafted recruiting plan, teachers can help students and their families prepare for a successful and rewarding experience playing music in middle school, high school, college, and beyond.

 COMMUNICATION SKILLS

Basic publicity and communication skills are vital to the health of a strong school music program. Sharing information about the successes of your program with parents, administrators, other teachers, and the community at large can be a valuable method of building a positive public image for your group. Standard media outlets such as newspapers or television or even social media and the Internet can be effective ways to stay in touch with parents and community members. It is also important to let campus and district administrators know about the good things that are happening in the music program. Don't feel embarrassed about bragging a little about the good things your students accomplish. Send a press release to the local paper announcing your first-division solo and ensemble medalists. Take that trophy your group earned at a band festival to the main office, and show it off to your principal. Touting your successes can be a great way to build and maintain a positive image in the school and the community.

Logistics The formal recruiting process requires careful planning and communication with a wide variety of people. As you begin developing a recruiting plan, work together to plan the details of scheduling with the various teachers and administrators who may be involved. Schedule school visits, recruiting concerts, aptitude testing, information nights, and so forth carefully to avoid any schedule conflicts, and be sure that everyone is aware of the final timetable.

Parents & Students Finally, provide clear channels of communication throughout your plan between the music teachers and prospective students and their families. Include clear information about when and why the events included in your plan will happen. Clearly communicate the details of selecting and obtaining an instrument. You can communicate this information through flyers, e-mail, post cards, or even social media and the Internet. Include contact information such as your name, phone number, and e-mail address in all of your recruiting materials. Parents will have questions, and they will want to have a point of contact for a person who can answer their questions.

SAMPLE RECRUITING PLAN

Taken on the whole, the recruiting process may seem like a long and drawn-out series of activities. Dividing the recruiting year into smaller segments allows you to spread your recruiting tasks across many months and gives you time to organize and collect the data you need to help prospective students and their families make informed decisions about joining your groups. Although there may be some variation in the order of these activities, here are some typical steps in a recruiting process.

1. *Coordinate and plan the overall recruiting calendar of events*. Take some time to carefully plan out specific dates, times, and locations for the various events in your recruiting plan. Make arrangements for the use of any classrooms you may need. If you are using classroom space after normal school hours, arrange for doors to be unlocked and for appropriate climate control so that the rooms are comfortable. If you are transporting students from one campus to another, arrange for transportation well in advance of each of these events. Be sure to make note of the overall school-district calendar as you select dates for recruiting events. Try to avoid days immediately before or after holidays, the end of the grading periods, or standardized testing dates. If you recruit students from different campuses, be certain to check the events calendars at each of those schools to avoid conflicts with PTA meetings, concerts, open houses, and so forth. Finally, don't forget to consult your own calendar. You would not want to schedule a recruiting event the week before your big festival performance! After you've created a rough draft of a recruiting schedule based on your coordination of all the various calendars, send a rough draft to your campus principal, the principals of other schools that you plan to visit, and to the music teachers at each of those schools for their approval. These folks are busy people, so be sure to get this information to them as far in advance of your first event as possible.
2. *Develop and deliver recruiting letters and pamphlets*. A brief, professional-looking recruiting letter or pamphlet should be sent to prospective students and their families before you begin your recruitment activities. Try to mail copies of these materials to each family at every school that sends students to your campus. Send additional copies of your materials to each campus, and ask that they be displayed in the main office and music classrooms.

These materials should have a very brief, but exciting, overview of the types of activities in which students will participate if they are in your classes. Middle school is often the first opportunity for students to choose elective classes. Briefly describe the types of electives that are available at your school and when they are offered so students understand the choices that are available. If students on your campus can take multiple electives, be sure to emphasize that fact. Many families are concerned about the financial commitment of participating in band. Explain the options of renting instruments, and inform parents about the possibility of playing school-owned instruments. You might also choose to outline the time commitment involved in studying an instrument. Keep your wording positive, and let students know that most students find that about thirty minutes a day is all it takes to make progress in beginning band. Be sure that recruiting materials include a list of the steps in the recruiting process so that parents can begin to plan and make arrangements to attend your various recruiting activities in the upcoming months. Be sure that contact information is on all of your materials. Lynn Cooper's (2004) *Teaching Band and Orchestra* contains some excellent examples of parent letters, teacher memos, and other recruiting materials.

3. *Perform early in the year for incoming students.* Many directors choose to present a holiday concert near the middle of the school year to keep the program visible to students who may eventually wish to join the program. Keep the concert fast paced and energetic, and try to include some audience participation. Let the students know that you will be coming back to demonstrate all of the instruments in a few months and to let them know how they can join in the fun!

4. *Conduct an instrument-demonstration recruiting concert.* Present a concert for all incoming students to get them excited about the music programs at your school. If your campus offers choir or orchestra, be sure work as a team so that each instructor can let incoming students know what their programs are all about. Younger students may be familiar with some of the more popular instruments like percussion and saxophone, but they may never have heard an oboe or bassoon or seen what a tuba looks like up close. Be sure to introduce yourself (and any other music teachers), and give a brief overview of the exciting things your students do in beginning band as well as in more advanced ensembles.

There are several options for the demonstration group you choose to use for the instrument-demonstration concert. Using an exhibition group made up of beginning-band students is an attractive option because these students are closer in age to the students you are trying to recruit, and many of your beginners will have friends in these lower grades. It is usually quite an honor for a beginner to be chosen to play in a concert like this. Alternatively, you might choose to have an advanced ensemble made up of older students perform for prospective students. Playing popular tunes and encouraging audience participation helps you make a strong connection with your listeners. Some teachers choose to feature chamber ensembles such as woodwind quintets and brass sextets. Using these two ensembles not only allows you to travel with a smaller group, but also it de-emphasizes two of the more popular instrument choices—saxophone and percussion.

Be sure to introduce each instrument in your ensemble during your demonstration concert. Briefly explain how each instrument works, and allow students to perform a very short tune that highlights the features of the instruments. Students may play movie or video game themes or other popular tunes to show off their instruments. Be sure that the students are well prepared and have practiced their tunes carefully in advance. Bring your recruiting materials to the concert, and outline the upcoming recruiting calendar so that students know what to expect and how they can begin to select an instrument. Some teachers like to have students try to make a sound on the instruments. If you decide to do this, be sure to instruct your student helpers on proper procedures for handling the instruments, and bring along some disinfectant spray.

maybe emphasize creativity in recruiting, discuss math vids in ohio

VIDEO AND INTERNET RECRUITING

In addition to live recruiting events, you might wish to develop and publish video materials that you can post directly to the Internet. A quick Google search will provide you with links to a multitude of recruiting videos that are already available. Should you wish to develop your own recruiting video, follow the same guidelines as you would for the instrument demo concert: give a brief overview of your program, and then introduce each of the instruments with a short tune that highlights the features of that instrument. If you use students in your videos, be sure to follow school-district guidelines about using their images on the Internet. You can publish your video recruiting materials on your campus or band website or on a video-sharing site such as YouTube.

5. *Conduct musical aptitude testing.* After you've introduced the instruments to your prospective students, work with your feeder schools to conduct some musical aptitude testing to help you gather data that can help you guide students as to which instruments they might be

"you know better than I do, list some good stuff quickly"

best suited. There are many published aptitude tests that make collecting and organizing this type of data easier. We'll talk more about specific musical aptitude tests later in this chapter.

6. *Send reminders about instrument night along with information on how to join the band.* Contact parents of potential students once again to remind them of the timeline for recruiting, and let them know specifically about your upcoming musical instrument exploration night. Some sample letters and flyers are available in David Vandewalker's (2010) *Everyday Stuff Every Band Director Needs to Know.*

7. *Conduct an instrument exploration night.* Invite parents and students to attend a session in which they can try different instruments and explore each of the instruments up close. This will allow you to conduct some physical aptitude testing (more on this later) to help students and their families make informed choices based on their physical characteristics and their musical aptitudes. One of your jobs during this event is to help students and their parents understand that each child possesses physical aptitudes that might make a particular instrument more or less difficult than others. Just as one student may have the physical makeup to play point guard in basketball instead of center, another student might have a face that is more suited to the tuba than to the trumpet. Hopefully, by the end of the evening, your students will be able to provide you with information indicating their top selections for which instruments they wish to play. As we'll discuss later, allowing students to select two or three instruments also allows you flexibility in making assignments to keep a balanced instrumentation.

   This event is also a great time to provide parents more information about obtaining instruments. You might choose to invite representatives from local music stores to present specific information about the instruments and services they offer. Many music stores offer rental plans that can be advantageous to students and their families. This event is also an excellent opportunity to warn families of the potential dangers of purchasing instruments online from lesser-known manufacturers. Some of these instrument manufacturers produce instruments assembled with inferior craftsmanship or design that is less than desirable for beginning-band students. This event is a great occasion to provide equipment and instrument lists to each family. Chapter 11 contains more information about specific instrument and equipment recommendations.

8. *Follow up with students and families about instrument choices and assignments.* After students make their instrument selections and after you have made the final decision about which student will play what instruments, you'll need to inform your students and their families

communication

about their final placements. If you have carefully explained how each student's musical and physical aptitudes are carefully matched to the requirements of each instrument, you will find that most students select an appropriate first or second choice. Send information about exactly which instrument brands and models are recommended, and include information about accessories and equipment (including a method book) that may be required. Include contact information for local music stores, and encourage families to shop locally for their convenience both now and when repair time comes. Let families know when the instruments they will purchase or rent from local stores will be delivered. Remind parents that allowing the students to assemble or play the instruments without professional guidance may result in damage to the instrument or the formation of poor playing habits that might be difficult to change after they have been established.

GATHERING DATA

In order to help everyone involved make informed decisions about which instruments suit each student best, you will need to collect some different types of data. Collecting contact information allows you to keep track of individual students and gives you ways to contact families. Gathering data about students' academic performance and behavior may help you make some decisions about placing students. You can also gather information about a student's musical and physical aptitude. All of this information will be useful as you help everyone involved make informed decisions about which instruments to play.

Student Information

The most essential student information you'll need to collect includes the name, student identification number, and primary or homeroom teacher for each student from every school in the grade level you're recruiting. Often, you can obtain this data from a campus secretary, an administrator, or from the school-district database. You may also want to collect the home address and phone number for each student. Remember that all of this data is confidential and should only be shared with school-district personnel who are directly involved in the recruiting process. Some directors would like to know if students have prior experience playing an instrument, such as piano or guitar. Other directors might want to know what instruments a student might be interested in playing. Other directors prefer to wait and allow the students to learn more about all of the instruments before initially committing choices to paper.

TEACHER EVALUATIONS AND GRADES

Some directors collect data on the academic performance, behavior, and attendance for each student. These directors attempt to assign instruments so that the high- and low-performing students in each of these areas are evenly distributed among all of the sections of the band. It is important to remember that teachers' comments and grades assigned in elementary school are relatively subjective and should be interpreted with caution. Some band teachers would rather not be influenced by another teacher's comments. A few elementary teachers may not feel comfortable sharing specific comments about student behavior while others appreciate the opportunity to express their concerns. It is up to you to decide if you value this data and could use it to help you place students on various instruments.

Musical Aptitude Tests ✱ *you know better than me, but let's keep the discussion mostly under the book's leaders*

Many directors find that assessing a student's aptitude in various musical skills is helpful when guiding students to make decisions about the instruments they choose to play. Assessing a student's aptitude or his or her preference for a particular sound might help you make those types of decisions. Several published aptitude and preference tests are readily available for purchase. The "Selmer Music Guidance Survey" is a tool that attempts to help teachers assess a student's musical aptitude by measuring a student's ability to detect differences in pitch, triads, melodic lines, and rhythmic figures. For each of these areas, a student is presented with two examples and then asked to determine if the two examples are the same or different. Edwin Gordon's "Musical Aptitude Profile" measures aptitude in these areas in a similar way. Both of these tests are easily graded and provide guidance for students and directors by highlighting areas of potential strength or weakness that might impact study on specific instruments.

Some research suggests that students will be more motivated to progress on an instrument if they find the tone quality and tessitura of that instrument pleasing. Gordon's "Instrument Timbre Preference Test" attempts to assess this type of data. In this test, students are presented with many pairs of melodies played with contrasting timbres in various ranges. Students must select which of the two timbres they prefer in each pair. By analyzing the results of these choices, directors can guide students to instruments that match the timbres they favor.

APTITUDE VS. ABILITY

It is important to note that each of these tests measures a student's *aptitude* rather than a student's *ability* in music. Aptitude is a measure of *potential success* in an area. Just because a student has a strong aptitude in an area does not guarantee success, and a weaker aptitude does not prevent a student from being successful in an area. For example, a student may have a very strong aptitude for science, but unless that student applies herself and does the work needed to progress in that field, she may quickly be outpaced by a hardworking student with a weaker scientific aptitude. A measure of musical aptitude should therefore be used only to guide students in making informed choices as they select an instrument. Aptitude tests should never be used to exclude students from participation in a music program. Work ethic, determination, and desire go a long way in assuring improvement on any instrument.

Physical Aptitude Tests

Assessing the physical makeup of potential students can help you enlighten them about which instruments might be best suited to their physiology. Even though most beginning-band students have a bit more growing to do, you can still get a good idea of students' physical traits. Having parents attend your instrument-demonstration night may give you an idea of how a particular student might develop as he or she matures. A student who is very small now but with a mother and father who are both over six feet tall might just grow into that tuba! Letting parents see what you do in these sessions also helps them understand that you are objectively evaluating the characteristics that will help the students be as successful as possible.

Here are some features you may wish to assess:

- *Overall physical stature.* Tall or short? Big person or tiny?
- *Hand and finger size.* For example, be sure that students can reach the keys on the saxophone without hitting the side keys, or check to see if a student with thin fingers is able to cover the tone holes of the clarinet.
- *Are the students right- or left-handed?* Left-handed students might feel more comfortable on horn since the valves are operated with the left fingers.
- *Finger coordination.* In general, woodwind players need more well-developed fine-motor coordination in both hands. Here are some tests to determine the relative degree of fine-motor coordination:

○ Have a student face you and place her palms on a table or on her knees. Have the student lift one finger at a time, several times, starting with the thumbs and moving to the pinky fingers.

○ Have the student touch the tip of her thumb to the tip of her first finger. Next, move the thumb to the middle finger, then to the ring finger, and then to the pinky. See if they can do this quickly with both hands simultaneously. Don't allow students to slide from one finger to the next.

○ Advanced test! Touch the thumb to the first finger in the right hand while the thumb touches the pinky finger in the left hand. Move across to the next finger in each hand from right to left and back again.

- *Teeth alignment.* Do students have overbites? Are the teeth straight or crooked?
- *Braces.* Do the students have orthodontic braces? Does it appear that they will need braces in the future?

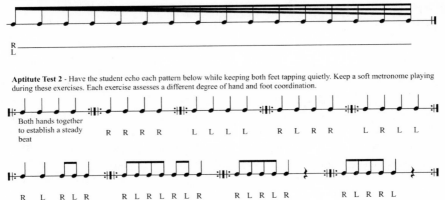

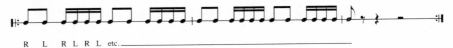

Figure 10.1.   Percussion aptitude tests

- Prospective percussionists need to demonstrate both gross- and fine-motor coordination skills. Start by having the students keep a steady beat by patting both hands on their knees. Keep a metronome going quietly, and then have students complete the following assessments. Model each pattern first, and have the student echo each pattern back to you (see fig. 10.1).

Carefully record your findings in each of these areas for each student who wishes to join the band on an individual record. As we'll see later, this information will allow you to help students and their families make decisions about which instruments best suit their natural tendencies and abilities. Cooper's *Teaching Band and Orchestra* (2004) contains some examples of ways to organize this data.

MATCHING STUDENTS WITH INSTRUMENTS

Keeping in mind that aptitude is merely an indicator of potential success, you can use the data you've collected about each of your students to help guide your students and their families to the instruments students may be able to play most naturally. Certain instruments lend themselves to skills and physical features, so it helps to match our students potential for success with those elements. Using this data, we can help guide students as they select instruments.

Using a Student's Musical Aptitude Test Scores

One of the ways that we can help students in selecting appropriate instruments is by using the results of musical aptitude tests. If at all possible, try to distribute students with high overall scores throughout each of the instrument families. You would not want all of your high-scoring students to play clarinet and all of your low-scoring students to play saxophone. As we mentioned earlier, a musical aptitude score should never be used to exclude a student from participating in band, but directors can use these scores to help guide students away from instruments that may require a great deal of extra work in order to be even minimally successful. For example, you might want to steer a student who scored poorly in the rhythm subsection of an aptitude test away from percussion or tuba; these instruments require a high degree of rhythmic stability and awareness. Students who score poorly on the melodic or pitch segments of the test might struggle to become successful on instruments such as the horn, trombone, or instruments in the double-reed family where fine discrimination of pitch is a prime skill. Keep in mind that a student's desire to play an instrument, coupled with hard work and determination, might allow a student to be successful on any instrument regardless of aptitude. Matching a student's strength with the characteristics of an instrument will make progress on that instrument much easier.

Using Physical Aptitude Data

The physical structure of the mouth, the shape of the lips and teeth, the size of the fingers and hands, and the overall coordination of each student are important elements that can be assessed in order to help students and their families choose appropriate instruments. Again, many of these apparent physical limitations may be overcome through students' efforts, but the students and their families need to understand the challenges that lie ahead of them and extra effort that may be involved to overcome these potential limitations.

The shape and size of the lips is a primary factor when deciding which wind instrument a student should select. Students with thick lips should be guided away from the flute, trumpet, and horn. Students with very thin lips should be steered away from low brass. Students whose top lip arches down to a point in the middle (often called a "teardrop" in the lips) should be steered away from the flute.

Students with uneven teeth or who wear orthodontic braces should be guided away from trumpet or flute—especially if they have thinner lips. Students with short fingers or small hands might have trouble with some of the larger woodwinds like saxophone or bassoon, and students with particularly skinny fingers might have trouble covering the tone holes on the clarinet. Students with very short arms might have difficulty playing the trombone. Students who have poor fine-motor coordination might struggle with playing a woodwind instrument. Students who have gross-motor coordination problems might find playing percussion instruments difficult.

There are always exceptions to each of these guidelines. Many professional trumpet players, for instance, have thick lips. Some professional percussionists were extremely uncoordinated adolescents. Evaluating each student's natural abilities and characteristics helps us set our instrumentalists up for the easiest route to successful achievement.

PERSONALITY AND INSTRUMENT SELECTION?

Some teachers believe that some personality types are particularly suited to playing certain instruments. The association between personality type and success on individual instruments has not been scientifically studied, and it is most likely the weakest indicator of potential success, but some teachers believe that these factors may help students make decisions about which instrument they play. Here are some of the more common descriptions of personalities for each of the instruments:

- Flute, trumpet, and percussion: strong personalities, achievement driven, like to show off
- Clarinet: sociable, like working in groups
- Double reeds: enjoy working with hands, work well individually
- Saxophone: sociable, like competition
- Low brass: hard workers, like to engage in physical activities

Student Choices

After you've collected musical and physical aptitude data and the students have had a chance to learn more about each of the instruments and after they have been counseled as to how their natural abilities match up with each instrument, the students are ready to select which instruments they would like to study. As we mentioned earlier, the students should be asked to provide you with two or more choices of instrument they would like to play. What if a student's aptitude doesn't match the requirements of the instrument? What if a student with a teardrop lip lists flute as his or her first choice? Remember that the musical and physical aptitudes of each student are merely indicators of potential success. Explain your concerns, and be sure that the students understand that they might be required to work even harder than their classmates to progress at the same rate if they select an instrument that does not match their natural strengths or physical makeup. In the end, a student's desire often outweighs any potential limitations. If you've kept careful notes about the musical and physical aptitudes of each student, you will be able to discuss placements objectively with parents and students.

Making Student Assignments

After you have collected your students' informed choices, you can begin to assign students to instruments. At this point, you will need to manage both your students' choices and the instrumentation needs of your school. Begin the sorting process by assigning the students to their first instrument choices. After you've initially placed your students by their first choices, you need to consider your instrumentation needs and the number of school-owned instruments that may be available. You may have many students who indicate a couple of popular instruments as their first choice, so you might need to make a few adjustments to keep the instrumentation balanced. Many band programs track instrumentation and enrollment trends for students entering beginning-band classes all the way through the graduating high-school seniors. The beginning-band class is the best place to maintain balanced instrumentation throughout the band program.

As we discuss in chapter 12, you may not wish to start students on every instrument. Some directors start students on common instruments such as flute, clarinet, trumpet, and trombone, and then move students from these instruments to the others. If you have ten students who want to play the tuba, and you only have five tubas available, then you either need to move some of the students to their second choice or find a way to come up with five more instruments (if your overall instrumentation would support that decision).

So how do you decide which students to move from their first choice to their second choice? You might start by looking at your notes from your assessment of each student's musical and physical aptitudes to determine if their second choice might be better suited than their first choice. Say, for instance, that you have many students who listed trombone as their first choice, but you need to move some of them to their second choice for balanced instrumentation. Looking through the musical aptitude scores of the students who listed trombone as their first choice, you notice that four of the students who listed trombone scored very low on the pitch discrimination portion of their musical aptitude test. Trombone players need to have a keen ear for fine variations in pitch in order to be successful, so those four students might be better suited on a different instrument. Perhaps you spot a player who listed trombone as his first choice, but your notes indicate that the student has small, thin lips. You also notice that the same student listed trumpet as his second choice. The physical structure of the student's lips indicate that he might naturally excel at the trumpet but struggle on trombone, and making that switch would help solve your instrumentation problem. Taking time to sort through these issues carefully during the recruiting process can save energy and prevent frustration in the following months and years.

HELPING CREATE A VISION OF THE FUTURE

Remember that recruiting is not something that directors do in a couple of months before school starts; successful band teachers are recruiting all the time. You will continue to recruit your students even after they have decided to be in your ensembles. The most crucial time to recruit students is often *after* they have joined your classes in the beginning-band year. Remember that one of the greatest motivators for retaining your students is to give them a feeling of success. If you set your students up for success by assigning them to instruments on which they will naturally excel, and if you lead them to playing sounds on their instruments easily and quickly, then they will be motivated to continue.

Try to feature your beginning-band students in a concert as soon as possible during their beginning year. A concert may introduce your students to the thrill of performing for an audience even if you play simple rote tunes using only three or four notes. You can also use these early-year concerts to educate your students' families about practice methods, class expectations, and to show off the great things you've accomplished in the band class up to that point. Many beginning-band method books have accompaniment CDs that would make a nice addition to these types of concerts, or you might develop your own background tracks using programs like Band-in-a-Box or GarageBand.

Help create a vision of the future for your students and their parents. Be sure that they understand the possibilities and benefits of participation in music later on in their lives. By helping students and their families look to the future, toward the types of activities and experiences that they will encounter when they join your advanced ensembles and begin performing at contests, travel to festivals, and the other exciting music events at your school, you create excitement for their musical futures. Emphasize that participation in band is a great way to bridge the gap between middle school and high school because it helps students to instantly have a network of friends who share the common experience of band. Let students know that instrumental music can be enjoyed throughout college regardless of their major. Emphasize that music can be a lifelong avocation and a fulfilling hobby regardless of their chosen career. In this way you are constantly recruiting lifelong participants in, and advocates for, the arts.

FIELD EXPERIENCE CONNECTIONS

1. Ask your cooperating teacher if he or she has a recruiting calendar or plan. Is there a performance for the feeder school? How does he or she help prospective students choose which instrument they will play?
2. Which instruments do your cooperating teachers recommend to incoming band students? Is there an official list of recommended instruments and accessories? How do the teachers at the school let students and families know about their recommendations?
3. How does your cooperating teacher make instrument assignments for beginning band? What is the process for communicating those choices to parents? What is the process for communicating instrument choices to administrators who make up band schedules?
4. Locate a school-district calendar from a local community. Work out a recruiting calendar using the steps outlined in the "sample recruiting

plan." See if you can plan your events so that you avoid the last week of any grading period, standardized testing days, and school-holiday weeks.

REFERENCES

Colwell, R. J., and M. P. Hewitt. 2011. *The teaching of instrumental music.* Upper Saddle River, NJ: Prentice Hall.

Cooper, L. G. 2004. *Teaching band and orchestra: Methods and materials.* Chicago: GIA.

Gordon, E. 1984. Instrument timbre preference test. Chicago: GIA.

Gordon, E. 2001. The musical aptitude profile. Chicago: GIA.

Selmer music guidance survey. n.d. Elkhart, IN: Conn-Selmer, Inc.

Vandewalker, D. W. 2010. *Everyday stuff every band director needs to know.* Marietta, GA: Vision.

WEBSITES

GarageBand. www.apple.com/ilife/garageband.

National Association of Music Merchants (NAMM). *A practical guide for recruitment and retention.* www.nammfoundation.org/music-achievement-council/practical-guide-recruitment-retention.

PG Music. Band-in-a-Box. www.pgmusic.com.

Selmer Music Guidance Survey materials. www.atssb.org/execsec/SMG.

11

Selecting Great Equipment

Bart was wrapping up the last instrument exploration night of the year. He had set up this event to help his students and their families select an instrument and to give them some more information on how to acquire an instrument for their upcoming beginning-band year. Bart was quite impressed with the number of parents who showed up to look at the various instruments available for rental from the local music store. Bart was sure that it wouldn't take him long to contact the parents of the few students who hadn't shown up that night. He wanted to be sure that they had made arrangements to have an instrument before classes started next fall.

Just as Bart was locking up the band hall, a woman with two young children tagging along walked into the school. The woman had a dusty, old flute case tucked under her arm as she approached Bart's office.

"Oh, I'm so glad that I caught you," began the woman. "I just got off work, and we had to catch the bus to the school. We were afraid we'd miss instrument night."

"Well, I'm glad you made it," replied Bart as he introduced himself. The woman looked very tired after a long day at work. Bart asked the woman to sit down at the table he'd set up in the band room. "What can I do for you?"

The woman nudged the smaller of the two children she had brought with her forward. "This is my daughter Marlie, and she has decided that she wants to play the flute."

Bart quickly glanced at the young girl and instinctively evaluated her lip shape and hand size. "Looks good so far," thought Bart.

"And we're so lucky," continued the woman. "I found my old flute from high school in the attic so we don't have to buy a new one! There's no way we could afford that!"

Bart had already made a mental note of the old case cradled under the woman's arm as she had entered.

"There isn't a chance that old instrument will play a note!" thought Bart to himself.

The woman blew the dust off the lid and opened the case. Inside sat the oldest, most tarnished flute that Bart had ever seen. The few pads that had not already fallen out were dry and cracked, and the end plug screw in the headjoint spun around like a top. Several of the keys were bent. Bart searched for a name brand on the instrument. At last he spied a faded name etched into the main body that read "Ingersol." Bart had never heard of that brand before. Bart closed the case and looked at the woman, then at her daughter, and then back to the woman.

"What do you think?" the woman asked. . . .

Using good quality accessories, instruments, and supplies greatly contributes to the speed and ease in which students can develop on their instruments. Proper equipment helps students develop solid fundamental playing skills, and regular maintenance of the instrument plays a major role in the success, motivation, and musical self-esteem. The wrong setup on a woodwind, brass, or percussion instrument makes it difficult or impossible to play with proper fundamentals and often leads to feelings of frustration and dejection. Even students who are able to use a pre-owned instrument (perhaps one belonging to an older sibling, parents, or other friend or relative) need guidance in selecting quality accessories and maintenance supplies.

BASIC CONCEPTS

For all wind instruments, the mouthpiece setup is of paramount importance. Adjustments made to the mouthpiece setup affect the resistance between the airstream and the instrument as well as the embouchure; this resistance naturally affects the sounds produced and the feedback the players receive as air moves through the instrument. A proper mouthpiece will make a poor instrument sound better and make it easier to produce a sound. A poor mouthpiece on a great instrument will make it difficult even for the best performer to play even the best instrument well.

The mouthpiece, ligature, and reed setup must be suited to promote ease of playing and proper embouchure development for wind players. For most woodwind players, a single mouthpiece, reed, and ligature setup may be prescribed for all students. Because of the variability of lip shapes in most young students, several brass options may be recommended for players on these instruments.

Even the best equipment needs proper care. Teach instrument care and maintenance in all your beginner classes, and be sure students have the proper equipment to keep their instruments in great playing condition. Dirty tone holes on woodwinds and filthy mouthpiece shanks on brass instruments can distort pitch and change the feeling of resistance between the airstream and the instrument. In the percussion section, improperly adjusted drum heads lack clarity and definition. Remind students that taking care of their instruments will help them perform better and advance more quickly.

WOODWINDS

The woodwind family is divided into instruments that make sounds by blowing across the edge of an open hole (flutes), the single reeds (clarinets and saxophones), and the double reeds (oboe and bassoon). In this section, we will discuss important aspects of selecting proper mouthpieces, ligatures, reeds, and care supplies for each of the woodwinds. We will also discuss some guidelines for selecting instruments.

Mouthpieces

Students who play single-reed instruments may select different mouthpieces to help change the resistance of the air as it moves through the instrument. Mouthpiece selection affects volume, pitch, timbre, resistance, and even control. By selecting mouthpieces that are best suited to the characteristics of most beginning students, directors can help develop proper fundamental habits in their students with the least effort.

There are several parts to a mouthpiece, but the two that affect the resistance of the instrument most are the lay (sometimes called the facing) and the tip opening. The tip opening is the space between the tip of the reed and the tip of the mouthpiece (figure 11.1). The lay extends from the tip of the mouthpiece to the point where the reed comes into contact with the mouthpiece. In general, the longer the lay of a mouthpiece, the smaller the

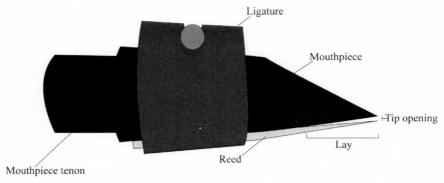

Figure 11.1.   Woodwind mouthpiece parts

tip opening. A mouthpiece with a long lay and a small tip opening offers the players a lot of resistance and requires soft reeds. A mouthpiece with a short lay and a large tip opening offers very little resistance and requires harder reeds.

For beginning-saxophone and beginning-clarinet students, it is important to select a mouthpiece that is relatively free blowing yet stable enough to produce a good sound throughout the range of the instrument. Most students will use their beginner mouthpieces throughout their first three or four years of playing, so it is important to select a mouthpiece on which it is possible to easily develop solid playing fundamentals but is flexible enough to serve them as they play more advanced music. Some of the most popular beginner mouthpieces, based on the guidelines above, are listed below.

Table 11.1.   Clarinet mouthpieces

Brand	Model	Tip Opening*
Hite	Premiere	1.09
Leblanc	LC3	1.14
Vandoren	5-RV Lyre	1.09
Vandoren	M-13 Lyre	1.02

*measurements are given in millimeters and are approximate

Table 11.2.   Saxophone mouthpieces

Brand	Model	Tip Opening*
Hite	Premiere	1.75
Rousseau	5R Classic	1.78
Selmer	C*	1.70

*measurements are given in millimeters and are approximate

Woodwind mouthpieces may be made of plastic, hard rubber, crystal, or even wood. Most good beginner mouthpieces are made of hard rubber. It is important to note that hard rubber mouthpieces can melt, so they should only be cleaned with warm (not hot) water. Clarinet mouthpieces have a thin section of cork around the mouthpiece tenon that fits into the barrel. A small cloth or a paper towel can be placed around the cork of the clarinet mouthpiece when cleaning to keep the cork dry.

Many clarinet and saxophone instructors recommend using mouthpiece cushions. These thin pieces of plastic can be affixed to the top of the mouthpiece opposite the reed to cushion the teeth to reduce the vibrations that players feel when playing. Mouthpiece cushions also provide a feeling of security for players and prevent the mouthpiece from sliding around or slowly slipping out of the mouth.

Ligatures

The function of the ligature is to hold the reed to the mouthpiece. Ligatures can be made of metal, plastic, leather, string, or other materials. The best ligatures keep the reed secure yet still allow maximum vibration of the reed. The material of the ligature affects the tone quality of the instrument as well as the ease with which the performer is able to produce a sound. Many stock ligatures that are provided as standard issue with instruments are poorly constructed and make it more difficult to play. For beginners, the best ligatures are durable, easily adjusted, and produce a satisfactory tone. Ligature screws usually point to the right as viewed from the player's perspective regardless of whether the screws rest on the top or the bottom of the mouthpiece. There are hundreds of ligatures from which to choose, but some of the most popular with directors of beginning instrumentalists include:

Clarinet
- Bonade: inverted or traditional
- Luyben
- Rovner: dark

Alto Saxophone
- Bonade
- Rovner: dark

Reeds

Reeds for clarinet and saxophone players are usually matched to the lay and tip opening of the mouthpiece. For beginners, as with the selection of the mouthpiece and ligature, care should be taken to provide options that balance ease of blowing with enough resistance to produce a characteristic, centered sound. Since reeds are usually plant material that has been shaped by machines, they are notoriously inconsistent; not every reed in a box will play well. Students should be taught how to select and make minor adjustments to reeds. Because the musculature of the embouchure is underdeveloped in the initial stages of instruction, softer reeds are often recommended for the first few months of study. Beginner-clarinet and beinner-saxophone students start using only the mouthpiece and barrel and then move on to work on the middle ranges of the instrument. As students develop strength in their embouchures and expand their playing range, they will gradually move to a reed that is more suited for their mouthpiece that will produce a more satisfying sound in all registers. This does not mean that "harder is better" in all cases. Remember that each mouthpiece lay and tip opening call for a certain strength reed; hard reeds are not appropriate for some mouthpieces.

There are many different reeds that young students on single-reed instruments may use. Some of the most commonly recommended reeds for the first few weeks of school include:

Clarinet:
- La Voz medium
- Mitchell Lurie 2½
- Rico Royale 2½
- Vandoren 2

Alto saxophone:
- La Voz medium
- Rico Royale 2½
- Vandoren 2

Bassoon and oboe players use double reeds to produce sound on their instruments. The double reed is most often a single piece of cane that has been split, tied together, and then shaped and cut to produce a matched pair of reeds that vibrate together to produce a sound. Double-reed selection for beginners is a particular challenge. Many manufactured reeds are inconsistent and difficult to play for many beginners. Players who start on reeds that are too hard or too open often develop poor habits that are extremely difficult to fix in later months. These students are often blamed for bad sounds when they actually have developed poor habits through months of playing on inadequate reeds or instruments.

Beginning double-reed players need beginning-level reeds. If you are not comfortable making and adjusting double reeds yourself, locate a local reed maker who can make four or five reeds that are specifically adjusted for beginners. These reeds should be relatively free blowing with as little resistance as practical yet still produce a great sound.

Care kits

Care kits for beginner-woodwind instruments should have all of the items needed to clean and maintain the instrument. These kits are often available as pre-assembled packages from instrument companies or local music stores. If the ideal care kits are not commercially available, it may be left to you to assemble the necessary parts. Care kits should be purchased by each of your students whether their instrument is new or used. Each care kit should also include a name tag for each instrument.

The flute care kit is the most basic of the woodwind kits; only items needed to clean the instrument are required:

- Cotton cleaning cloth (a handkerchief or bandana will work)
- Metal cleaning rod (should be included with the instrument)
- Name tag

Some flute instructors request that students purchase finger or thumb guides (such as the ones designed by Bo-Pep) as a part of the kit. These guides, when properly attached to the flute, help establish and maintain proper hand placement and position. Critics argue that daily addition and removal of the guides can scratch the clear lacquer on flutes and that these guides amount to a crutch that is difficult for students to adjust to when the guides are removed.

Double-reed students need equipment to store their reeds safely in addition to general cleaning and maintenance items. Double-reed kit items include:

- Plastic case for reeds
- Silk swab
- Cork grease
- Empty prescription bottle for soaking reeds
- Name tag

Clarinet care kits usually require the greatest number of accessories. These kits should include recommended reeds, ligature, and mouthpiece as well as equipment for cleaning and oiling the bore and keys of the instrument. Wooden clarinets can crack unless bore oil is applied once or twice a year. Pivot screws should be oiled very sparingly—about once every six months. Specific directions should be given to students in the use of all care-kit materials. A typical clarinet care kit might include the following items:

- Recommended mouthpiece
- Mouthpiece cap (often included with mouthpiece or ligature)
- Recommended ligature

- Clear or black mouthpiece patch
- A box of recommended strength and brand of reeds
- Reed case to hold four reeds
- Silk cleaning swab
- Cotton oiling swab (for oiling the bore of the instrument)
- Key oil
- Bore oil
- Thumb-rest cushion
- Cork grease
- Name tag

Saxophone care kits should include recommended mouthpiece, ligature, and reeds as well as cleaning and lubrication supplies. Pivot screws should be lubricated sparingly—about once every six months. A standard neck strap is generally included with the instrument, but used instruments are sometimes missing this important item. Standard neck straps are generally thin and lack padding. Your students will appreciate the recommendation of a padded strap. Some typical items in the saxophone care kit include:

- Recommended mouthpiece
- Recommended ligature
- Mouthpiece cap (often included with mouthpiece or ligature)
- Box of recommended brand and strength reeds
- Clear or black mouthpiece patch
- Reed guard to hold four reeds
- Key oil
- Cork grease
- Silk cleaning swab
- Padded neck strap (standard, nonpadded neck strap is usually included with the instrument)
- Name tag

Instruments

As with mouthpiece and ligature recommendations for beginners, instruments for new students should balance durability with stable performance characteristics. These instruments should stand up to wear and tear as young students get used to manipulating their new instruments with their changing bodies. Some beginner models have features that compensate for smaller fingers and hands to make playing easier for young students.

In the first part of the twenty-first century, the musical instrument industry is undergoing an exciting era of expansion and change. Many of the best foreign and domestic instrument companies are shifting their production to China and other countries located in the Pacific Rim. As these new countries continue to improve their production of instruments, some of the old "tried and true" manufacturers are meeting with increased competition. Time will tell if these new brands and models will be able to compete with the traditionally recommended models in terms of quality and durability. Certainly an investment in a musical instrument is a large one, and great care must be given in evaluating and ultimately recommending whether or not these new models and brands will work for your students.

It is important for you to communicate to your band families the importance of purchasing or renting musical instruments wisely. In general, instruments purchased at discount stores do not hold up well and are difficult or impossible to repair. Some parents relate well to analogies comparing purchasing "cheap" computers or cars to renting or purchasing inexpensive musical instruments—you usually get what you pay for! It is impractical to provide lists of every acceptable beginner instrument to your families. Offer to inspect any instrument that is not on your recommended instrument list before a family invests in a purchase.

Flutes

Beginner flutes often have closed tone holes (sometimes referred to as "plateau" style) so students do not struggle to cover open holes. Some flute players feel that open tone holes sound better, but some professionals play on flutes with closed tone holes. Care must be taken to insist that flute players using plateau key systems use proper playing technique and avoid the habit of closing the key work with the edges of the fingers. One popular option is the use of plastic or metal plugs inserted into the tone holes of the open-hole flute. These plugs provide the forgiveness of the solid plateau arrangement until students have achieved the consistency to remove one or more of the plugs in the open-hole flute.

A good option for beginner flutes, especially those used by players with smaller hands, is the offset G key. In the traditional layout, all of the six primary tone holes in the flute are aligned with each other. Flutes with an offset G layout place the third key of the right hand closer to the palm of the player so that it can be more easily reached. Even some professional models feature this ergonomic arrangement.

Most beginner-level flutes are nickel or silver plated (as opposed to solid silver) and have a playing range down to a low C. Some intermediate and most advanced flutes are solid silver and extend the range down to a low

B. Some commonly recommended flute brands and models for beginners are listed below:

Table 11.3.   Beginner flutes

Brand	Model
Armstrong	103
Emerson	EF6
Gemeinhardt	3
Pearl	Quantz 525E
Pearl	Quantz 665E
Yamaha	YFL200AD
Yamaha	YFL281
Yamaha	YFL261

Double Reeds

Because of their relative expense, schools most often own the instruments of the double-reed family. Durable double-reed instruments are often made of plastic or composite material. The key work on these instruments is generally tough and withstands use by young students. The key work on these instruments should remain in adjustment and may be easily adjusted by directors when needed. Some brands and models of double-reed instruments that are often recommended for beginners include:

Table 11.4.   Beginner oboes

Brand	Model
Fox	333
Fox	330
Selmer	104B
Yamaha	YOB241

Table 11.5.   Beginner bassoons

Brand	Model
Fox	Renard 51
Selmer	1432B

Clarinets

Most good beginner clarinets are made of wood or composite material. Wood clarinets sound better, but regular (annual) oiling of the wood bore of the instrument is required to avoid cracking of the instrument. Some beginner-model instruments feature adjustable thumb rests so that players with different hand sizes can be comfortably accommodated. Key work on beginner-model clarinets is most often nickel or silver plated and is generally difficult to bend accidentally. Overall pitch stability and ease of response are important factors to consider when selecting beginning models. Some brands and models that have been recommended in the past include the following:

Table 11.6.   Beginner clarinets

Brand	Model
Buffet	E-11
Buffet	E-12
Leblanc/Normandy	4
Selmer	CL211
Selmer	1310S
Ridenour	Lyrique RCP-146
Yamaha	YCL450N

Saxophones

As with other beginner-model instruments of the woodwind family, saxophones for beginners should be durable, reliable, and fairly consistent in pitch, response, and feel. Good beginner saxophones are always made of metal that is coated with a thin, protective layer of clear lacquer. Poor saxophones are notoriously difficult to play in tune; many less expensive models are difficult to play at all! As with all instruments, if a family wishes to provide a saxophone that is not on your recommended list, you or another expert should carefully inspect the instrument so that the student and the family understands how their selection might affect playing progress. Used horns are often missing neck straps, mouthpieces, or ligatures, so careful inspection of instruments that are not purchased or rented from reliable music stores should be inspected carefully as soon as possible as the school year begins.

Some brands and models of beginning-level saxophones that directors recommend include:

Table 11.7.   Beginner saxophones

Brand	Model
Jupiter	667GN
Selmer (USA)	AS500
Selmer (USA)	AS600
Yamaha	YAS200AD
Yamaha	YAS-23

BRASS INSTRUMENTS

The brass family is represented in the beginner band by the trumpet and French horn in the high-brass section and the trombone, euphonium, and tuba in the low-brass section. Because of their relative expense, many schools provide French horns, euphoniums, and tubas for students. Students who play school-owned instruments usually pay a nominal fee to help offset the cost of normal repairs and maintenance of these items. The students pay for damage that is caused by abuse or neglect. As with the woodwind section, brass mouthpieces and instruments should be carefully selected to promote ease of playing and greatest opportunity for success.

Mouthpieces

Brass mouthpieces come in a multitude of shapes and sizes and are generally labeled to help describe the various dimensions of the cup and rim of the mouthpiece. It is important to understand the numbering and lettering variations of different brands and mouthpieces to help guide each player in the selection of the best mouthpiece. The three primary variations

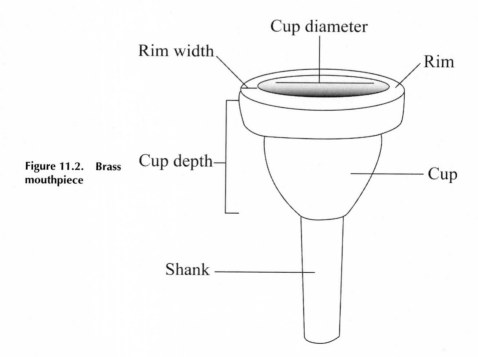

Figure 11.2. Brass mouthpiece

in mouthpieces for the beginner are the cup depth, the cup diameter, and the width of the mouthpiece rim (fig. 11.2).

The cup diameter is one of the most important for beginner mouthpieces. In general, the larger the cup diameter, the fuller the sound will be. The cup depth influences the sound and feel of the mouthpiece. A deep cup tends to help the player produce a larger, darker sound, and a shallow cup often makes higher register notes easier to play. The width of the rim affects comfort, flexibility, and endurance. In general, most beginners should use a mouthpiece that provides the best balance among each of these measurements: medium diameter cup, medium cup depth, with a medium rim. Because each of your students will come to the brass section with different sizes and shapes of lips, it is important to match the size of the player's lips with the appropriate size mouthpiece.

The Bach and Schilke mouthpiece numbering systems for identifying the dimensions of brass mouthpieces are used by most mouthpiece manufacturers. Unfortunately for the non-brass player, they are almost completely opposite in the way they identify mouthpiece measurements. The Bach system designates the cup diameter with the first number. Larger numbers indicate smaller diameters, and smaller numbers indicate larger diameters. The letter that usually follows the number in the Bach system represents the cup depth starting with "A" representing the deepest cup up through "E" or "F" at the shallow end. A Bach 3C has a larger diameter and deeper cup than a Bach 7D.

The Schilke system also uses numbers and letters. In the Schilke system, larger numbers represent mouthpieces with wider cups; smaller numbers represent mouthpieces with narrower cups. The letter in the Schilke system represents cup depth, but this system also works opposite of the Bach system: "A" represents a shallow cup while "E" represents a deep cup. The Schilke system also adds a second set of numerals that represent the rim shape with "1" signifying a rounded rim and "5" representing a flat rim. If no number is present, the mouthpiece features a standard rim.

Mouthpieces are like a glove in that what may fit one person may not work at all for another. It is best to have a couple of sample mouthpieces for each instrument so that students can experiment to find the perfect fit for the individual player's needs. Many directors find the most success by recommending two (or sometimes three) mouthpieces that feature rims, cup diameter, and cup depths that are in the "medium" range of each brand.

Some recommended brass mouthpieces for beginners include:

Table 11.8. Beginner-brass mouthpieces

Instrument	Brand/Model
Cornet/Trumpet*	Bach 7C, 5C, 5B, 3C Conn 23B Schilke 9
Horn	Bach 7, 10, 11 Holton Farkas MC, Conn 2, Yamaha 30C4 Giardinelli C8
Trombone**	Bach 12C, 11, 7C, 6.5AL, 301 Schilke 48
Euphonium**	Bach 6.5AL, 12 C Schilke 46D Yamaha 48D
Tuba	Bach 22, 24AW Conn Helleberg 7BConn Yamaha 66

*Cornets require a mouthpiece with a shorter shank than trumpets; other measurements are identical.

**Trombone and euphonium mouthpieces come in large- and small-shank versions; other measurements are identical.

Care Kits

Regular maintenance for brass instruments includes lubrication of the moving parts and polishing the instrument. Brass care kits should include a soft cloth for polishing the clear lacquer that covers the metal of the instrument, a mouthpiece brush, and a flexible cleaning snake. Remind students to never use brass or silver polish on their instruments.

Trumpets and euphoniums should use light valve oil. French horns and tubas with rotary valves should use rotor oil. Trombone players either use slide oil to lubricate their main slide or a combination of slide cream and water. In the latter setup, water is usually applied to the main slide with a small spray bottle. As you might imagine, proper use of the water bottle should be taught and reinforced regularly with young trombonists. All brass instruments need slide grease for their tuning slides. Students should be taught how to clean and oil their valves, how to give their horns a bath, and how to clean their mouthpieces. Even a small amount of dirt built up inside the lead pipe or shank of a brass instrument dramatically affects the tuning and response of the instrument.

Some teachers advocate adding a device called the BERP (which stands for Buzz Extension Resistance Piece). This device attaches to the lead pipe of brass instruments and allows students to buzz their mouthpieces in a natural playing position. The BERP also adds a bit of resistance to the mouthpiece, creating a feeling that is more similar to the full length of the assembled instrument.

Instruments

The best beginner instruments are durable, easily maintained and repaired, and hold up to the typical use of young players. Good beginner-brass instruments balance ease of playing with consistency in tuning and response across the range of the instrument. Some instruments have features that help students with smaller hands, arms, and bodies hold and manipulate the instruments with greater ease.

Trumpets and Cornets

There is some debate as to whether students should start their study on the cornet or the trumpet. The cornet has a conical bore that produces a mellower sound than the trumpet. Because of their bore, cornets are a bit more forgiving in terms of response and articulation but lack the bite and clarity of the trumpet. Although the cornet and trumpet are the same length, the shape of the cornet makes it a little easier to handle for students with smaller hands. Some teachers argue that students cannot produce a characteristic trumpet sound on a cornet and should therefore start on the instrument most of them will eventually play in band—the trumpet!

Whether you choose to use cornets or trumpets, good beginner instruments have adjustable rings on the third valve slides so that students with larger or smaller hand sizes can find a good fit. Good instruments also have a first-valve adjustment by way of a trigger or, more commonly on beginner horns, a thumb saddle.

Beginner cornets and trumpets that many band directors have found to work well with beginner students include:

Table 11.9.   Beginner cornets

Brand	Model
Bach	CR300TH
Conn	34A
Getzen	381
Jupiter	520M
Yamaha	YCR2310II

Table 11.10.   Beginner trumpets

Brand	Model
Bach	TR300H
Blessing	BTR-1270
Blessing	BTR-XL
Conn	23B
Getzen	390
Getzen	490
Jupiter	606MRL
King	601
Yamaha	YTR2335

French Horn

As mentioned earlier, many schools purchase French horns for students to use as they play in school ensembles. Many directors choose single F horns rather than double horns with the separate B♭ set of tubing for their beginners simply because of the weight factor. A double horn weighs more and is bulkier for young students with small hands. Some beginner instruments feature a mechanical linkage that activates the individual valves as opposed to the traditional string linkage. Mechanical linkages are noisier and are sometimes a bit more sluggish than string linkages, but they are usually more durable for young students. Some brands and models of horns that many directors select include:

Table 11.11.   Beginner French horns

Brand	Model
Conn	14D
Holton	602
Holton	652M
Holton	Farkas-H378
Holton	Farkas-H379
Yamaha	YHR314II

Trombone

Beginner trombones are usually small-bore instruments with or without an F attachment. The F attachment is helpful for students with shorter arms in that they can play some of the longer slide positions using alternate fingerings. F-attachment horns are heavier and more expensive than single trombones. Directors have recommended the following trombone brands and models:

Table 11.12. Beginner trombones

Brand	Model
Bach	TB200B
Bach	TB301
Conn	23H
Conn	88H*
Getzen	351
Getzen	451
Jupiter	438L
King	606
Yamaha	TSL354

*F-attachment instrument

Euphonium and Tuba

The euphonium and tuba are generally school-owned instruments. Beginner models usually feature piston valves that are a bit more durable than rotary valves. Some instruments feature a fourth valve, which provides alternate fingerings to help improve intonation and flexibility as well as extend the lower range of the horn.

As with most school tubas, beginner models are pitched in BB♭ . Some manufacturers offer a three-quarter-size version of the tuba that is only a little larger than the standard euphonium. Students have a much easier time manipulating these smaller tubas. If your budget allows, these smaller instruments are well worth the investment. Some recommended euphoniums and tubas are shown in tables 11.13 and 11.14.

Table 11.13. Beginner euphoniums

Brand	Model
King	628
Yamaha	YEP201

PERCUSSION INSTRUMENTS

Since the beginning percussionist must become fluent in both mallet percussion and the snare drum, beginners should be required to purchase a kit that has both instruments. Beginning-percussion kits generally have a practice bell kit with 2½ octaves, a practice pad, and an instrument stand that attaches to both. These instruments often come in either a backpack-style or rolling case for ease of transport to and from school.

Table 11.14.   Beginner tubas

3/4 Size	
Brand	*Model*
Bach	1107
Jupiter	378
King	1135W
Yamaha	YBB105
Full Size	
Bach	1108
Bach	1109*
Jupiter	382
Jupiter	482*
Yamaha	YBB201
Yamaha	TBB321WC*

*Indicates a 4-valve instrument

While some beginner kits feature full-sized snare drums, the practice pad is a good alternative for both classroom and home use. A practice pad provides the response and feel of a snare drum membrane without the volume of the full drum. Even if your beginner-percussion section is relatively small, you will appreciate the use of practice pads in class. Students have little trouble transferring skills learned at the practice pad to the battery instruments of the percussion section.

The beginner bell sets sold in percussion kits are notoriously poor instruments. Their keys are smaller than almost any other mallet instrument, and the screws that are used to attach the keys take up a great deal of the effective playing area. Most bell kits also have the names of the notes stamped into the keys. Electrical tape can be used to cover up the letter names so that students do not rely on these for note reading.

Students should be instructed on the care and cleaning of the instruments in their kit as well as the instruments that they use in the school's percussion section. The threaded inserts that attach the practice pads and bell kits into the metal stands can be stripped if they are tightened too much. The percussion section probably is the most expensive investment in your band room; teach your students to respect and care for the instruments the school provides. Some of the most popular percussion kits are listed below:

Table 11.15. Beginner-percussion kits

Brand	Model
Adams Percussion	Academy Series practice xylophone (no pad included)
CB Percussion	8674
CB Percussion	8676
Innovative Percussion	IPPK32
Ludwig/Musser	M651
Pearl	PK800
Vic Firth	V8705
Yamaha	Percussion Pack

Mallets, Sticks, and Accessories

Beginning-percussion students should be expected to provide snare sticks and mallets appropriate for their bell kits. A snare stick featuring a medium shaft with a standard wood tip is appropriate for most beginners. A small, plastic mallet with standard-length handle is best for bell kits. Each percussion student should have a small metronome.

Some percussion instructors require students to purchase a pair of medium-hard xylophone mallets, a pair of medium yarn marimba mallets, and a set of general timpani mallets. While these mallets will probably get more use in the following years of playing, it is a good idea to get students into the habit of providing these basic mallets for themselves. When compared to the equipment and accessory needs of other instruments, these additional mallets are not an unreasonable expense.

QUESTIONS FOR DISCUSSION

1. How would you handle Bart's situation described in the story at the beginning of this chapter? Imagine that one of your band parents comes to you with an old, dusty case with a very old instrument. What information or advice would you share with this parent?
2. How might musical self-esteem be affected by the condition or quality of an instrument? What steps can a band director take to help?
3. Why are mouthpiece and instrument brands so important? Why provide recommendations for students at all?
4. Imagine that you have two separate music stores in your area. Both stores feature reliable, friendly, and helpful employees and owners, but only one of them carries the brand and model that you recommend for your students. What are some ways that you might handle this situation?

5. Go online and find rental and purchase prices for the instruments listed in this chapter. Find retail prices for the care-kit supplies listed in this chapter.
6. How can you help keep the expense of playing in band from negatively affecting students and their families?

FIELD EXPERIENCE CONNECTIONS

1. Ask your cooperating teacher how they communicate recommended equipment and care-kit information to students' families.
2. Pick up a copy of the recommended instrument and care-kit supplies for the school to which you are assigned. What other recommendations might you make?
3. See if you can spot students who are struggling in beginning-band classes. How much of their struggle is caused by equipment problems (mouthpiece, reed, instrument, etc.)? What are some things you might do as a band director to help students who are struggling because of equipment problems?

WEBSITES

Instrument Manufacturers

Blessing. www.ekblessing.com.
Buffet. www.buffet-crampon.com.
Conn-Selmer (manufactures Armstrong, Bach, Conn, Emerson, Holton, King, Leblanc, and Selmer brands). www.conn-selmer.com.
Fox. www.foxproducts.com.
Gemeinhardt. www.gemeinhardt.com.
Getzen. www.getzen.com.
Jupiter. www.jupitermusic.com.
Pearl Flutes. www.pearlflutes.com.
Ridenour. www.ridenourclarinetproducts.com.
Yamaha. www.yamaha.com.

Mouthpiece Manufacturers

BERP. www.berp.com.
Conn-Selmer (manufactures Bach, Conn, Holton, King, Leblanc, and Selmer brands). www.conn-selmer.com.
Giardinelli. www.giardinelli.com.
Schilke. www.schilkemusic.com.
Vandoren. www.vandoren.com.
Yamaha. www.yamaha.com.

Woodwind and Brass Accessories

Luyben ligatures. www.luybenmusic.com.
Rovner ligatures. www.rovnerproducts.com.

Single- and Double-Reed Resources

Rico Reeds (distributes Rico, La Voz, and Mitchell Lurie reeds). www.ricoreeds.com.
Vandoren reeds. www.vandoren.com.

Percussion Kit Resources

Adams Percussion. www.adams-music.com.
CB Percussion. www.cbpercussion.com.
Innovative Percussion. www.innovativepercussion.com.
Ludwig/Musser. www.ludwig-drums.com.
Pearl Drum. www.pearldrum.com.
Vic Firth. www.vicfirth.com.

12

Philosophy, Curriculum, and Planning

The final bell signaling the end of the last day of classes at Phillis Wheatley Middle School rang through the band hall as the last of Mark Timmons' students scurried out of the band hall doors in pursuit of summer adventures yet to come. Mark looked back on his first year of teaching middle-school band. He was happy with how the school year had gone; he was also surprised that it had gone by so quickly! Overall, Mark felt that his students had done well, and he was looking forward to his first real summer vacation—one that did *not* include summer school—in several years.

Quincy, one of Mark's favorite beginning-band students, ran past the band-hall office on the way out of the building. "Have a great summer, Mr. Timmons!"

"You too, Q!" Mark replied with a grin. "Stay out of trouble!"

Mark sat down and thumbed through his lesson plan book one last time for the year. It seemed like only yesterday that his classes were opening up their instrument cases for the first time. Mark glanced over the assignments he had jotted down over the past 182 days of classes.

As he sat back in his chair at his desk, a set of stapled papers fell out of the front of his plan book. On that packet was a neatly typed list of goals he had developed for his students during the week of in-service meetings before classes had started last fall.

"Well look at you!" Mark said to the papers, "I guess I forgot about this."

Mark thumbed through the sheets and laughed.

"All twelve major scales . . ." He laughed again and then looked around to see if anyone had heard him. "That was a nice goal. Never quite got to that, I guess."

Mark had gotten caught up in the cycle of planning for the next concert with his advanced band and plowing through the method book with his beginners. He never quite got around to teaching everything he had jotted down on his list of goals for the year. All the great ideas and goals that he had for his students . . . somehow all of that just got brushed aside in the constant push to move forward through the details of each day.

Mark put the plan book into his desk, turned out the lights in the band room, and made the walk to his car from the band hall for the last time until August.

"I guess we'll try harder next year on those scales."

Hopefully, you have developed—or will begin to develop—some long- and short-range goals and expectations for your students. These goals may be performance goals, expectations for behavior, attitudes toward music, or notions about what your students should understand about various musical terms and ideas. While method books and the literature you select for your students can provide materials that may help them learn the knowledge, skills, and dispositions necessary to become proficient musicians, it is up to the director to help shape and select music and activities that help our students become good musicians and citizens. Even the best ideas and ambitions we have for our students can get moved to the back burner unless we engage in some thoughtful long- and short-range planning. How do we decide which knowledge, skills, attitudes, and activities are important or beneficial to our students? How do we select materials and plan for instruction in a way that ensures that what we want our students to learn is presented in the most efficient way? This chapter looks at some of the reasons teachers need a well-developed philosophy of teaching—and more specifically for music teachers, a philosophy of music education—in order to help them make decisions about both long-term and day-to-day decisions regarding how their programs operate. Your philosophical orientation influences the goals you select for your students and your expectations for their experiences and activities in which they will engage and will guide you as you make more detailed plans and decisions on a daily basis.

ORIENTING YOURSELF: DEVELOPING
A PHILOSOPHY OF MUSIC EDUCATION

At some point in your undergraduate educational experience, you most likely were asked, or will be asked, to formulate a philosophy of education. The term "philosophy" used in this sense is more of a personal orientation toward teaching or a set of beliefs about education that guides you as you make decisions for the classroom. In this regard, a philosophy of education can be viewed as a sort of mission statement that guides teachers as they move through the various decision-making processes that are involved in designing long-term and short-term plans for students. A philosophy of music education helps define who you are as a music teacher. This philosophy fundamentally determines your disposition toward music learning and teaching, and it influences your beliefs about the knowledge, skills, attitudes, activities, and approaches that are most important in learning and teaching music. Having a well-defined philosophy that articulates what is important in your teaching helps guide you in decisions such as: *What classes do I offer? In what order should I present material?*

A solid philosophy of music education can also help you make tough decisions whenever a crisis occurs. Say, for instance, that your principal were to come to you and tell you that you need to cut your budget by 10 percent or that you need to eliminate one of your music classes from the schedule. A clear philosophical statement about what is important to you in your music teaching can help you answer a parent who asks, "Why can't my daughter just play in the school's jazz band without being required to be in the concert band as well?" Your philosophy of music education can help you make informed choices and guide you to decisions that fit your situation best.

So how does one go about developing a philosophy of music education? One approach is to ponder your answers to some questions that may, on the surface, seem to be easy to answer:

What is music?
What is "good" music? Which music should be taught in schools? Before you answer "all kinds of music," do you really mean that? What about popular music? What about rap music? What about mariachi music?
Who should teach music?
Who should study music? Before you answer "everybody," really think through this answer.
When can a person begin to learn an instrument?
Why should music be taught in schools? Why not after school? Why not in professional studios?
How should music be taught? How is music learned most efficiently?

After you've pondered these questions for yourself and debated them with your colleagues, you might begin to flesh out your answers and fashion them into a philosophy statement. Remember that your philosophy of music education is not written in stone; you can—and most likely will—revise your statement several times over your career. You may revise your thinking based on your experiences as a teacher, but you should always have a firm philosophy in place that guides your decisions and day-to-day actions in the classroom.

It should be noted that many great minds have considered these questions in substantial detail. Two of the foremost modern thinkers in the philosophy of music education are Bennett Reimer (*A Philosophy of Music Education*) and David Elliott (*Music Matters: A New Philosophy of Music Education*). Their thoughts on the questions listed earlier in this chapter are well developed and carefully articulated in their writings. The National Association for Music Education also weighs in with major philosophical ideas presented in the "National Standards for Music Education." While these sources do not always agree with each other, they can be fantastic inspiration for your own philosophical ideas.

SETTING GOALS AND BENCHMARKS

Your philosophy of music education can guide you as you make decisions about goals for your students. Your philosophy and goals can help you set standards of development to help measure your students' progress in order to assess your teaching and your students' advancement. By setting specific goals for your students, you help define more clearly the knowledge, skills, and dispositions you want your students to develop as they move through your program.

WHAT'S A DISPOSITION?

A disposition is a tendency for something or someone to act in a particular way under certain conditions. If a person has an "optimistic" disposition, they will tend to look on the bright side when confronted with adversity. This does not mean that optimistic people *always* react in the same way; even optimistic people can be overwhelmed by tragic events just as a "greedy" person may have moments of great charity! Dispositions are sometimes referred to as "attitudes," but that term has developed a negative connotation in some circles (as in the statement, "Man, that girl has an attitude!"). As important as musical knowledge and skills are, we should also make a conscientious effort to help students develop dispositions favorable toward music. Remember that most of our students will not be professional musicians, but all of them can become lifelong supporters, patrons, and participants in the arts in some way. Developing positive dispositions toward music can influence students and those with whom they come in contact for years to come.

Most teachers are familiar with setting short-term goals in the form of daily or weekly lesson plans. Long-term planning and goal setting includes the objectives we set for our students over the course of the semester, year, or their entire experience in a music program from entry point until graduation. What are your goals and ambitions for a student who has progressed all the way through the music program at your school? Do you have goals for a student who has moved through the entire band program from beginner band through high-school graduation? To help you begin to shape these goals and benchmarks, consider what a typical student should know and be able to do at the end of various periods in his or her musical development. What skills should a sixth-grade percussionist have? What should a second-year bassoonist be able to do? These benchmarks not only help you plan what to teach, they also give you a way to measure your students' progress. Benchmarks also give you a way to assess your teaching approaches. Are you getting done what you planned to accomplish? If not, is it because of your planning? Is your sequencing faulty in some way? Are you leaving some key element out of your instructional plan?

Calendar events and performance opportunities help determine some of our program goals and long-range planning. For example, you may develop a "unit" goal based on an upcoming concert, or you may develop a series of lessons in anticipation of activities leading up to a solo and ensemble festival. Perhaps you are preparing for an assessment of a particular skill such as performing a certain series of scales. These long-term plans may overlap; you may begin your plans for the holiday concert as you are wrapping up a review of major scales. In practical terms, you will need to outline preparations for various performance events, but many of your long-term plans should be driven by your overall program goals and the benchmarks you have set for your students and not exclusively by the calendar. In other words, you are not just moving through "contest music time" and then on to "spring concert music preparation" and so forth. While concerts and contests are significant events, and you do need to prepare for them, keep in mind the philosophy of teaching music through preparation of the pieces we perform at these events. Take a long look at your overall goals and benchmarks, and then work to ensure that you have addressed the knowledge and skills that you feel are important in a consistent way across the year as you develop your long-range plans.

As with the philosophical issues discussed earlier in this chapter, a lot of people have given a great deal of thought to curriculum in instrumental music. These groups and individuals have considered the topics and concepts we might teach to our students in very organized ways. One of the earliest codified curriculum efforts was the Manhattanville Music Curriculum Project. This project took fundamental elements of music and layered them into an ongoing curriculum in which students would continually revisit topics in greater and greater complexity as they moved through the program. Another philosophical influence upon music curricula was the Tanglewood Symposium. This conference brought together representatives from music, the social sciences, businesspeople, and other educators to help develop and update a philosophy of music education. The materials developed as a part of the Tanglewood Symposium led, in part, to the development of the National Association for Music Education's "National Standards for Music Instruction." The curriculum ideas that grew out of the Tanglewood Symposium, including its influence upon the "National Standards," are an effort to codify what students should know and be able to do at various stages in their musical development in vocal and instrumental music from kindergarten through high school. The "National Standards" have been very influential upon several state and local school-district music benchmarks; a quick Google search of "instrumental music benchmarks" shows many examples of this influence. Other state curriculum guides reflect the overall spirit of the "National Standards" in their acknowledgment of the importance of including musical knowledge and skills beyond performance skill on various instruments (see, for example, the "Texas Essential Knowledge and Skills for Fine Arts"). The Canadian Band Association has developed another useful set of specific benchmarks for instrumental musicians at various stages of development.

The "Comprehensive Musicianship through Performance" (CMP) model is less specific as far as specific benchmarks for specific grade levels, but the overall philosophy of the model emphasizes that teachers use various musical works to teach musical concepts and to shape dispositions toward music in an organized and purposeful way. Patricia O'Toole's (2003) *Shaping Sound Musicians* and Robert Garofalo's (1983) *Blueprint for Band* are thorough overviews of the CMP model. Another excellent resource for exploring the knowledge, skills, and dispositions music students can develop can be found in the "What to Teach" chapter of Robert Duke's *Intelligent Music Teaching*.

The goals and benchmarks we set for our students, carefully aligned with the performance calendar for the year, influence our long-range plans. These long-term plans then help us create weekly and daily lesson plans. Each lesson plan is, in reality, a series of micro-plans that include an objective, an activity (or activities) to help students achieve the objective, and an assessment that helps the teacher evaluate how well the students have accomplished the objective.

LONG-TERM PLANNING

After you have a general idea of what your students should know and be able to do at various times during their musical development and after you have your performance obligations penciled into your calendar, you can begin to outline some preliminary long-range plans. These plans may vary in length from as few as three weeks up to a year. These long-range "units" may be driven primarily by our list of benchmarks for a particular skill (students will perform all twelve major scales by memory at quarter note = 112) or by a calendar event (the winter concert is December 15). You might be tempted to start filling in your long-range plan by outlining what your students would do on the first day of the plan, but most people find that they do best by beginning at the *end* of the plan. Place the "due date" for the completion of the "unit" on which you are working in pencil on your calendar. This might be the day(s) you plan to assess your students on scales or the date of the winter concert. Next, be sure to pencil in any rehearsal dates you might lose because of holidays, field trips, school testing, or other events. Once you have these events penciled into your calendar, you have a good idea of the number of days you can set aside to work toward your goals. As you complete your planning—especially with concert pieces—keep in mind the *whole-part-whole* idea: begin by giving your students a "big picture" overview of the things you will be working on during this time frame. Next, zoom in to work on specific details during the middle days of your plan. Finally, zoom back out to put the details your students have worked on into context at the end of your plan. Long-range plans are generally not as specific as daily lesson plans; you might include an entry such as "work on the details of the slow section of 'Holiday Tune 1'" on a particular date. Your long-range plans are flexible so that you can adjust your teaching based on your students' response to your instruction (they may move faster or slower than expected) or to unforeseen changes to the schedule (fire drill anyone?). These long-range plans help you set up a framework for your short-term planning.

SHORT-TERM PLANNING

Short-term plans include weekly lesson plans, daily lesson plans, and plans for individual activities within your daily plans. Using your long-range plans as a guide, complete an outline for the specific activities your students will complete on a given week. The elements you choose to include on your weekly plans are directly influenced by your long-term plans. Which scales will you work on during each particular day this week? What sections of the music will you address? How will you isolate various aspects of the music to work on potential problems? How do you plan to assess your students on a particular skill? As with long-range plans, don't feel like you are locked into the details your weekly plan; feel free to adjust and adapt your plan if your students progress slower or more quickly than expected.

PLANNING LESSONS

Your weekly plans allow you to make your most detailed planning in your daily lesson plans. When working to complete daily lesson plans, keep in mind that the students' mental energy is usually highest at the beginning of the rehearsal. Consider rotating the order of activities so that you do not always begin with the same exercise or the same musical work each rehearsal. Most likely, each daily lesson plan will be made up of a series of individual micro-plans for various goals and activities within each lesson. For example, you may start with a micro-plan that takes the class through warm-up activities, then move to a micro-plan for working on applying a specific skill to a line out of the beginning-band method book, then move on to a micro-plan for working on a particular segment of a specific musical work, then wrap things up with a run-through of a class favorite (ending with a "fun" piece is often rewarding and motivating for students).

Each of these micro-plans for the various goals and activities of the class should have three parts: (1) a clear objective, (2) a detailed list of activities, and (3) some type of assessment to gauge the success of the activities in accomplishing the goal of the lesson. Each of these parts of the micro-plan is presented in detail below.

Objective

The objective for a micro-lesson states what you want your students to know or be able to accomplish at the end of your instruction. In order for your objective to be most effective, it needs to satisfy two requirements. First of all, your objective should be *student centered*. In other words, state the objective in terms of what the *students* will know or be able to do rather than listing what the *teacher* will do. For example, instead of saying, "The teacher will lead the students in scales," you might write:

The students will perform the B♭ and E♭ scales two octaves in eighth notes with two mistakes or fewer at quarter note = 112.

The second element of a clear objective is that it should be *stated in terms that are observable.* The students must demonstrate their understanding or their ability to accomplish your objective in some way. The students need to produce something tangible that you can listen to, read, or see that demonstrates their mastery of the objective. Careful wording will help you develop objectives that are observable; it is impossible for us to see a student "understand" or "appreciate" something, but we may be able to think of a way that students can *demonstrate* their understanding or appreciation of a musical topic.

If you have trouble coming up with an objective or writing an objective for your lesson plan, you might want to start by identifying a specific problem in the music or a specific skill you want your students to accomplish. For example, you may notice over the course of a rehearsal that your students play out of tune at letter *D* in a particular piece of music, or your students might have trouble playing a particular rhythm in bar 74. Turn these problems around by stating them in terms of what your students would do or perform if they were successful in these spots in the music. Using the example above, we might say:

> *The students will play in the key of concert A♭ with accurate intonation by eliminating acoustic beats in all whole-note chords at letter D.*

Other objectives might arise from reviewing the benchmarks you have set for your students, looking over your state or local curriculum guides, or by consulting a reference such as Duke's (2010) *Intelligent Music Teaching* or the "National Standards for Music Education."

Activities

After your objective has been stated in clear, observable, student-centered terms, it is time to develop activities that will help your students accomplish your goal for the micro-lesson. Great activities have three common characteristics:

1. *Each part of the activity is directly related to the objective.* Everything the students do as a part of the activity should be directly related to the goal of the lesson. There are no extra, unrelated steps or activities in the lesson. This means that, even if an activity may be fun or engaging, if is not related to what you need to get done, it should be left for another lesson. For example, including a clapping activity when our goal is to work on balancing volume between sections is an unrelated activity. Even though clapping and counting rhythms can be a valid and valuable activity, it may not be the most direct way to address ensemble balance.

2. *Begin with what students already know or are able to do, and then add new material.* Start from the familiar—something with which everyone can be successful—and then try to relate new material to the knowledge and skills students already have. In this way, we keep in mind the Pestalozzian principle of moving from the known the unknown (see chapter 2).

3. *Move in small steps toward your objective by adding one new thing at a time.* One of the most common mistakes novice teachers make is that they move too quickly or skip key steps when progressing toward a goal. As accomplished musicians, we sometimes fail to comprehend all of the small details that go into executing seemingly simple skills or concepts in music. Be certain that each step toward your objective adds just one new component. For example, having your students "hiss" a rhythm successfully and then attempting to play the same rhythm as printed in a piece of music might skip some important steps such as playing the rhythm on one note, hissing the rhythm while we read the music, reading the music while playing on one note, and so forth.

Assessment

After you have selected and sequenced an appropriate set of activities, you will need to plan on how your students will demonstrate their achievement of the objective you have developed. Consider several questions to help you develop your objective:

1. *WHAT will your students do to demonstrate that they have achieved your objective?* If your objective is written in terms that are specific, observable, and student centered, then your assessment will naturally flow directly from your objective.

2. *HOW or WITH WHAT materials will they demonstrate their understanding of the objective?* Will they perform a certain passage? Will they complete a worksheet or other written activity?

3. *If you are using a specific piece of music, WHERE in the music will they demonstrate their understanding of the objective?* What measures will they perform to show you that they have accomplished their objective? You will be able to focus your attention on specific musical excerpts to gauge your students' success if you are specific as to which portions of the music allow them to demonstrate their understanding of musical skills and concepts.

4. *HOW WELL will your students demonstrate their accomplishment of the objective?* How many of them will answer correctly? How fast will they perform? How many mistakes will they be allowed to make and

still be considered successful? How many tries will you allow them to make in an effort to be successful?

Here is an example of a well-constructed assessment based on the scale example above:

The students will perform (what) *the B♭ scale passages in measures 9–16* (where) *in "Holiday Tune 1"* (with what) *with two note mistakes or fewer* (how well) *at quarter note = 112* (how well).

Each of your daily lesson plans will probably have at least two types of activities that are directly related to each other—a set of skill-development and warm-up routines and work on specific repertoire. As mentioned in chapter 8, warm-ups can be categorized as exercises to get the lips, fingers, and minds going; cyclical warm-ups developed from our long-range goals and benchmarks; and ad hoc tasks derived from the requirements of the tunes upon which you are working. Recall that "warm-up" activities need not be restricted to the first few minutes of the rehearsal period; they can be utilized anytime various skills need to be isolated prior to their application to individual pieces.

When developing micro-plans to address performance problems on individual pieces within your daily lesson plans, keep the *whole-part-whole* idea in mind. Begin your rehearsal of a particular piece or passage with a run-through of the piece or passage upon which you will be working. Next zoom in to work on the details of the piece using your micro-plan's objective, activities, and assessment as a guide. Finally, plan to zoom back out to put the passage back into the context of the entire piece or segment of the tune.

Finally, be sure to list prominently any announcements that the class needs to hear in your lesson plans. It is often best to write out your announcements in a consistent way in the same place each day in addition to verbally delivering your announcements. Many directors also post their announcements on their websites in addition to delivering them in class.

EVALUATING YOUR PLANS

Great teachers are reflective practitioners in that they look back on what they have done in their lessons and assess their effectiveness. This reflective practice includes a careful inspection of our long- and short-range plans. After each lesson, or as each week draws to a close, or as you wrap up another year, ask yourself the following questions: Did we reach our goals? Why or why not? What features of my plan went well? What could we have done differently? An honest assessment of your plans will help you be an effective teacher and allow you do build upon your strengths and learn to adapt to improve your weaknesses. Invite others to review your plans to give you their insight. Your mentors, colleagues, and campus administrators may have valuable tips to help you adapt your plans to be most efficient and a comprehensive teacher.

SCHEDULING AND STAFFING

One of the most important aspects contributing to the success of the school band program is the structure and scheduling of classes. Successful band directors make educationally sound decisions about which instruments they offer their beginner students and which band performance opportunities they provide. As the music expert at your school, you should have major input into the course offerings and scheduling of classes within the program.

WHICH INSTRUMENTS TO OFFER?

One of the first decisions you will have to make is which instruments are taught in the beginning band. This decision affects how many different class periods you will need, which books and supplementary materials you might use, and how to best assign instructional staff. One philosophy of instruction proposes that only flute, clarinet, trumpet, trombone, and percussion be offered in the initial stages of instruction. As students progress, teachers help students make decisions about switching to the other instruments. This switch generally happens during the first year or sometime near the end of the first year's instruction.

Starting only these five primary instruments has several advantages. Directors often find that they can be more organized when they focus on only a few instruments at a time. Students are not distracted by instruction given to students on other instruments and can move at a quicker pace. Directors may also become more familiar with the work habits and personalities of students they might consider switching to other instruments. By taking these factors into account, directors can avoid having a section full of fast-moving students or a section that always seems to fail courses.

There are, of course, disadvantages to this approach. Students who switch instruments after the initial instruction period on one of the "core" instruments miss up to a year of instruction on their primary instrument. While these students usually progress much faster than they did on their initial instrument, they will still need time to develop good embouchures, hand positions, tone quality, and technical facility. In some cases, this switch involves learning a new clef for note reading. Students also miss out on hearing the other instruments that are not offered. A "band" without tubas and low reeds can be disappointing for students and audiences and certainly does not model a mature ensemble sound.

A second, more traditional approach is to offer all of the common band instruments to students. In this approach, each student begins on his or her primary instrument from day one. Some directors use a hybrid approach in that they start *most* of the common instruments (flute, clarinet, oboe, bassoon, alto saxophone, trumpet, horn, trombone, euphonium, tuba, and percussion) and then add "color" instruments of the woodwind family (bass clarinet, low saxophones) in the second year. Chapter 10 outlines some ways in which you can help beginning-band students and their families select appropriate instruments.

HOMOGENEOUS VS. HETEROGENEOUS CLASSES

After determining which instruments you will offer to your students in the first year of instruction, it is time to decide how you will group students within the classes you teach. You may wish to schedule your classes so that all the students in each class play the same instrument (homogeneously) or so that many different instruments are combined within each class (heterogeneously). This decision may be driven in part by your schedule flexibility and the availability of staff to teach each class. If you are the only director, and beginning band is only offered one period a day, then you probably will be forced to teach a heterogeneous class!

The most efficient way to teach beginners is in strictly homogeneous classes. This arrangement allows teachers to maximize their instructional time and focus only on the specific pedagogy of each individual instrument. While this arrangement is the ideal, it requires flexibility and puts demands on staff and scheduling resources. If every instrument were offered to beginners and taught in individual classes, it would take over ten class periods to teach every beginner class!

SOME WAYS TO DIVIDE CLASSES

In reality, most directors work to provide hybrid homogeneous classes by grouping instruments with similar pedagogical concerns. For instance, it is often appropriate to group the low-brass students (trombone, euphonium, and tuba) in a class together. Even though trombones have separate issues, such as manipulating their slides and legato-tongue technique, these instruments have enough commonalities to justify their grouping: they all read bass clef, they play in the same general tessitura, fingerings and slide positions are practically identical, and they produce their tone in a similar way. What about adding bassoons to the group? What about a separate class for the trombones? What about offering a class that groups all the brass together? The possibilities are practically unlimited as long as you have a pedagogically sound reason for grouping students.

If your facilities and staffing allow, it is often practical to offer two or more beginner classes during the same instructional period. Think "outside of the box" of the band room when considering teaching spaces; cafeterias, stages, book rooms, and other rehearsal halls are all possible places you could meet with a beginner group. Consider grouping sets of classes so that they can be combined when needed. You may wish to have a trumpet class that meets at the same time as the clarinet class; these instruments read the same clef, are both pitched in B♭, and play in the same relative tessitura in most beginner music.

If you can't manage to get students separated into the groups you want, it is important to meet with them on a regular basis outside of regular class time to cover important fundamentals that are difficult to address during their normal band classes. Give parents as much advance notice of these meetings as possible, and expect to have a few scheduling conflicts. Most students will enjoy this extra time in band if you stress the importance of meeting their individual needs.

HOW SCHEDULING REALLY WORKS

It will be up to a school administrator (usually a principal or guidance counselor) to set the final class schedule for the school. It is important that you communicate your needs and requests to this person early and often. The scheduling administrator will need to know the name of each class, which period each class meets, the instructor for each class (if multiple directors), as well as the first and last names (and ID numbers if your school uses them) of the students that need to be placed in the class.

Many middle-school campuses utilize a "teaming" concept in which large populations of students are divided into smaller groups that share specific teachers in the core subjects such as math, science, reading, and social studies. In this arrangement, elective classes are restricted to specific time slots allowing the core teachers to meet as a team during these elective blocks. When working with team-based scheduling, it will be especially important that you provide information to your administrators as quickly as you can *before* the teams are formed. Often a student's instrument selection will determine the team in which a student is placed. If the "bluebird" team has electives first period, and you offer percussion first period, all of your percussionists will be on the "bluebird" team. You will win a friend and carry great influence with your scheduling administrator by providing as much assistance and information as you can in a timely manner.

OTHER COURSE OFFERINGS

The core organization of your program is the concert band, so be sure to remember to include your primary performance ensembles in your schedule! After the first year of instruction, most directors place students in a performing ensemble. Some directors choose to offer ability-based ensembles while others place students into ensembles by grade level. While scheduling a grade-based class is sometimes easier, it has many disadvantages. In grade-based classes, students who learn at a slower rate may inhibit the progress of high-achieving students. Younger students often benefit from the leadership and maturity of older students in mixed-grade classes. You should develop and be able to articulate an educationally sound philosophy of how you would like to see your performing ensembles grouped. In addition to the "traditional" band class, you may wish to offer other opportunities for students in your school as time permits, such as jazz band, small ensemble classes, music-theory courses, and even music-technology opportunities. Some of these courses can be offered to students who are not enrolled in a performing ensemble.

GETTING HELP

When making decisions about which courses to offer and when to teach them, keep in mind the professional skills and expertise of other members of the music staff in your school district might have. If you are a woodwind expert, it might make sense to team teach with another director on another campus who is a brass expert. Perhaps you could arrange to teach some of this colleague's woodwind classes or sectionals in exchange for teaching your brass classes. Is there a high-school director who is a brass expert that might teach some or all of your brass classes? Is there an elementary teacher who is a percussion expert? If there are two or more directors assigned to your campus, making decisions about who will teach which class may be easier.

If you have directors in your district who are primarily assigned to teach on a high-school campus, work with them to come up with an effective team-teaching approach. Remind them that a solid foundation established at the beginning stages of instruction will pay off for them in only a couple of years. High-school directors can retain students in their programs if they become a familiar face at their feeder schools. You might offer to work with the marching band or cover weekly sectional rehearsals for them in exchange for their assistance.

QUESTIONS FOR DISCUSSION

1. If you've already completed a philosophy of education statement, take it out and review what you have written. Does it reflect who you are as a teacher? Would you change your statement now that you have had more time to reflect upon these statements?
2. Discuss the philosophy questions listed on page 247 with some friends or classmates. How do your views differ from those of your colleagues? How would you handle it if a music supervisor had different views from yours on the answers to these questions?
3. Role-play—philosophical situations—principal cuts budget, parent asks about jazz band vs. concert band.
4. Write an objective, activity, and assessment for a musical skill on your primary instrument. Assess your objective using the criteria listed on pages 252 and 253.
5. Think back to your own experience in school music programs. Did your teachers schedule courses for efficient student progress? What factors may have influenced their decisions? What would you have done differently? Why?
6. Develop an argument for or against the following statement: "In our school district, we will only start beginners on flute, clarinet, trumpet, or trombone."
7. Create a class schedule based on seven periods each day. Justify how you have scheduled your classes. Can you make a schedule work with six periods? Remember to schedule a conference period and lunch for yourself!
8. What are some combinations of instruments that might go well together in a class? Justify your answer with specific pedagogical reasons.
9. What are some other "nontraditional" performing ensembles or classes you might offer students? What knowledge and skills do directors need to teach these classes? Where can teachers develop the "chops" to teach these classes?

FIELD EXPERIENCE CONNECTIONS

Arrange an informal three-minute talk with your cooperating teacher about scheduling band classes. Here are some possible questions you might ask:

1. Are you happy with the way your band classes are scheduled at your school? Why or why not?
2. Who makes the master schedule at your school? How do you keep in contact with that person regarding the scheduling needs of the band?
3. In your school district, do the band directors team teach? How do you decide who can/will teach what courses?

REFERENCES

Blocher, L., and R. Miles. 1999. *Scheduling and teaching music*. Springfield, IL: Focus on Excellence.

Boyle, J. D. 1992. Program evaluation for secondary school music. *NASSP Bulletin* 76 (544): 63–68.

Draper, A. 2000. The times are changing. *Teaching Music* 7 (4): 30–37.

Duke, R. A. 2010. *Intelligent music teaching*. Austin, TX: Learning and Behavior Resources. See "What to Teach" chapter.

Elliott, D. 1995. *Music matters: A new philosophy of music education*. New York: Oxford University Press.

Garofalo, R. 1983. *Blueprint for band*. Fort Lauderdale, FL: Meredith Music.

Gary, C. L., and M. L. Mark. 2007. *A history of American music education*. Plymouth, UK: National Association for Music Education.

Hinckley, J. 1992. Blocks, wheels, and teams: Building a middle school schedule. *Music Educators Journal* 78 (6): 26–30.

Latten, J. E. 1998. A scheduling-conflict resolution model. *Music Educators Journal* 84 (6): 22–25, 38.

Lehman, P. R. 1989. Assessing your program's effectiveness. *Music Educators Journal* 76 (4): 26–29.

Mark, M. 1986. *Contemporary music education*. New York: Schirmer Books.

Music Educators National Conference. 1995. *Scheduling time for music*. Reston, VA: Music Educators National Conference.

Music Educators National Conference. 1986. *The school music program: Description and standards*. Reston, VA: Music Educators National Conference.

O'Toole, P. 2003. *Shaping sound musicians*. Chicago: GIA.

Reimer, B. 2003. *A philosophy of music education*. 3rd ed. Upper Saddle River, NJ: Prentice Hall.

Van Zandt, K. 2001. Is it curtains for traditional ensembles? *Teaching Music* 8 (5): 24–29.

Walker, D. E. 1998. *Teaching music: Managing the successful program*. 2nd ed. New York: Schirmer Books.

WEBSITES

Canadian Band Association. CBA national curriculum and standards publications. www.canadianband.ca/standards.html.

Comprehensive Musicianship through Performance. www.wmea.com/CMP.
MENC: National Association for Music Education. National standards for music education. www.menc.org/resources/view/national-standards-for-music-education.
Texas Education Agency. Texas essential knowledge and skills for fine arts. http://ritter.tea.state.tx.us/rules/tac/chapter117/ch117b.html#117.33.

13

Rules, Procedures, and Classroom Management

Brian could hear the roar of his sixth-grade low-brass class crescendo steadily as he sifted through the mound of paperwork on his desk in a valiant effort to find his grade book. For weeks the pile of papers on his desk seemed to grow like something out of a science fiction movie. Brian shuffled through the papers, practice charts, reeds, and parts from a disassembled flute in an effort to find the missing grade book.

"I know that grade book is somewhere in this pile," thought Brian, panicking.

Mrs. Brown, the school's assistant principal, was on her way down from the office to complete her second observation of Brian's teaching for the year. The first observation had not gone well. When Mrs. Brown met with Brian after the first observation, she recommended that he develop clearer procedures to address the classroom-management issues that were becoming a nuisance for the administrators in the front office.

"Brian, it seems like every day you send three or four students to my office for every little thing," Mrs. Brown had said in their conference earlier. "At this point, I just talk to the kids you send to me and then send them right back to your class. We can't keep calling parents and giving school detentions for every little offense."

Brian had been upset that Mrs. Brown and the other principals were not doing anything to help him when he referred students to the office. He felt as if most of his classes were out of control and even dreaded coming to school some days. He wished he could just concentrate on teaching music to kids—something he enjoyed a great deal! But recently, the students' behavior was sucking that joy of teaching music right out of him.

At this moment, however, he just wanted to find his grade book so that he would be ready for his observation. The roar of the low-brass class was starting to reach a fever pitch. Brian heard something—perhaps it was a drumstick—hit the office window. He called off his search for the grade book, grabbed his cup of coffee, and stormed out of the band office. When Brian got through the band-room doors, he saw students running everywhere. Music was flying through the air, and two students were wrestling with each other in the back of the room near his brand-new tubas. Brian had finally had it. He leaned his head back and shouted, "Shut up!"

The class immediately grew quiet as Mrs. Brown walked through the door with her clipboard. . . .

OVERVIEW

I can recall having vivid nightmares each year just before school started that included scenes such as the one described at the beginning of this chapter. While none of my classes were ever quite as bad as I dreamed, I sometimes struggled as a young teacher juggling the many responsibilities of planning my lessons, managing the grades and paperwork generated by my large classes, and managing students' behavior as I taught each group of students. You might be the greatest instrumentalist in the world, but if you can't manage people, activities, and disruptions, you will never be as effective as you could be. Teaching music offers special challenges above and beyond what most other classroom teachers might encounter. The good news is that most of your students want to be in your classes and want to play their instruments. Music is fun, and students get to be active participants as they learn in your class, so you immediately have an advantage over some of the other teachers in your school. Even the smallest accomplishments can motivate beginning-band students; opening instrument cases for the first time or learning a new note can be a thrill for beginners.

This chapter outlines three major areas that will help develop and maintain a successful classroom climate. These areas include (1) developing a rapport with each of your students, (2) being organized and professional, and (3) communicating clear expectations of your procedures and expectations for class to your parents, administrators, colleagues, and students.

ADDRESSING THE NEEDS OF BEGINNING-BAND STUDENTS

In chapter 5 of her book *Managing Your Classroom with Heart*, Katy Ridnouer (2006) outlines eight areas in which middle-school students need support. These areas include confidence, connection with the curriculum, a model of self-control, a sympathetic ear, a sense of possibility, order, respect, and acceptance. I've used these recommendations, based on the social and developmental needs of adolescents, to frame the particular needs of music students.

Confidence

Students need to have a confident leader and need to develop confidence in themselves. To become a confident teacher, plan carefully, prepare well in advance of your classes, and organize your classroom so that you establish a solid foundation for yourself and your students. We'll talk more about the details of planning and organizing later in this chapter. Often just by *looking* and *sounding* more confident you *feel* more confident—even when you have butterflies in your stomach! You can give the appearance of confidence by using a strong voice, making eye contact with your students, and establishing a strong, balanced, open posture. Many teachers inadvertently raise the pitch and speed of their voice as they speak louder or when they are in a stressful situation, but those changes often make them sound less confident. Teachers look less confident when they exhibit a weak posture. Slouching or standing in a defensive-looking position makes you look less confident or even fearful.

Our students need to develop confidence in themselves as well. As a teacher, your ability to instill confidence in your students, as performers and as individuals, is an important part of your job. To develop your students' confidence, give them tasks that allow them to be successful. Guide your students in giving their peers positive feedback when critiquing other students' performances in class. Create an environment in which students are free to give and accept constructive criticism to each other. Confidence in the music classroom can even translate to confidence in other areas of academic performance and in social circles.

A Connection with the Curriculum

Developing a connection between your students and with your musical curriculum may seem pretty straightforward at first; students hear music all the time, and they already have some experience with music, right? We need to realize that the connections between what we do in band class and what students experience in their lives is not always so obvious for our students. One of the strongest connections we can help our students build is the one with their instrument. Often students hold preconceived notions of what it might be like to be a saxophone player or a drummer, but sometimes we need to help them develop excitement about being an oboist or a euphonium player. Our students' initial images of what is involved with being a saxophone player or a drummer may not match the reality of what goes on in middle-school band. Developing students' role identification as a band member and as a performer on their particular instruments is an important part of developing positive connections with the instrument they choose to play and with what we do in the band class. Students with strong, positive associations with the activity of making music in band class and with their role on each of the instruments are more likely to continue to pursue involvement with musical activities.

We should also enhance the connections between our music class and what goes on in the lives of our students. Being in touch with what students watch on television, the video games they play, the movies they watch, and the sports they're interested in can help us connect our presentation of material in the music class with what they experience outside of school. We can also draw from and contribute to connections between other school subjects and what we do in the music classroom. For instance, if students are studying weather in science class, we might point out that temperature affects pitch on our instruments. If the students are studying Australia in social studies, then you might want to teach them the song "Kookaburra" and about talk the bird that inspired that tune. This interdisciplinary approach to teaching is an important part of many state curriculums and is a powerful benefit of music classes; some students will only understand academic subjects if they are presented in the context of their music class.

A Model of Self-Control

Modeling desired behavior and attitudes can be an important way to develop positive classroom conduct. Our students need to look to us as a model of how responsible adults relate to each other and handle conflict or stress. As a teacher, you sometimes will be the only adult in some of your students' lives that models self-control and respect. If you respond to a student's misbehavior in a calm, businesslike way, you may serve as a stark contrast to other adults who may handle these types of situations by yelling at them or even abusing them physically.

Your students will mirror your behavior in the classroom, and you can use that to your advantage. Act in ways in which you want your students to behave. For instance, if you want your students to be on time, then you should start class promptly. If you want your students to speak respectfully to you, then you should model respectful speech when addressing your students. Of course, one can look at it from a negative perspective as well; if you don't want your students to eat in the band room, then don't lead class with a cup of coffee on the podium and a doughnut in your hand.

Students can also serve as models for each other. Try to catch other students doing the right thing, and reinforce that behavior with positive statements. Publically praise positive behavior with statements such as, "I love how the front row is giving me great eye contact while I'm speaking." Giving sincere, positive reinforcement to students who are doing what you want them to do will often influence those who are not behaving as you wish. Pointing out correct behavior is often more effective in correcting negative behavior than addressing the negative behavior directly.

A Sympathetic Ear

Students need to know that you care about them as individuals. Building positive rapport, especially with middle-school students, can help you maintain a productive and positive work environment. Developing relationships with students might begin with acts as simple as greeting students as they enter your classroom or as you see them around school. Try to get to know your students' interests and activities and support them when you can. Take a few minutes to drop by your students' soccer or basketball games and watch them play. Get to know what movies or television shows your students watch or what kinds of music they listen to during their free time. Making these connections makes you seem more approachable and gives you material that you can use to develop positive conversations and relationships with your students. Make it a point to try to connect in some way with all of your students. It's often easy to get to know the outgoing, gregarious students, but the shy students are often lost in the background. Reach out to the quiet students; sometimes you may be the only person that takes the time out of the day to acknowledge them in a positive way.

When it comes time to discipline students, you can help develop a positive rapport by being consistent and fair. Many successful teachers adopt a businesslike model when addressing classroom-management situations: they are polite, firm, and objectively address behavior issues quickly before moving on with class. Students will develop trust and respect for you as a teacher more quickly if they observe that your actions are consistent and fair.

A Sense of Possibility

Great teachers are always aware of the potential that lies in the future for their students and help their students look to the possibilities in their musical abilities. Great teachers encourage and motivate their students to improve by showing their students that they believe in them and have high expectations for them. Teachers can be a primary motivator for future study in music in high school, college, and beyond. Making statements like, "When you're in band in high school . . ." or "When you go to college you'll play . . ." allows you to plant subliminal seeds of music participation that will possibly bear fruit well beyond your class. Some of your students will begin to visualize themselves going to college only after they hear it from you. We can also give our students a sense of what is possible about achieving in their lives outside of music. By showing students what it's like to work hard to achieve a goal, to work together to make something meaningful, you give them valuable life skills that translate into success in any endeavor.

Order

Students value a secure and predictable classroom experience when they step into your room. Despite what students might tell you, young people value order and structure in school in a time of their lives that is often unstable and erratic. Order, structure, organization, and stability are important skills that musicians call upon as performers and ensemble members. These skills are therefore necessary intertwined with the ways the band classroom works.

The structure and organization of the band class begins with creating solid, well-thought-out plans and procedures. First, be sure to plan each lesson and activity carefully. Consider what you will do as a teacher and what your students will do in each step of your lessons and activities (see chapter 12 for more detailed information on planning). Think from a student's point of view as you move through your activities. Consider carefully what you want your students to be doing along each step in your plan. Of course you should be flexible and allow yourself the freedom to vary from your plans based on how your students are performing, but as a great person once said, "It is better to have a plan and not need it than to need a plan and not have it."

In addition to planning each lesson and activity carefully, you'll also want to develop a plan for the daily routine of the class. What activities will signal the start and end of each class? How will students enter and leave the classroom? What is the general order of activities on a typical day? While it's important to avoid boredom induced by following the exact, same routine each day, we need to have a default plan that we follow with some regularity to provide some degree of predictability in our classrooms. If students know that mouthpiece buzzing usually follows breathing exercises, for instance, then they can be more prepared to be successful in your class.

After you have your daily routines and your lesson plans and activities organized, you'll need to be sure that all the materials and technology you will need are ready. Be sure that any instruments and accessories that you need to teach are ready to go. Have your music and lesson plans organized so that you can refer to them easily. If you use technology, such as a metronome, a computer, a projector, or sound system, be sure that you know how to work each item, and have a backup plan in case they don't work. Your room should also be organized so that you and your students know exactly where they can find the materials and equipment they need for class. Later in the chapter we'll discuss ways to organize items such as instruments, paperwork, music, books, and backpacks.

Don't expect your students to automatically understand the routines and procedures of your classroom. They may not immediately know where they should store their equipment or submit their paperwork. Give your students clear instructions and allow them a chance to practice the routines and behaviors you expect in your classes. For example, you might want to have your students practice coming into the room quietly and putting their instruments away in the correct place. You might want to have your students practice particular behaviors when the conductor steps up on the podium. Put a positive spin on practicing these procedures by explaining to your students that these are the types of things we do as musicians in order to be organized, use our time efficiently, and protect our valuable equipment.

Respect

By providing students with clear procedures and routines in the music classroom, you allow students to develop respect for each other, for themselves, and for property and equipment. Remind students that their music classes are typically larger than any of their other classes, so it's important that we develop social skills that allow us to work with each other. Our classroom procedures allow us to show respect for each other as human beings and as fellow musicians in large ensembles. The music room also contains expensive and delicate property that can be easily damaged. Some of this property belongs to individual students, and some of it belongs to the school, but everyone needs to understand that all of us need to follow certain rules to avoid damaging equipment. The way you handle class procedures and routines shows the students that you respect them as individuals as well as a part of a musical team.

Acceptance

Students want to be accepted as individuals and as members of a group. If you are fair and consistent as a teacher, and if your students are successful and enjoy what they do, then other students will want to be a part of your group. As the group leader, you can provide acceptance into the group for your students from the very first day of classes. Students need to know that they are valued as individuals and not just as performers in your ensemble. They also need to know that you continue to value them even when they make poor decisions behaviorally. By separating a student's behavior from our dealings with her as a person, we allow our students to start each day fresh.

AN OUTLINE OF BASIC RULES AND PROCEDURES FOR THE BAND CLASSROOM

So why do we need rules in the band room anyway? Don't students just want to play their instruments? As we mentioned earlier, the nature of adolescents, coupled with the number of expensive instruments and equipment typically found in most of our band classrooms, call for some basic rules for the band classroom. Being clear to students and parents about your expectations for how things should work in your class will help you and your students face these special challenges. Use positive wording, logical consequences for rules infractions, and positive reinforcement for desired behavior to create an environment in which students can learn more quickly and efficiently as they develop the skills they need to become productive musicians and ensemble members.

Be sure that students and parents know the expectations for behavior, procedures for entering and leaving the classroom, how to properly care for their instruments, as well as the consequences for not adhering to these guidelines and procedures. One of the ways that you can provide students with a clear explanation of your expectations is by developing a band handbook. Outlining procedures and philosophies in a handbook helps to minimize questions and confusion. Have a signature page at the back of your handbook allowing your students and parents to acknowledge that they have read and agree to the policies outlined in your handbook. Sample handbooks can be found in the websites listed at the end of this chapter as well as in appendix A.

Some teachers prefer to use what Jim Fay and David Funk, in their book *Teaching with Love and Logic* (1995), have described as a principles-based method of designing classroom rules and guidelines for behavior. Fay and Funk explain the differences between a *principles* and *systems* approach to creating classroom rules and guidelines. In a principles-based system, we give our students the opportunity to adhere to a set of values that we feel are important for learning and making music together rather than ask our students to follow a list of very specific rules. A systems-based approach might have a very specific rule that addresses a single behavior such as *do not touch another person's instrument without permission.* A principles-based system might have a more general rule such as *treat school and personal equipment and property with respect.* By working within a principles-based system rather than a systems approach, we're teaching our students to be responsible citizens and ensemble members; the focus is on the general behavior rather than adherence to a set of specific rules. The *principle* expressed in the rule *treat school and personal equipment and property with respect* addresses the issue of touching other students' instruments but could also apply to taking care of music stands or deal with students vandalizing the band room. In a principles-based classroom-management system, one selects the core values that outline how students should behave or act in your class rather than creating a long list of rules.

One of the problems with a rules-based system is that trying to list all of the rules for every situation that you may encounter in a band classroom is an extremely difficult task. Try to think of all of the possible rules you could come up with for desired behavior in a music classroom. You might come up with items such as *no running in the band room* or *don't chew gum in class* or, perhaps, *keep your hands to yourself.* As you soon discover, if you tried to list every possible rule that covered every possible infraction, your list of items might run into the hundreds! What if you left out an important rule? Instead of having our students learn a bunch of rules, we might ask them to adhere to a few common values and principles that cover a wider variety of behaviors.

As you work to develop the core principles that are important in your music class, try to utilize positive phrasing to help your students visualize desired behavior. Frame your rules and procedures using positive statements that describe what you *want* your students to do rather than by describing what you *do not* want your students to do. This may seem like a trivial difference in semantics, but let's take a look at how words can be very effective in influencing what we visualize. What if I asked you *not* to think of a pink elephant? You probably had, at least for a fleeting moment, a brief visual image of some type of elephant floating through your mind, and I placed that image in your mind by asking you *not* to think of it! In terms of classroom behavior, consider the difference between a positively stated rule such as *always move about carefully in the band hall* and a rule like *no running in the band hall.* When your students read or hear the first, positively worded statement, they may visualize a calm, careful atmosphere, while the later statement may cause them to visualize students running wildly through the classroom. Keep the statements in your behavior guidelines simple, brief, and to the point with positive wording when possible.

Here are some possible ideas for some basic classroom rules based on principles of behavior expressed using positive sentences:

1. Respect others and their property.
2. Care for personal and school-owned instruments and treat equipment with respect.
3. Raise your hand and be recognized before speaking.
4. Be prepared with all supplies and equipment for each class.
5. Move about carefully in the music room.

Can you think of other rules you might add? Would you take away any of these rules? Remember that the rules must be consistently enforced, or they will lose their effectiveness, and you will lose your credibility. Don't include a rule unless you really agree with its principles and are willing to monitor and enforce it.

LOGICAL CONSEQUENCES

When a student violates a rule or procedure, there should be a logical consequence that follows her actions. Logical consequences allow students to connect their actions with specific consequences. Let's say that a couple of your students were roughhousing before school in a practice room and accidentally broke the glass in the practice-room door. You would most likely be very angry and might even assign them to after-school detention for the rest of the semester. While the students would surely not enjoy serving detention for that period of time, eventually the *reason* that they were serving detention would fade from their minds, and your punishment would not be as effective. Now consider *why* you might be angry over the incident involving the broken door: you may feel upset that the students acted irresponsibly without your supervision before school, or you might be upset with having to spend your budget funds for repairing the door. A more logical consequence for the students might revolve around the under-lying issues of why you're upset with the whole affair. Perhaps you could require the students to pay for part of the repair for the door and revoke the before-school practice privileges for these students. If a student violates one of your principles-based rules, the consequences of violating that rule follow logically from the infraction.

Some teachers like to have a standard set of consequences for minor disruptions or rules infractions that are easily handled on a day-to-day basis. Since most students really want to participate in your class, and they want to play their instruments, some of these standard consequences are based on their desire to play and participate in class. If the misbehavior continues, further measures such as student and parent conferences are utilized. Here is an example of a set of consequences for minor classroom misbehavior:

1. *Remind the student of the rule.* This is often all that it takes to correct most students' misbehavior—especially if you are consistent in enforcing your rules and they know that you consistently apply your consequences.

2. *Student loses the right to participate in class momentarily* (for example, the student removes her mouthpiece and places it on the floor). This period of time is generally very short—perhaps two or three minutes. Remember you *want* your students to play and are genuinely disappointed that they are no longer able to participate.

3a. *Student loses the right to participate in class for the remainder of the class.* After class, you should meet with the student to discuss the issues and work out a plan to modify the behavior in question. Record this meeting in your discipline log (see the next section for details on meetings and discipline logs).

3b. *For persistent misbehavior, student loses the right to participate for the remainder of the class. Parents are contacted by phone or personally.* Record this meeting in your discipline log.

3c. *If, even after meeting personally with the student and with the parents, the student continues to be a disruption to your teaching, the student meets with a school principal.* At this point, a serious conversation needs to happen among all the parties involved as to whether or not the student really wants to participate in your class. Bring copies of your discipline log to this meeting so that you can document the steps you have taken to address persistent misbehavior.

Of course there are some instances where a major disruption needs to be addressed at once. It is good to have an "emergency clause" to handle behaviors such as destruction of property, theft, fighting, and other serious offenses. If a student engages in this kind of destructive behavior, they are immediately removed from class, the parents are contacted, and the school administrator is involved in handling the consequences.

Students are also motivated by rewards for their great behavior. Allowing a class to play their favorite song or scheduling a "request day" where students get to choose they songs they get to play in class are great ways to motivate your class to behave well. You might recognize outstanding individuals by choosing a student of the week for each class or each section. The students could be recognized by name during class, on a poster prominently displayed in the band hall, or even with prizes such as a special snack, drink, stickers, or other small prizes. Be sure to check with your principal to see what kinds of prizes and rewards are allowed at your school and are appropriate for your community.

WHEN THINGS GO WRONG IN CLASS

Even if you've prepared carefully, organized your classroom and materials, and developed a solid set of rules and procedures for your classroom, you will inevitably have to deal with disruptive students from time to time. Students often experiment by testing the limits and your enforcement of classroom rules. How you deal with classroom-management issues that arise in class can reinforce the behaviors you desire in your classroom and allow you to be a more effective teacher.

Carry out any corrective discipline efficiently, maintaining the student's dignity, and remembering that every rule violation is a teaching opportunity—not only for the student involved but also for all of the students in your classroom. When disruptions do occur, try to deal with them in such a way that your valuable instructional time is not lost. Sometimes *nonverbal* intervention is the best way to deal with disruptions. Say for instance, two of your flute players are chatting on the left side of the class. You might be able to address this behavior merely by making eye contact with the students. Another silent but effective way to deal with a minor disruption like this would be to simply move closer to the students and continue on with your lesson. More than likely the students will understand your nonverbal cues in these situations.

When you do need to address the behavior verbally, tell the student what you want her to do in positive terms such as, "I need you to remain seated over here until the end of class." Some teachers find that giving students small, positive choices is a great way to avoid a power struggle with students. Of course, you'll want to limit the choices that you offer your students by giving them a set of options that you can be happy with regardless of the option they choose. For example you might give them the choice between finishing their music theory worksheet now or completing the worksheet during after-school detention; either way, the worksheet gets done.

If there is a classroom-management issue that escalates to the point where you'll need to speak with the student individually, meet with that student outside of class time. This allows the student to save face in front of her peers and saves valuable instruction time. Remember that the situation causing the problem is not up for discussion with the student during your class. You will never win a verbal battle with a student over a classroom-management issue in front of her peers, so don't engage your students in those types of battles.

There are several resources that address specific, challenging behaviors in the classroom. *Teacher-Tested Classroom Management Strategies* (Nissman 2009) lists many common classroom misbehaviors and how teachers can deal with them. A list of 124 challenging behaviors, their motivations, and helpful interventions is available on The Master Teacher website. This site even offers a classroom-management reference application for mobile devices.

YOU'RE NOT ALONE! DEALING WITH PERSISTENT PROBLEMS

When dealing with persistent or especially troubling behaviors, it is important to remember that you can get help and assistance from your campus administration, other teachers, and parents. Be sure that your campus principal knows your classroom-management plan, procedures, and consequences. Give your campus principal a copy of your handbook for approval before you distribute it to your students and their families. Assign logical consequences for classroom-management issues in your classroom first before referring discipline problems to the principal. If you deal with minor infractions yourself, your principal will know that any students you refer to the office have already been dealt with according to your classroom-management procedures and probably represent serious or persistent issues. Principals can be a great resource in dealing with persistent classroom-management issues.

If you have a particular problem with a certain student, check with the student's other teachers to see if similar issues are manifesting themselves in other classes. If your campus uses a team-based approach where a larger population of students is divided into smaller groups of students who have the same set of core teachers, see if you can meet with the entire teaching team assigned to that student. Often if a student is acting out in your class, they are having similar issues with their other teachers.

If you're lucky enough to have other band teachers on your campus, be sure that you each agree on the rules and consequences for behavior. If you have other music teachers who visit your campus regularly, be certain that they understand and support your classroom-management plan. Consistency across all the staff members is an important aspect of an effective behavior plan.

STUDENT AND PARENT CONFERENCES

Despite your best efforts in the classroom, you will eventually need to meet individually with students or their parents. Often these meetings allow you to better understand the underlying issues related to the behavior in the class. These meetings also allow you to clearly state your concerns and help you and the parent or student agree on the best way to move forward. Here's one approach to handling a conference with a student or parent.

1. *Describe the problem objectively.* Tell the student or parent what you observe in nonjudgmental terms. Use terms such as, "I notice that . . ." or "I feel like . . ." At this point, you are merely describing your view of what has happened in the class.
2. *Let the student or parent talk about the problem.* During this stage, you are trying to uncover the underlying cause of the problem. You're gathering data at this point, so feel free to ask questions if there are issues that are unclear.
3. *Describe to the student or parent what you feel like your understanding of the problem is.* Check with the parent or student to see if your impression of the underlying problem is accurate. You might say something like, "It sounds to me like you are upset because of your chair placement." Be sure that the student or parent agrees with your description.
4. *Try to reach an agreement on how you can work together to solve the problem.* Come up with a solution that addresses the underlying issues surrounding the problem. For instance, if a student is talkative in class because a particular student distracts her, you might agree to change her seat assignment. If a student fidgets in a distracting way during class because she is restless, you might suggest a special task that allows her to move around the room each day.

Most of the time, the parents are very willing to listen to what you have to say and want to work with you to solve any problems. If you have a parent that is particularly upset or angry, you might want to have another teacher, a counselor, or a principal sit in on the meeting. If at any point a parent is rude or abusive verbally, kindly end the meeting and request that the parent come back when he or she is able to discuss the situation calmly.

Parents will be more willing to work with you in stressful situations if they have met you before the conference and understand your rules and procedures. Communicate your expectations through your handbook, and make it a point to try to meet with your parents *before* any negative classroom-management issues arise. You might be able to visit with them at an open house, at a reception after a concert, or just with a friendly phone call or e-mail message conveying a positive experience with their students. Always document your student and parent conferences so that you can keep track of your visits with each other and your plans for correcting the behavior and so that you can show administrators or parents the steps you've taken to correct any problem issues at hand. See appendix B for a sample discipline log.

MANAGING THE FLOW OF STUDENTS AND PAPERWORK

Part of managing the band classroom is dealing with large numbers of students, their equipment, and the paperwork that they generate. Moving into and out of the classroom is especially challenging for young students with instruments. Have a location in which students can store their instrument cases, and have a plan for how they should deliver and pick their instruments before and after school. Each instrument should have a secure, assigned spot where the instrument can be found at any time during the day. This may be in an instrument slot, a locker, or even a marked spot on the floor of a closet. Have a plan for what students will do with instrument cases, backpacks, and textbooks during class. Will they put them back in their lockers? Will they place them under their chairs?

The seating arrangement for your beginner-band classes is an important consideration. You should be able to move around freely in front of, behind, and in between your students as much as you can within the constraints of your teaching space. Have your students set up so that they can play their instruments efficiently. Students should be able to sit with great posture with their music stands at arm's length from their bodies. Remember to consider students with special needs, such as those with a hearing or vision impairment, as you arrange seating assignments. If you choose to seat your students according to playing ability, consider seating the less-advanced students closer to you. If you have multiple rows of students, you might consider seating your best students in the back rather than in the front. This arrangement allows you to work with your weaker students more directly and allows these students to hear the best players more easily. Consider alternating strong students with weaker students so that the stronger students serve as models for the less-advanced students.

Organize the classroom to support your teaching needs. Some teachers have a "command center" set up at the front of the room with items such as a metronome, method books, seating charts, lesson plan book, instrument, pencils, and so forth. Often, this equipment must be mobile and set up on a rolling cart to allow the teacher to move from room to room. Organizing your materials in this way will keep you from losing valuable instructional time searching for the things you need to teach your classes.

Work to develop efficient ways to handle common classroom interruptions. Be very efficient when taking attendance each day. With a very small class, you might be able to just glance at the students and get an accurate accounting of who is present. For larger classes, you might need to create a seating chart. If a chair is empty, it is easy to refer to the chart in order to find the missing person's name. Some teachers laminate a list of their students or a seating chart and mark absences with a dry-erase marker each day to help speed the attendance-taking process. Create a plan for handling restroom breaks and nurse visits. Develop procedures for common tasks such as sharpening pencils and for when and how students may get reeds or take care of broken equipment. The broken instrument is a unique interruption that instrumental music teachers face. As with classroom-management situations, it is important not to lose valuable instructional time trying to figure out how to fix a broken instrument. If an instrument can be fixed in a few seconds (such as popping an easily accessed wood-wind spring back into place) then the repair can be dealt with immediately. If the problem is more involved (removing a rod on an instrument to move a more intricately positioned spring back into place), then the student should just finger along silently until the end of class when you can take the time to assess the repair individually.

Managing the flow of paperwork is another important issue that music teachers often find challenging. You will need to pass out music, paper-work, or return assignments to your students. If you have time before class begins, you can place paperwork or music parts in the seats of the students' chairs prior to their arrival. If you need to pass out paperwork during class time, be as efficient as possible. For example, hand papers to students on each end of the rows rather than starting on one side, or make a game of seeing which row can finish passing out their papers first. If a student is absent, place her name on the paper, and then place that paper in your lesson-plan book or class folder to remind yourself to deliver the paperwork to the student when she returns.

Students will also need to return paperwork and messages to you. Many teachers like to purchase a hanging wall file to create an "in-box" for any paperwork that needs to be returned. Utilizing an in-box allows you to sort through and organize papers outside of class time and helps prevent you from inadvertently misplacing the many papers that come your way.

These rules and procedures are merely methods for dealing with the complexity of managing adolescent students along with the intricacies of keeping track of large amounts of money, paperwork, and equipment. Re-mind your students that the rules and procedures are merely principles of common courtesy and respect and are ways to make life in the band room a bit more manageable for everyone involved.

FIELD EXPERIENCE CONNECTIONS

1. Can you think of some times in which your music teachers enhanced your self-confidence? Can you think of some instances in which a mu-sic teacher might negatively impact a student's self-confidence? How can directors develop confidence in playing?

2. Think of some typical directions you might give in a music classroom. Stand in front of a partner or a mirror and say these directions using variations in the pitch, rate, and volume of your voice. Repeat these directions using different postures and facial expressions. How do your voice, face, and body affect how your words are perceived?

3. How well do the teachers at your school model the behavior they expect from their students? Are they good role models? Why or why not? Without giving any names, can you provide some specific examples?

4. Investigate the instrument storage situation at your school. What features do you like? What would you change? Look up the pricing for various storage solutions for band equipment, and share this information with your colleagues.

5. Think of some behaviors you would *not* want to see in your band classroom. Make a *positively stated* rule that might address that behavior. Can you make your rule general enough to cover a wide variety of potential misbehaviors?

6. Does your school have a behavior-management plan? Your classroom? List the rules and the consequences. What do you like about the plan? How might you change the rules or consequences if you were in charge?

7. Ask your cooperating teacher if the school has an emergency plan for fire, disaster, or intruder. Be sure you know the plan!

8. Why do you think some students quit band? Why don't most students continue playing for the rest of their lives? Why do you think people might put their instruments away forever after middle school or high school? How might we encourage students to be lifelong performers? Is this even important?

REFERENCES

Breaux, E. 2005. *Classroom management simplified*. Larchmont, NY: Eye on Education.

Curwin, R. L., and A. N. Mendler. 1999. *Discipline with dignity*. Alexandria, VA: Association for Supervision and Curriculum Development.

Fay, J., and D. Funk. 1995. *Teaching with love and logic*. Golden, CO: Love and Logic. For more information about Love and Logic skills for the classroom, go to www. loveandlogic.com.

Haughland, S. L. 2007. *Crowd control: Classroom management and effective teaching for chorus, band, and orchestra*. Lanham, MD: Rowman and Littlefield Education.

Lemov, D. 2010. *Teach like a champion: 49 techniques that put students on the path to college*. San Francisco: Jossey-Bass.

Nissman, B. S. 2009. *Teacher-tested classroom management strategies*. Boston: Pearson.

Ridnouer, K. 2006. *Managing your classroom with heart: A guide for nurturing adolescent learners*. Alexandria, VA: Association for Supervision and Curriculum Development.

WEBSITES

Association of Texas Small School Bands. Band handbooks. http://www.atssb.org/handbook.asp.

Love and Logic. www.loveandlogic.com.

The Master Teacher. Classroom management. http://www.disciplinehelp.com.

Texas Music Educators Association. Music educator toolkit. http://www.tmea.org/resources/teaching-resources/educator-toolkit.

14

Assessment

Mrs. Marmon was furious! The normally pleasant president of the school's Parent-Teacher Organization was fuming as she sat across the table from Alison Brock in the school's conference room. This was Alison's first parent-teacher conference, and it was not starting well. The principal was running late, and now Alison found herself sitting alone in the room with the angry Mrs. Marmon.

The principal's secretary poked her head into the doorway of the conference room. "Mr. Storm is dealing with an issue at the bus loop in front of the building. He'll be right here."

"Mrs. Marmon?" asked Alison meekly. "Can I get you some coffee from the teachers' lounge?"

"I'm fine," Mrs. Marmon snorted.

Alison could hear the clock ticking on the wall as the two sat in an uncomfortable silence.

Late yesterday afternoon, Mr. Storm had summoned Alison to his office to let her know that Mrs. Marmon wanted a conference with her to discuss the new grading system Alison had implemented for the new nine-week grading period. Alison had changed her original grading system and felt that she needed to begin recording some performance-based assessments so that the grades students received actually reflected how well the students were progressing. The former band director, Mr. Duran, had given almost all of the band students high marks in band just for showing up and participating in class. Mr.

Duran always used to say, "These kids have enough to worry about; they shouldn't have to sweat their grade in band."

Alison had spent a restless night trying to come up with a solid justification for why and how she was assessing her students in a different way. Now, as she sat clutching her grade book across the table from the angry Mrs. Marmon, Alison wondered if changing a system that parents and students seemed to like was the right thing to do. . . .

The terms "assessment" and "evaluation" have always been prevalent in the education field, but over the last twenty years, they have taken on an even greater significance with the renewed emphasis on high-stakes, standardized testing in public schools. Educators tend to throw these terms about without stopping to think about what they mean and often fail to consider the place of assessment and evaluation as a vital part of the daily instructional process. What are the purposes of assessment in music? What do we do with the data we collect from our students? How can we develop meaningful assessment tools and techniques that become a part of the teaching process in music classes? These questions drive the discussion throughout the remainder of this chapter.

WHAT IS ASSESSMENT?

Educators often think that the term "assessment" refers only to a written exam or some type of standardized test. They may think that an "evaluation" is primarily a review of their performance on the job. In reality, *assessment* is the collection of data in order to make some type of decision based on the data collected. In the band class, we might listen to our students perform a line from the beginner book, and then, based on how the students perform, decide to address some type of performance problem we heard during the performance. When we do this, we have assessed their performance—we collected data from their performance, then made a decision based on that data to work on some performance problem. On a more formal basis, we might give our students a written quiz on key signatures. After we look over the quizzes, we might discover that our students are very good at recalling key signatures using flats, but have more difficulty recalling key signatures including sharps. Based on that data, we decide to spend more time the next week reviewing the rules for determining key signatures using sharps. As you can see, assessment is a basic part of what we do every day as music teachers: we present material, we collect data based on our

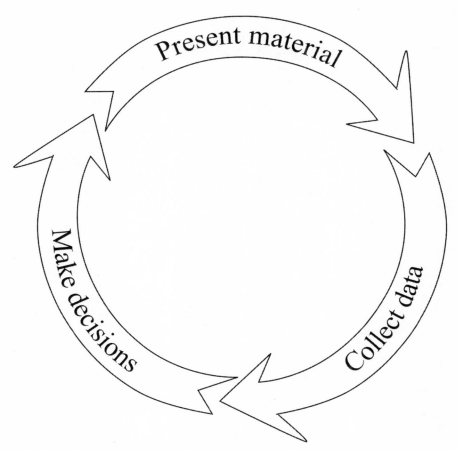

Figure 14.1. Assessment as a part of the teaching process

students' performance in relationship to what we've taught, then we make decisions based on our analysis of the data (fig. 14.1).

The term *evaluation* is used when we give some type of *value* to the data. If we were to convert our students' performance of their method-book line into a numerical grade, for instance, we would be evaluating those students' performance. While assessment is a part of our daily experience as teachers—it is a part of the natural cycle of teaching—we can choose representative formal assessments to help evaluate our students' progress. These formal evaluations can be used to help shape our students' future behavior and performance, or we can use them as a way to help measure their progress toward our students' goals.

PURPOSES OF ASSESSMENT

Teachers use assessments and evaluations for two primary purposes. Teachers may choose to use assessments to help their students change behavior or improve their skill in some way toward a goal. Since the purpose of this type of assessment is to evaluate where students stand in relationship to a goal as well as to give them some ways in which they can improve their performance, we call this type of assessment *formative assessment*. Formative assessment occurs as we move through the various learning stages as we acquire new knowledge and skills. As an example, we might give our students a formative assessment in which they would play particular segments of a piece of concert music two weeks before a big performance. Effective formative feedback to students following this assessment would help them know what their strengths were as well as give them concrete suggestions to improve their performance. Notice that the formative assessment would also give the teacher a good idea as to what performance elements would need to be addressed in subsequent lessons. Formative assessment can be a valuable tool in your instructional tool belt to help your students understand exactly what you are looking for in their performance skills and knowledge. The key to effective formative assessment is wrapped up in the nature of the feedback you give your students; without effective feedback, your students cannot use this type of assessment to improve their performance. We'll discuss feedback as a part of the assessment tool a little later in this chapter.

At some point, as we wrap up our instruction on a particular topic, we may wish to give our students some type of *summative assessment*. Summative assessment gives our students feedback as to how they have done in relationship to the goals and standards we have set for them. These "final grades" usually are more formal and occur at the end of a unit of instruction. To continue the example we used above, you might choose to give one final assessment on the performance music to serve as a grade. This grade would let students know "how they did" on a particular set of skills you have identified as important to their performance. If the summative assessment is based on your formative assessment, and your instruction is based on the feedback you received from your formative assessments, your summative assessment will most likely indicate improvement toward your goals. The assessment and evaluation flow using formative and summative assessment can be a part of our instructional plan as we present material to our students. What specific knowledge and skills should we assess? How do we convert our assessments into grades? What tools can we use to complete our assessments and evaluations?

WHAT TO ASSESS?

Our philosophy of music education as well as our list of goals and benchmarks (see chapter 12) can help us identify knowledge, skills, and dispositions that we feel are important. These items, along with the specific knowledge and skills needed in the musical materials we select for our students, helps us identify the items we might choose to assess.

KNOWLEDGE VS. SKILL

What is the difference between *knowledge* and *skill? Knowledge* refers to our ability to recall facts and information about a particular subject. We know *about* musical topics and can recall musical facts and particular musical information. For example, we recall that the classical-style period occurred in about 1750 to 1800. We know the fingering for A♭ on the euphonium. We know the names of the notes in the G-major scale.

Skill refers to the ability to put some type of knowledge into action. We may know the fingerings for the G-major scale on trumpet, but we need a set of specific skills in order to actually manipulate our fingers, embouchures, and air to perform the scale accurately. Knowledge and skill are intricately related—the more skill we have in a particular area, the greater our knowledge, and more knowledge about a topic can improve our skill.

We may choose to assess our students' knowledge on a particular topic. We may give them a quiz on key signatures or have them write in fingerings for certain notes. Assessments based on students' knowledge tend to be in the form of written tests. Naturally, our assessments of performance skill tend to be carried out through playing tests. Remember that knowledge and skill are intimately related. You can assess both knowledge and skill by formatting your assessments by using prompts such as, "Play the major scale that has two flats." Stating your question in this way requires students to recall which scale has two flats and also requires them to demonstrate specific performance skills.

DO YOU GRADE ON IMPROVEMENT OR ACHIEVEMENT?

Your philosophy of music education will help you decide whether or not to evaluate your students on elements other than musical knowledge and skill. One of the first philosophical dilemmas teachers run into is whether or not to evaluate effort and improvement. When you evaluate your students' performances, should you assess them in relationship to their accomplishments against a standard or upon their improvement upon their prior performance level? What if you have a student who performs at a level that is below most of the others in the class, but through hard work and extra effort, has shown marked improvement? Should she get the same grade as a student who performs at the same level but has not worked very hard? Should you give grades for attendance? Should you give bonus points for bringing in school supplies? The answers to these questions can be guided by your philosophy of music education.

Some music teachers choose to seat their students in ability groupings based on performance skills. These "chair tests" can be motivational to students; some students will practice much more in preparation for these competitive evaluations. One disadvantage to these types of assessments is that there can be a negative connotation to being labeled "last chair" in a section. Even if a student is improving and has performed well, she may be developing more slowly than the rest of the class. It would be unfortunate to have a negative experience with a chair test be a factor in her deciding not to continue to put forth the effort to improve and enjoy musical activities. Another disadvantage of seating students based on their ability is that this arrangement can segregate your best performers from your weakest students. Your most accomplished performers should be able to positively influence your weakest students whenever possible. Students should understand that chair placement and grades in band are not necessarily related; depending on your grading system, a student may be "last chair" and still make a good grade in band, and a student may be first chair and still make a poor grade in band if she does poorly on the other requirements for the class.

ASSESSMENT TOOLS

While we may be able to gather and informally assess our students by listening to their verbal responses in class or by hearing their performances, eventually you will want to use more formal assessment tools to help assign grades and to provide formative and summative feedback. You could listen to your students, give them some informal feedback, and then assign them a grade, but if you want your assessments to be more meaningful, structured checklists, rating scales, and rubrics can be effective tools with which to perform these tasks. In addition to using these tools, you may wish to collect portfolios of your students' works, have them complete journals or other reflective assignments, or even use technology to help students understand how they are progressing in your classes.

Holistic Grading

As an accomplished musician, you are able to listen to a student play a piece of music or an exercise and judge that student's performance in relationship to your own standards of how that tune or exercise should be performed. You might base your opinion of that student's performance on your own experiences, your knowledge of what students of a particular experience level should be able to play, or you might have a standard set of performance criteria that you have developed over time. When you listen to a student play and then give that student a grade based on your overall impression of the performance compared to a set of standards, you are engaging in *holistic grading*.

Let's say you are listening to a group of beginning-band students play scales. The first student plays the first scale and plays all the right notes with a steady pulse and has a good, characteristic sound. You think to yourself, "OK, that was pretty good—probably an A, but I had better leave room for someone who might perform better. I'll give this student a 97." The next student plays and gets all of the right notes, keeps a steady pulse, but has a very weak and stuffy sound. Would you give this student a lower grade than the first student who performed? How much will you deduct for having a stuffy sound? How will you communicate to the students why they received a particular grade? What about a student who plays with a great sound, steady pulse, all the right notes, but stumbles a few times when playing the descending portion of the scale? As you can see, this type of grading is particularly subjective; this scheme is open to your interpretation and is based on your overall impression of the performance. While it is not an invalid way to assign grades, there are some different tools we might use to help us be more objective in our assessments.

Checklists

One of the most basic tools we might use to objectively assess our students is the checklist. Start by listing the *criteria* that you feel are most important to successfully perform or complete the task that you have assigned for your students. List these elements in a checklist. Continuing with the scale-test example, we might decide that tone quality, steady pulse, and

correct notes are three important criteria, so we would list these three elements in a checklist. If the skill is demonstrated successfully, the student
gets a check; if the performance element is missing, the student does not
receive a check. You might have a separate set of checks for each scale performed. The more checks a student receives, the higher his grade would be.

While a checklist may be a fairly objective way to assess your students,
you can probably already see that there are a few weaknesses with this
assessment tool. Some things that we choose to assess are easily graded
using a checklist: your instrument is either clean or not; you either placed
your instrument on the floor safely before opening your case, or you did
not. One of the problems with checklists is that there is an "all or nothing" element involved; you must make a judgment that a student either
does or does not have a "characteristic tone quality" in our scale-assess-
ment checklist example below. What if our student has a particularly offensive tone quality? Using this system, a student who has a minor flaw
in her tone quality might receive the same "grade" for her performance
as the student who has the offensive tone. You may choose to give the
student with a minor tone flaw a check, but then they would receive the
same "grade" as the student with an excellent tone quality. The second,
less obvious, problem with checklists is their ambiguity. What exactly
does "steady pulse" mean? If a student does not get a check in that box on
a particular scale, what does that mean? How can you help your students
improve in that area? As you can see, we may need to refine our checklists
when we move beyond basic skills (fig. 14.2).

Scale Test

Name: _____   Date: _____

☐ Plays with a characteristic tone quality.

☐ Maintains a steady pulse.

☐ Plays correct notes.

Figure 14.2.   Checklist example

Rating Scales

One way to address the "all or nothing" issue with checklists is to assign each item on our list a range of possible scores based on the degree with which a student accomplishes the goals assessed. Using a rating scale, we can decide the degree to which a student might demonstrate "characteristic tone quality" or "steady pulse" on each of the scales. Continuing with the example we began above, we might give the student with a severe tone production problem a "1" rating while we give our student with minor inconsistencies in her tone quality a "3." Using rating scales allows us to put a finer point on our assessments in various areas, to give more subtle shading to our assessments, rather than merely checking to see if the skill is absent or present. The problem remains, however, that our students may not be able to explicitly interpret our ratings. Students may be left with questions such as, "Why did you assign me a '2' on *note accuracy*?" or "How can I get a '4' next time?" (fig 14.3).

Scale Test

Name: ________________ Date: ________________

Plays with a characteristic tone quality.	4	3	2	1
Maintains a steady pulse.	4	3	2	1
Plays correct notes.	4	3	2	1

Figure 14.3. Rating scale example

Rubrics

A rubric is a type of rating scale in which each element that is being assessed is described in some detail based on the level of success the student shows in that area. For example, we might have four degrees of success in our rating scale for *tone quality* where the best score is a "4" and the lowest score is a "1." To convert this rating scale into a rubric, we would need to break apart our concept of tone quality into its constituent parts and describe what each level of competency might look or sound like. The ratings for the four levels that address tone quality might look something like this:

Rating 4 – *Excellent.* The student performs all scales with a clear, characteristic tone quality.

Rating 3 – *Good.* The student performs most scales with clear, characteristic tone quality, but there are minor flaws at times.

Rating 2 – *Needs some improvement.* The student performs scales with some flaws in tone quality. See written comments below for suggestions on how to improve your tone quality before the next playing test.

Rating 1 - *Needs much improvement.* The student has many tone quality problems today. Please visit with the director to see how you can work to improve your tone quality before the next playing test.

By looking across the statements that describe each level of competency in each area that is assessed, the students should have some idea what specific skills they need to improve. You may choose to add additional notes at the bottom of the feedback forms to put a finer point on your recommendations for improvement or to provide additional information.

Here is another example using the concept of "correct notes" as an assessment item:

Rating 4 – *Excellent.* The student performs all of the correct notes on each assigned scale.

Rating 3 – *Good.* The student performs all of the correct notes on most of the assigned scales. Spend more time practicing the scales with which you are having trouble. Play the more difficult scales at a slower tempo.

Rating 2 – *Needs some improvement.* The student performs mostly correct notes on all of the scales, but each scale has some minor flaws. Spend more time practicing all of your scales. Play all of your scales at a slower tempo.

Rating 1 – *Needs much improvement.* The student performs with many note errors on all of the assigned scales. Spend much more time working slowly through your scales.

To develop a rubric, think of a descriptive statement that describes the successful completion of *one* element of an item that you choose to assess. A statement such as "Plays all of the right notes and rhythms in the musical selection" does not allow you to consider accurate note playing and accurate execution of the rhythms as separate elements. What if the student played all of the right notes but none of the correct rhythms? Using this statement might prevent you from begin able to give accurate feedback since you would have to assess both notes and rhythms in a single statement. After you have written your sentence describing a successful performance, you can edit that statement to reflect the other levels of proficiency on your rubric. The "RubiStar" link on the 4Teachers.org website has many excellent examples and tools for constructing and grading rubrics.

Scale Test

Name:_____   Date: _____

Assessment area	Excellent (4)	Good (3)	Needs some improvement (2)	Needs much improvement (1)
Tone quality	The student performs all scales with a clear, characteristic tone quality.	The student performs most scales with clear, characteristic tone quality, but there are minor flaws at times.	The student performs scales with some flaws in tone quality. See written comments below for suggestions on how to improve your tone quality before the next playing test.	The student has many tone quality problems today. Please visit with the director to see how you can work to improve your tone quality before the next playing test.
Correct notes	The student performs all of the correct notes on each assigned scale.	The student performs all of the correct notes on most of the assigned scales. Spend more time practicing the scales with which you are having trouble. Play the more difficult scales at a slower tempo.	The student performs mostly correct notes on all of the scales, but each scale has some minor flaws. Spend more time practicing all of your scales. Play all of your scales at a slower tempo.	The student performs with many note errors on all of the assigned scales. Spend much more time working slowly through your scales.

Figure 14.4.   Rubric example

As you can see, rather than telling a student that they received a "98" or a "72" on their scale, using a rubric can help students understand exactly what they need to work on in each area that is being assessed to help them improve their future performances. This kind of feedback also helps parents and family members understand your grading system as well. Be sure to let your students see what your checklist, rating scales, or rubrics look like in advance so that they can be prepared for your assessment (fig. 14.4).

Portfolios

Some teachers have their students assemble a portfolio of representative work as a part of a long-term assessment of their progress. A portfolio is a collection of representative work that shows a student's progress across a long time frame or is a collection of a student's best work. Artists, architects, and fashion designers often assemble a portfolio to help show off their work to potential clients or employers. You may have a portfolio of your best lesson plans and teaching videos that you assemble to present to potential employers as you search for your next teaching job. If you choose to assemble a portfolio showing how students have progressed over time, you might select representative works from each student at various points across the school year (or even over several years). Depending on your goals for the portfolio, you might include written examinations, practice records, audio or video recordings, assessment sheets, or creative works, such as compositions and arrangements in the collection. If you are assembling a "greatest hits" type of portfolio that showcases a student's best work, then you should involve the student in collecting the best works for inclusion into the collection. Portfolios can help your students enjoy the progress they have made over time and can help you develop a longitudinal view of your students' progress.

Journals

Having students complete written journals is a great way to help you assess your students' understanding of musical concepts and can be an effective method of assessing your students' dispositions and feelings related to the musical material with which they work. Many teachers who use journals have their students write entries based on writing prompts they give to their students. An example of a prompt might be,

If I were in charge of the band program, the first thing I would change would be . . .

You might have a more specific musical prompt such as,

Describe at least two ways you might work on your weakest areas in your spring concert music.

Other teachers leave the journal more open ended and allow the students to write more generally about their experiences in class or in their practicing. Some teachers like to read about students' general thoughts, feelings, or creative ideas in journal writing. Other teachers like to see more specific documentation of practice activities or responses to specific questions. Journals may be written by hand or completed using a secure, online journal or blog. Reading all of your students' journal entries on a weekly basis is labor intensive for the instructor, but it can be a tremendously powerful window into your students' thoughts and feelings. Many students will only communicate to you in any kind of depth through these types of journal activities.

Practice Records

Many teachers require their younger students to complete some type of practice record. Requiring your students to complete a practice record reinforces the idea that practice time is important and should be completed regularly. Many students feel a sense of accomplishment when they check off their daily practice list—particularly when they can see that increased practice often results in better playing skills! Other students have trouble keeping track of their practice sessions, fail to practice regularly, or simply fail to complete the practice-recording task.

There are several approaches to assessing students' outside-of-class practice. Some teachers require that students complete a certain number of minutes of practice each week onto a practice record or chart. For example, a student who practices 180 minutes a week (30 minutes a day with a day off each week) might receive a 100 in the grade book for that week. What if a student finishes everything she needs to get done in less time? What if 30 minutes a day is not enough for a particular student? Rather than have their students record specific times for each practice session, some teachers ask that students complete an activity checklist each week. These checklists help students understand *how* and *what* to practice during their practice sessions and can give parents things to look and listen for as they monitor practice sessions at home. A practice checklist for the first week of classes in beginning band might include a grid where parents initial each day of the week that the students have completed a list such as:

1. Practice whole-note breathing exercises five times.
2. Play ten block notes on your mouthpiece and barrel. Listen for solid starts, steady middles, and clean endings for each note.
3. Practice saying your musical alphabet forward *and* backward for a family member. See how fast you can go with no mistakes!
4. Practice "Note Name Exercise" with the metronome set at 60. If you can say each line with no mistakes, bump up the metronome to 65. Your goal for the week is *no mistakes with the metronome set at 70!*

Whether you choose to use practice records, checklists, or some other method of keeping track of outside-of-class practice time, be sure to include some type of parent signature on the form. This helps parents understand how much time their students are spending working to improve their skills and also allows them to see your expectations for your students.

Technology Assessment Tools

There continue to be several valuable assessment technologies that can help teachers evaluate student progress and performance. Many web-based and software-based music theory, history, and performance packages are available for your students, and several of these packages feature comprehensive assessment tools. One of the most exciting uses of this technology is the assessment feature included in SmartMusic. Smart-Music is an intelligent accompaniment software package that allows the computer to follow the students' performances. The assessment feature monitors the students' pitch and rhythmic accuracy on selected pieces of music, including lines from many of the most popular beginning-band and orchestra method books. This tool gives the students feedback by showing incorrect notes and rhythms in red on the music that is displayed on the computer screen.

You can also use audio and video technology to help you assess your students. Recording audio from your students is relatively easy with a laptop or desktop computer set up in an office, storage area, or practice room. Free programs such as Audacity allow you to record and edit simple audio files. You can easily instruct your students how to record themselves in order to submit audio files to you for assessment. Free video capture and editing software is available for both Windows and Mac operating systems. Using video recordings of your students allows you to assess the visual aspects of posture, hand position, and embouchure that may not be as easily assessable using audio only.

External Assessment: Music Contests and Festivals

Getting feedback from adjudicators and other music professionals at contests and festivals can be another way to help your students assess their skills. For young students, solo and small ensemble contests can be particularly valuable and helpful developmentally. Just hearing the same things you have been telling them over and over said by a different person will help students sometimes. Even though the feedback from the contest judge is valuable, remember that the goal is not a rating or a medal or a trophy but is the experience gained from the preparation and the skills developed along the way.

Whether students get their feedback from the assessments a contest judge gives them or from an evaluation we give them following a particular assignment, consider assessment a part of the regular instructional process. Carefully crafted educational assessments can help us give specific feedback to help our students solidify specific details about the knowledge and skills we would like them to develop. Purposeful assessment, whatever form it takes, can be a valuable tool in your instructional tool belt.

QUESTIONS FOR DISCUSSION

1. Should grades in band be based on achievement or improvement? Should we factor "effort" into our grades we give our students? Defend your answer.
2. If your assessments are based on the knowledge and skills necessary to be a successful musician, is it possible to make a failing grade in band class? What if a student failed to complete all of the tasks you required in band and then failed your class? How would you defend your decision to fail a student in band?
3. Select a set of performance skills from a beginning method book that you would like to assess. Write a checklist, rating scale, or rubric to use as an assessment tool based on that line.

FIELD EXPERIENCE CONNECTIONS

1. Sit in on an assessment or evaluation of students at your school. Keep your own set of grades using one of the tools illustrated in this chapter. How do the results of your assessment compare with your cooperating teacher's?
2. Ask your cooperating teacher about how grades are determined for beginning-band students. Is the scheme different for students in other grade levels? Why or why not?
3. Does your teacher factor in improvement in her grading system? Why or why not?

REFERENCES

Colwell, R. J., and M. P. Hewitt. 2011. *The teaching of instrumental music.* 4th ed. Upper Saddle River, NJ: Prentice Hall.

Cooper, L. G. 2004. *Teaching band and orchestra: Methods and materials.* Chicago: GIA.

Doane, C. 1994. Middle school music assessment strategies. In *Music at the middle level: Building strong programs,* ed. J. Hinckley, pp. 135–146. Reston, VA: Music Educators National Conference.

Farrell, S. R. 1997. *Tools for powerful student evaluation: A practical source of authentic assessment strategies for music teachers.* Ft. Lauderdale, FL: Meredith Music.

Feldman, E., and A. Contzius. 2011. *Instrumental music education: Teaching with the musical and practical in harmony.* New York: Routledge.

Frakes, L. 1994. Assessing musical growth according to your goals. In *Music at the middle level: Building strong programs,* ed. J. Hinckley, pp. 147–150. Reston, VA: Music Educators National Conference.

Jagow, S. 2007. *Teaching instrumental music: Developing the complete band program.* Galesville, MD: Meredith Music.

Mertler, C. A. 2003. *Classroom assessment: A practical guide for educators.* Los Angeles: Pyrczak.

Navarre, R. 2001. *Instrumental music teacher's survival kit.* Paramus, NJ: Parker.

Pizer, R. A. 1990. *Evaluation programs for school bands and orchestras.* West Nyack, NY: Parker.

Roberts, Henry M., and Daniel H. Honemann, Thomas J. Balch, Daniel E. Seabold, and Shmuel Gerber. 2011. *Robert's Rules of Order Newly Revised,* 11th Ed. Boston, MA: Da Capo Press.

WEBSITES

Audacity. http://audacity.sourceforge.net.

RubiStar. http://rubistar.4teachers.org.

SmartMusic. www.smartmusic.com.

Appendix A

Sample Band Handbook

Superior Middle School

Wildcat Band Student Handbook of Policies and Procedures

Welcome to the Superior Middle School Band!

STAFF MEMBERS

Percy Holst	Director of Bands	sweet@mail.edu	555-1212 x101
Gustav Grainger	Assistant Director	posy@mail.edu	555-1212 x102
Band Hall FAX			555-1213

SUPERIOR MS BAND PROCEDURES

A. Every morning when you arrive at school, put your instrument in your assigned slot, and go to your locker when the first bell rings. Next, go to your first-period class. If you have band first period, you will need to bring study materials with you and quietly work until first period begins.

B. No band student will play an instrument before class begins. The entire class will warm up together. Likewise, students will not play instruments once the band directors have instructed students to put away the instruments.

C. Be sure that you return to the band hall after school to pick up your instrument so that you can take it home to practice.

D. Please DO:
- Have a name tag on your instrument at all times. Include the serial number, your name, and your address.

- Take your instrument home every night to practice.
- Turn in practice journals every Monday.
- Raise your hand and be recognized before speaking out in class.
- Bring your band notebook and pencil to class every day.
- Have proper respect for both teachers and fellow students.
- Cooperate with fellow band members, and share all responsibilities of being a good band member.
- Make a real effort to learn and improve daily.
- Keep food, drinks, candy, and gum out of the band hall.
- Avoid running and horseplay in the band hall.
- Keep your hands to yourself, and touch only equipment that belongs to you.
- Enter practice rooms, offices, or workrooms with permission only.
- Take care of school equipment, including music stands.
- Play your instrument only when instructed to do so.
- Have your friends who are not in band remain outside of the band hall.
- Use the band-hall phone only in emergencies.
- Use PENCIL, not ink, in band class.

GRADING

Each band member will be given a *cumulative* grade based on the following: performance, participation, rehearsals, practice records, playing, and written exams.

Participation grades include having correct equipment as well as participating in class. Performances such as concerts and the solo and ensemble contest are another part of the grade. Attendance is a critical part of the student's grade. Practice records will be turned in Monday of each week. Reports may be turned in late on Tuesday for a reduced grade. Practice records turned in after Tuesday are not accepted unless a student has been absent (see "Make-Up Work" section below).

Opportunities to receive extra credit will be given as assigned by the director. The point value and specific assignment will be at the discretion of the director.

MAKE-UP WORK

A. **Make-Up Work for Written or Playing Assignments Following an Absence**

Students are expected to make up any written or playing assignments missed while they were absent. Please consult the *Superior Middle School Student Handbook* for details regarding credit given. *It is the student's responsibility to contact the director concerning make-up work immediately upon returning to school after being absent for any reason.* A zero will be recorded for work that has been required by a director and has not met the timelines for the make-up work.

B. **Make-Up Work for Missed Concerts Following an Absence**
Students who miss a performance with an excused absence shall have the opportunity to make up that grade. An alternative assignment will be given by the director, and credit will be given following successful completion of that assignment. *Students with an unexcused absence from a performance will receive a grade of zero and will not have an opportunity to make up that assignment.* **Excessive excused or unexcused absences from performances will result in that student being removed from the band program.**

LATE WORK

Students may submit written work or perform playing assignments one class-day late for a deduction of 20 points. An assignment that is two class-days late shall receive a deduction of 40 points. After two class-days late, the grade for the assignment shall be zero. An assignment shall be considered late if it is not turned in or performed at the time designated by the director as the due time.

CONCERTS AND OTHER PERFORMANCES

Our students work hard in preparing what we feel are enjoyable performances. It is important that they are given the respect onstage that they so deserve. It is in this spirit that we offer these guidelines in an effort to increase everyone's enjoyment of the concert.

Concert Etiquette

1. Remove all hats upon entering the performance hall.
2. No food or drink is permitted at any time.
3. Turn off all cell phones, pagers, watch alarms.
4. Audience members are asked to remain quiet during the performance. Remember that the acoustics that allow you to enjoy the performance also enhance extraneous noise in the theatre.

5. Recordings are made of each performance, so if bringing small children, please sit near an exit or on the aisle in case you have to leave suddenly.
6. Remain seated. Do not leave or enter the auditorium while a group is performing. If you absolutely must leave before a group is finished, please wait and do so only between selections.
7. Applaud the performers onstage after a selection but not between movements of a song. In a formal concert setting, whistling and shouting are inappropriate.

Severe disruptions of a performance or class will be referred to the office immediately and will not receive the benefit of a warning.

DISCIPLINE PLAN

We expect all members of the Superior MS Band to follow the procedures and rules of the band without question. Remember that our rules are basically common sense and that each rule is set up to allow the band and its students to have safe, enjoyable, and successful educational experiences.

In the event that a student does break a band rule, the following consequences will occur:

1st offense–reminder of correct procedures and band policy
2nd offense–put instrument in lap, no class participation, and teacher conference
3rd offense–classroom isolation and phone call to parents
4th offense–parent/teacher conference
5th offense–parent/teacher conference with assistant principal

Note: Repeated office referrals will result in removal from the band program.

Severe breaches of policies and procedures (those actions that disrupt a performance or class or that jeopardize the safety of other students or sponsors) will be referred to the office immediately and will not receive the benefit of a warning. Remember that all Superior School District rules are in effect at all times when students travel with and/or perform with the band.

Remember our "rules" are really just a matter of being courteous and using common sense. We DO NOT anticipate having to call your parents. Treat others (including teachers) and their equipment with as much care and respect as you would like to be treated. Remember that a band is a team, and the actions of individual members affect everyone else in some way.

We look forward to working with you this year!

PRIVATE LESSONS

Individual private instruction is available to all students for a cost of $10.00 per each twenty-minute lesson. Lessons are NOT required to be a member of the bands. While private lessons are encouraged for enhanced musical growth, they do not guarantee higher placement in bands. We do, however, maintain a listing of many fine teachers who have been approved by the band directors and encourage the students to participate in the program should they so desire. An effort will be made to schedule any interested student.

UNIFORMS

1. Khaki-colored dress pants—no jeans. Pants must touch shoes.
2. White, button-down, oxford cloth, long-sleeved dress shirt.
3. Orange, short-sleeved Superior Middle School Band shirt. Buy this in the band hall.
4. Dark-colored dress shoes—all one color.
5. Black socks or dark hose.

Thank you for helping the bands look good! If you have a problem securing any part of the uniform, financially or otherwise, please call us.

INSTRUMENTS/EQUIPMENT

A. **USAGE FEE:** The band provides the more expensive instruments for students who do not own one. These instruments will be issued at the beginning of the school year. **There will be a non-refundable $75.00 rental/maintenance fee for these instruments.** Students who play more than one school instrument will be charged only one time. Students using a school horn for only one semester will only pay half of the fee ($37.50). This fee will help cover a minor portion of the necessary funds needed to service the instrument at the end of the year and to provide any necessary maintenance required during the school year. These fees *MUST* be paid or other arrangements made no later than December 1. If no other arrangements have been made, the student will not be allowed to use the school instrument. The band staff is *MORE THAN WILLING* to work with students and their families who need help paying these fees. Please do not hesitate to come to a band director to work out a payment plan or other arrangements.

B. **REPAIR:** Any student needing repair of an instrument should first inform the director before taking it in to be repaired. Often what looks like a major problem can be fixed easily by one of the directors; likewise, a simple-looking problem may require the services of a repair specialist.

C. **SUPPLIES:** Some basic supplies will be sold out of the band office. We do insist, however, that clarinet and saxophone players purchase a full box of reeds at once for the convenience of the band directors. A price list for supplies is posted in the band office. PLEASE BRING CORRECT CHANGE IF POSSIBLE or make checks payable to SUPERIOR TOWNSHIP MUSIC STORE. Supplies will be sold ONLY BEFORE AND AFTER SCHOOL HOURS.

D. **STORAGE:** All students are issued a locker at the beginning of school. Depending on the number of students in the band program, some students may have to share a locker. For the protection of the students, the band hall is monitored 24 hours a day by videotaped camera surveillance; however, band directors cannot assume responsibility for any instrument or equipment not locked in a locker. All students are required to keep locks on their lockers at all times.

E. **CASES:** All school-owned instruments include a protective case. Students must transport school-owned instruments inside the case to and from school. Students who fail to transport school-owned instruments inside the approved case will be charged for any damage the instrument incurs and may lose the privilege of using a school instrument.

F. **DAMAGE:** Damage due to abuse and neglect of any school-owned instrument/equipment will be repaired at the student's expense. A privately owned instrument is the responsibility of the student who owns it. Students should check with their parents to see that the instrument is included on their homeowner insurance policy. School-owned woodwind instruments, French horns, and baritones *must* be stored in a *locked* locker at all times when not in use at school. Abuse, neglect, or carelessness when using a school-owned instrument may result in the loss of the privilege of using a school instrument, and the student will be responsible for paying any repair bills that result from that abuse or neglect.

We are *extremely* fortunate and proud of our facilities and equipment here at Superior Middle School. Please take care to keep all stands, chairs, practice rooms, and so forth in the best possible shape, and report any damaged items to a band director immediately. Any vandalism or intentional damage to school property or to another band member's property will result in an immediate discipline referral (see "Discipline Plan" in this handbook).

Only band members are allowed inside the band hall. If you have friends who are not in band, they must remain outside the band hall while you pick up your instrument, and so forth. We do not have space for any additional visitors, and all of our equipment and materials will remain safer and in better shape without non-band visitors.

Food and drink other than bottled water are not allowed in the band hall, practice rooms, or instrument room at any time. Students who choose to violate this rule will receive consequences as listed in the "Discipline Plan" above.

All instruments should be kept in excellent playing condition and stored properly in a locker at all times. <u>Never leave an instrument in an open case or unattended.</u>

MISCELLANEOUS FEES AND EXPENSES

In addition to the Instrument Fee, students will be responsible for paying for various expenses and fees. Some of these items are required expenses, and some of these items are optional.

Some items that are *required* include: purchase of the official warm-up book (*Foundations for Superior Performance*), proper reeds, appropriate mouthpieces, instrument maintenance items (valve and key oil, cork grease, etc.), and flip-folders for pep rallies and football game performances.

CALENDAR OF EVENTS

AUGUST	19	First day of school
SEPTEMBER	02	Holiday
	05	Sectionals begin
	08	Fundraising begins
	11–12	School pictures
	12	Pep rally
	19	BMS vs. Scarytown football game performance
OCTOBER	03	Car wash
	04	Marching spectacular (with Superior HS)
NOVEMBER	07	All-City Band auditions
	14–15	All-Region Band auditions

DECEMBER	01	Region Band Clinic/Concert
	11	Winter concert, 7:00 p.m.
	12	Tuba Christmas, Fancytown Mall
FEBRUARY	05	Pops concert, 7:00 p.m.
	19	Percussion ensemble concert, band hall, 7:00 p.m.
	28	Solo and ensemble contest, Superior High School
MARCH	25	Spring concert, 7:00 p.m.
	22	Superior Community College Jazz Festival
APRIL	06–08	Concert and Sight-Reading Contest, Biggs High School
MAY	05	Band trip—Milly World
	07	Spring concert, 6:00 p.m.

SUPERIOR MIDDLE SCHOOL BAND

TRAVEL CONSENT/HEALTH FORM

PLEASE PRINT

Student Name:_____Grade:_____
          (last   first   middle)

Address_____Home Phone:_____

City:_____ZIP Code:_____

Parent/Guardian Names:_____

Father's Employer:_____Mother's Employer:_____

Father's Work Phone:_____Mother's Work Phone:_____

Father's Cell/Mobile/Pager No:_____

Mother's Cell/Mobile/Pager No:_____

In case parents cannot be reached, please notify: _____
                                        (name)   (phone)

List all allergies to food, medications, other (if "none" please state):

Special medical problems (if "none" please state):

List any medications that the student may carry (if "none" please state):

Date of last Tetanus injection:_____

Medical Insurance Provider:_____Policy Number:_____

Name of family physician:_____Office Phone:_____

Additional medical information or comments that the band sponsors would need to know:

Parents and students: After reading over the handbook, please date and sign this page and return it to the directors no later than:

FRIDAY, AUGUST 29TH

In case of an accident or sudden illness, or in the event I cannot be reached, I hereby authorize a representative of Superior School District to transport my child to a physician or hospital for treatment, or to activate 911.

We have read, understand, and agree to abide by the policies and procedures presented in this handbook and the Superior School District student code of conduct. We understand that any violation of the SSD code of conduct at any band function will result in disciplinary action through the school.

This form must be signed and returned to the Band Directors before the student will be permitted to participate in any off-campus activity.

Date_____Signature of Student_____

Signature of Sponsor_____Signature of Parent_____

Appendix B

Sample Discipline Log

Superior Middle School Band
Discipline/Contact Log

Date	Student's Name	Reason for log entry	Person contacted	Contact phone	Outcomes
April 18	Stephen Student	Stephen was tardy to class for the fourth day in a row.	Mother	555-1234	Mother will wake Stephen up earlier. Stephen will make up missed time during lunch next week.
May 2	Penelope Pupil	Penelope received a third warning for talking during class.	Aunt (guardian)	555-4321	Penelope will be assigned another seat away from her friends to discourage her from talking during class.

Figure B.1. Sample discipline log

Appendix C

Beginning-Snare Method Books

REFERENCES

Crockarell, C., and C. Brooks. 2010. *The snare drummer's toolbox*. Nashville, TN: Row-Loff Productions.

Wessels, M. *A fresh approach to the snare drum*. Prosper, TX: Mark Wessels.

Wylie, K. *Simple steps to successful snare drumming*. Flower Mound, TX: K. Wylie.

	A Fresh Approach to the Snare Drum	Simple Steps to Successful Snare Drumming	The Snare Drummer's Toolbox
Features	Wessels	Wylie	Crockerell & Brooks
	$16.95	$15.00	$15.00
	83 pages	74 pages	80 pages
	CD	CD	DVD
	DVD		
Rudiments	Single stroke roll	Single paradiddle	Double stroke roll
	Double stroke roll	Five stroke roll	Five stroke roll
	Multiple bounce roll	Nine stroke roll	Seven stroke roll
	Five stroke roll	Thirteen stroke roll	Nine stroke roll
	Single paradiddle	Seventeen stroke roll	Thirteen stroke roll
	Nine stroke roll	Multiple bounce roll	Seventeen stroke roll
	Thirteen stroke roll	Accent	Multiple bounce roll
	Flam	Flam	Paradiddle
	Flam tap	Flam accent	Flam
	Flam paradiddle	Flam paradiddle	Drag
	Double paradiddle	Flam tap	Flam tap
	Seventeen stroke roll	Flamacue	Drag tap
	Flamacue	Seven stroke roll	Single stroke roll
	Ruff	Drag	Flam accent
	Drag paradiddle	Ratamacue	
	Seven stroke roll	Double ratamacue	
	Single drag	Triple ratamacue	
	Flam accent		
	Ratamacue		
Rhythms/ Terminology	Quarter note	Note ratio chart	Whole note
	Eighth note	Quarter note	Half note
	Half note	Half note	Quarter note
	Sixteenth note	Whole note	Whole rest
	Note ratio chart	Dotted half note	Half rest
	Dotted half note	Dotted whole note	Quarter rest
	Dynamics	Dotted quarter note	Eighth note
	Dotted eighth note	Bar repeat	Eighth rest
	Eighth note triplets	Sixteenth note	Bar repeat
	Ties	Dynamics	Dotted half note
		Eighth note triplets	Dotted quarter note
		Sixteenth note triplets	Dynamics
			Sixteenth notes
			Sixteenth rests
			Dotted eighth note
			Thirty-second note
Other Percussion Instruments	Bass drum		Bass drum
	Crash cymbals		Crash cymbals
	Tambourine		Suspended cymbal
	Triangle		Triangle
	Suspended cymbal		Tambourine
			Accessories

Figure C.1.   Beginning snare methods

Appendix D
Beginning-Band Method Books

REFERENCES

Bullock, J., and A. Maiello. 1996. *Belwin 21st century band method*. Los Angeles: Alfred Music.

Feldstein, S., and L. Clark. 2001. *The Yamaha advantage*. Paoli, PA: PlayinTime Productions.

Lautzenheiser, T., J. Higgins, C. Menghini, P. Lavender, T. C. Rhodes, and D. Bierschenk. 1999. *Essential elements 2000*. with DVD. Milwaukee: Hal Leonard.

O'Reilly, J., and M. Williams. 1997. *Accent on achievement*. Los Angeles: Alfred Music.

Pearson, B. 2004. *Standard of excellence*. San Diego: Neil A. Kjos Music.

Pearson, B., and R. Nowlin. 2010. *Tradition of excellence*. San Diego: Neil A. Kjos Music.

Sheldon, D. A, B. Balmages, T. Loest, and R. Sheldon. 2010. *Measures of success: A comprehensive band method*. Fort Lauderdale, FL: FJH Music.

Sheldon, R., P. Boonshaft, D. Black, and B. Phillips. 2010. *Sound innovations for concert band*. Los Angeles: Alfred Music.

Smith, R. W., S. L. Smith, M. Story, G. E. Markham, R. C. Crain, L. J. Gammon, and J. Campbell. 2003. *Band expressions*. Los Angeles: Alfred Music.

Sueta, E. 1974. *Ed Sueta band method*. Bloomfield, NJ: Macie.

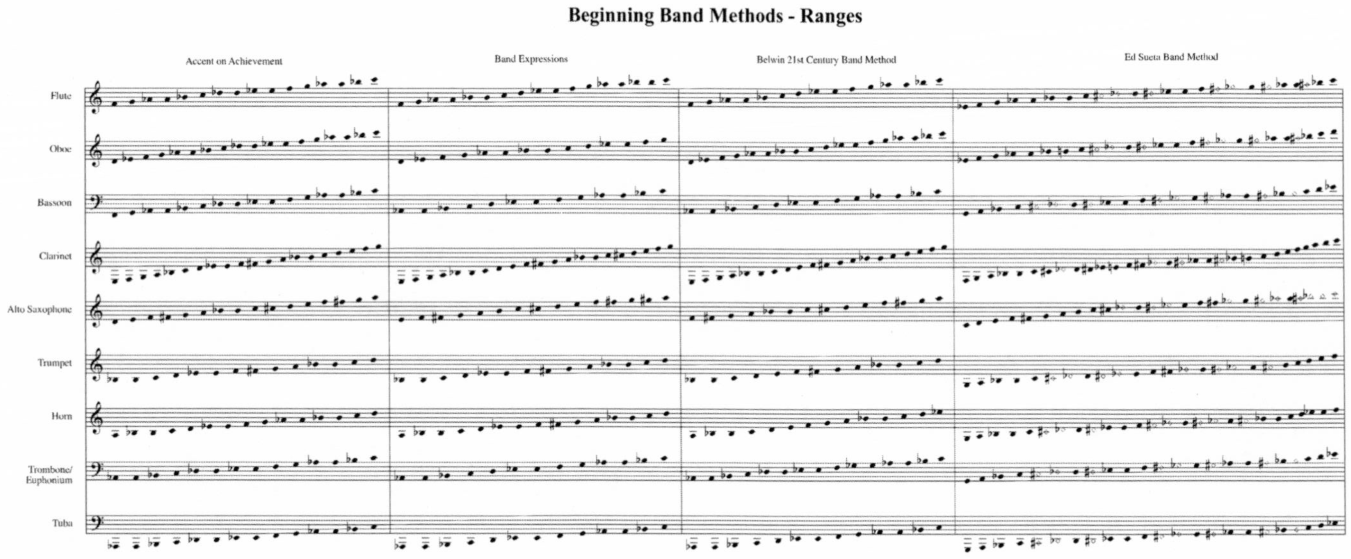

Beginning Band Methods - Ranges

Figure D.1a. Ranges1: Landscape orientation

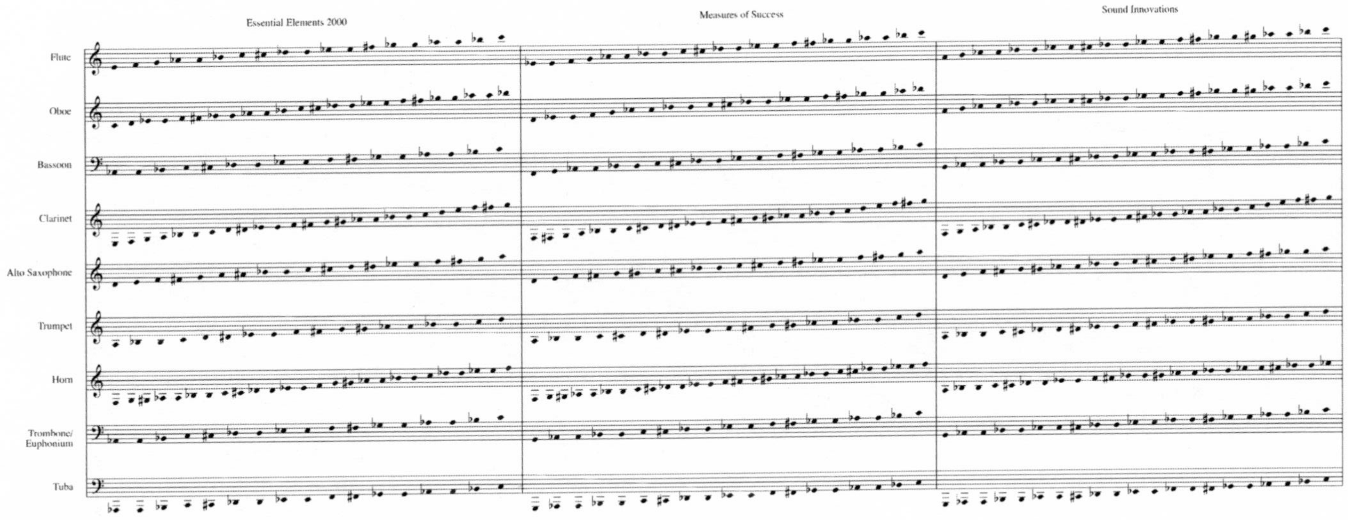

Figure D.1b. Ranges2: Landscape orientation

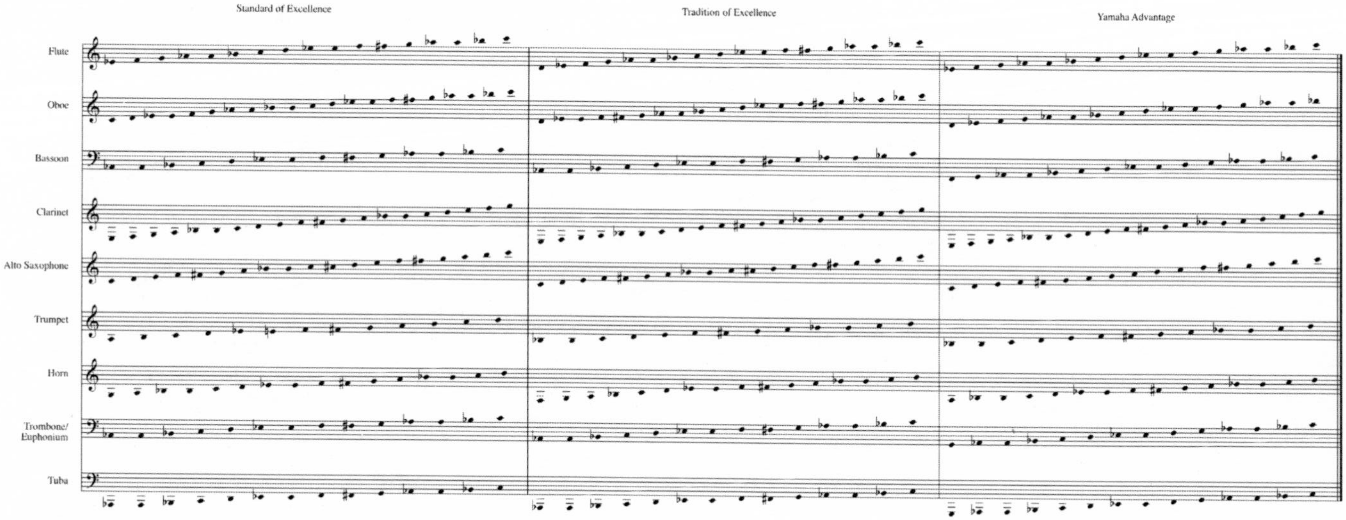

Figure D.1c.   Ranges3: Landscape orientation

	Length (approx. pages)	Lines (approx. pages)	Piano Accompaniment	CD	DVD	SmartMusic®	Color	Illustrations	Basic Fingering Chart	Alternate Fingering Chart	Assembly Instructions	Care Instructions	Practice Chart	Alt. Horn Pages	Alt. Oboe Pages	Rhythm Exercises	Counting System
Accent on Achievement	48	134	●	●		●	C	P	●	●	●	●				1,2	R
Band Expressions	58	210	▲	●		●	C	P	●	●	●	▲				1,2	R
Belwin 21st Century Band Method	30	60	●	▲		●	B	L				●	●	●	●		-
Ed Sueta Band Method	34	170	●	●			B						●	●	●	1,2	H
Essential Elements 2000 Plus DVD	48	190	▲	●	●	●	S	P		●	●	●	●	●	●	1,2	R
Measures of Success	56	190	●	●		●	S	D,P	●	●	●	●	●	●	●	1,2	R
Sound Innovations	56	205	●	●	●	●	S	D	●	●	●	●	●	●	●	1,2	R
Standard of Excellence	48	155	●	▲		●	S	D	●	●	●	●	●	●	●	1,2	-
Tradition of Excellence	48	140	●	●	●	●	S	P	●	●	●	●	●	●	●	1,2	R
Yamaha Advantage	50	168	●	●		●	C	P	●	●	●	●	●	●	●	1	R

▲ = Available separately

Color
B = Black and white
C = Full color
S = Spot color

Illustrations
D = Drawings
L = Line art
P = Photographs

Counting System
H = Hybrid (Too Too)
R = Standard (1 e & a)
- = No specified system

Rhythm Exercises
1 = Integrated separate lines
2 = Separate rhythm charts

Figure D.2.   Features: Landscape orientation

Appendix E

Sample Trip Itinerary

SUPERIOR MIDDLE SCHOOL BAND
BIG FESTIVAL CONTEST ITINERARY
WEDNESDAY, APRIL 7

7:45	Report to the band hall. Take any last minute potty breaks. Double-check to make sure that you have all the parts to your uniform. As soon as you have your equipment together, load large instruments under the busses. Small instruments (flutes, clarinets, oboes) should be taken with you to your seats. Remember to load your uniform under the bus. Bus 1 = Woodwinds Bus 2 = Brass and percussion
8:00	Roll check on the bus.
8:05	Depart Superior Middle School.
8:55	Arrive at Bigtown High School.
9:05	Unload equipment, and get dressed. Take any last minute potty breaks.
9:35	Gather near the warm-up area.
9:50	Warm up in the Bigtown High School Choir Room.
10:30	STAGE PERFORMANCE.
11:00	SIGHT-READING PERFORMANCE.
11:30	Change out of uniforms, and load busses.
11:50	Roll check on busses. Be sure to get on the correct bus.
11:55	Depart Bigtown High School for Fancypants Mall.
12:20	Arrive at Fancypants Mall for Lunch.

1:20   Roll check on busses. Be on time (early).
1:25   Depart Fancypants Mall.
1:55   Arrive at Superior Middle School. Hang up your uniform, and help unload all equipment. Remain in the band hall until the end of sixth period. You will need to report to seventh period after band class.

Index

accent (percussion stroke), 88, 93–94
accessory percussion, 108
acoustics
    battery percussion, 87
    keyboard percussion, 99
activities (as a part of a lesson plan),
    253–54
admission, review, and dismissal
    (ARD), 12
adult beginners, 14–16
andragogy, 14–16
aptitude:
    physical, 214–16, 217;
    testing, 210–11, 213–17;
    versus ability, 214;
articulation, 67–68, 169–70
assessment:
    as a part of a lesson plan, 254–55;
    defined, 282–83;
    formative, 284;
    purposes, 284;
    summative, 284;
    tools, 286–94;
        checklists, 287–88;
        holistic grading, 287;
        journals, 292;
        practice records, 292–93;
        portfolios, 291–92;
        rating scales, 288–91;
        rubrics, 289–91;
        technology, 293–94;
    what to assess, 285
audiation, 28–30, 36–40, 116, 121,
    135
auditory learners, 9, 11, 43, 123
aural skills, 36–37, 38, 108, 135–36,
    184

Bach mouthpiece sizing system, 235
baritone horn. *See* euphonium.
bass drum, 87, 102–04;
    setup, 102–03;
    striking spot, 102–03;
    stroke, 104;
    rolls, 102, 104
bassoon:
    assembly, 71–72;
    care kits, 229;
    embouchure, 59–60;
    fingerings, 153;
    first notes, 78;
    half-hole, 153;
    hand position, 72;
    instrument selection, 232;
    key names, 152;
    reed adjustments, 155–57;

About the Author

Si Millican teaches courses in instrumental music education at the University of Texas at San Antonio. Prior to his university work, he was a public school teacher in the Arlington, Lewisville, and Belton (Texas) school districts teaching at the high-school and middle-school levels. While at Lamar Middle School in the Lewisville school district, the Symphonic Band was a Texas State Honor Band finalist twice. At Belton High School, the Marching 100 advanced to the State Marching Contest twice and finished as high as sixth place in class 4A.

Dr. Millican remains an active clinician and adjudicator across the state of Texas and is on the Active Concert Band list of the Texas Music Adjudicators Association. He has a son and daughter in elementary school.

The author welcomes your questions or comments. Please feel free to contact him at si.millican@utsa.edu.